Kohut's Self Psychology for a Fractured World

Drawing from Kohut's conceptualisation of self, Riker sets out how contemporary America's formulation of persons as autonomous, self-sufficient individuals is deeply injurious to the development of a vitalizing self-structure—a condition which lies behind much of the mental illness and social malaise of today's world.

By carefully attending to Kohut's texts, Riker explains the structural, functional, and dynamic dimensions of Kohut's concept of the self. He creatively extends this concept to show how the self can be conceived of as an erotic striving for connectedness, beauty, and harmony, separate from the ego. Riker uses this distinction to reveal how social practices of contemporary American society foster skills and traits to advance the aims of the ego for power and control, but tend to suppress the needs of the self to authentically express its ideals and connect with others. The book explores the impact that this view can have on clinical practice, and concludes by imaginatively constructing an ideal self-psychological society, using Plato's *Republic* as a touchstone.

Informed by self psychology and philosophy, this book is essential reading for psychoanalysts, psychotherapists, and philosophers, seeking to revisit and revise constructions of both self and humanity.

John Hanwell Riker has been an award-winning professor of philosophy at Colorado College since 1968 and has published four books. He was the Kohut Distinguished Professor at the University of Chicago in 2003.

New Directions In Self Psychology Book Series

George Hagman

Series Editor

Since Heinz Kohut's *The Analysis of the Self* was published in 1971, psychoanalytic Self Psychology has developed into a theory and mode of treatment which is complex and multi-dimensional as well as vital and still evolving. Enlisting authors from a variety of disciplines, and under the editorship of psychoanalyst and social worker George Hagman, the *New Directions in Self Psychology: Clinical, Research and Cultural Applications* book series will examine the state-of-the–art in Self Psychology, providing an opportunity for authors to explore and extend the model in new directions.

Once limited to a small group centered in Chicago, Self Psychology currently has adherent organizations on every continent. Over the past half century, Self Psychology has influenced academic disciplines such as history, political science, art history, and social theory, as well as psychological research into child development, neuropsychology, addiction and psychopathology. Its influence on psychotherapy has been enormous, with many analytic and non-analytic models benefiting from its concepts such as motivational interviewing, grief therapies, addiction treatments, and person-centered counseling. Most importantly, Self Psychology has continued to thrive in the field of psychoanalysis, being elaborated and augmented by the contribution of many subspecialties such as motivational systems theory, intersubjectivity theory, relational psychoanalysis, systems theory and complexity.

The volumes in this series will be devoted to a variety of topics including, but not limited to, couple's treatment, addiction, depression and bereavement, intersubjective Self Psychology, adolescence, infant research, Relational Self Psychology, culture and historical theory. Specific clinical subjects will be highlighted such as the selfobject transference, rethinking resistance, new understandings of empathy, neuro-psychoanalysis, relationality, trauma, and grief. The editor invites contributions from across these areas of practice and the subject areas previously mentioned toward the promotion of vital culture of debate and experimentation in the field of Self Psychology.

For more information about this series, please visit: https://www.routledge.com/New-Directions-in-Self-Psychology/book-series/NDSP.

Kohut's Self Psychology for a Fractured World

New Ways of Understanding the Self and Human Community

John Riker

John Riker brilliantly examines Heinz Kohut's ideas of self with the astute eye of the philosopher. Riker, who is thoroughly versed in the literature, picks apart the critics of Kohut and shows how this remarkable psychological thinker offers hope for the healing of the modern soul.

Charles Strozier, author of *Heinz Kohut: The Making of a Psychoanalyst* and *The New World of Self: Heinz Kohut's Transformation of Psychoanalysis and Psychotherapy*

It is well known that one of the least clearly defined concepts in psychoanalytic self psychology is the concept of the self—until now. With this deeply probing and rigorous treatise on the self from the perspective of a seasoned philosopher who is well versed in Kohut's theories, Riker sets out to correct this deficit. He provides us with a comprehensive account of the structural, functional, and dynamic dimensions of the self which is equally illuminating to those of us who are well versed in self psychology as well as to those readers who want to learn more. Riker does not stop there. He draws on Kohut's ideas, applies them to Plato's *Republic*, and thereby imaginatively and boldly conceives of a world based on the ideal of empathy and interconnectedness rather than on reason and autonomy alone. It is an illuminating journey and a joy to read.

Peter Zimmermann, PhD, co-author of *Intersubjective Self Psychology: A Primer*

What a treasure John Riker is giving to contemporary intellectual culture with his epic new book! His book is in the rare scale of psychoanalysts like Erik Erikson and Erich Fromm, in their broad visions of the potential power of psychoanalysis to humanity.

Raanan Kulka, founder and director of the Human Spirit-Psychoanalytic-Buddhist Training Institute, Israel

Kohut's Self Psychology for a Fractured World

New Ways of Understanding the Self and Human Community

John Hanwell Riker

Routledge
Taylor & Francis Group

LONDON AND NEW YORK

Designed cover image: Sculpture of Narcissus by Maria Battista.
Website: mariabattista.com.

First published 2024
by Routledge
4 Park Square, Milton Park, Abingdon, Oxon OX14 4RN

and by Routledge
605 Third Avenue, New York, NY 10158

Routledge is an imprint of the Taylor & Francis Group, an informa business

British Library Cataloguing-in-Publication Data
A catalogue record for this book is available from the British Library

ISBN: 978-1-032-30149-5 (hbk)
ISBN: 978-1-032-30150-1 (pbk)
ISBN: 978-1-003-30365-7 (ebk)

DOI: 10.4324/9781003303657

Typeset in Times New Roman
by SPi Technologies India Pvt Ltd (Straive)

Sophia, Derek, and Ethan: Beloved Children

Contents

Preface

The most important thing that any society does is to construct its members to be the kind of human beings who can satisfy the material, cultural, and social needs of that society. Crucial to this construction is society's concept of what it means to be an ideal human being and live an ideal human life. Contemporary society is organized around the capitalist economy and needs to construct persons who can efficiently run the machinery of our highly technological, productive, mobile, ever-changing economic world. As such it has invented the ideal of being an autonomous, self-sufficient, rational individual who is willing to abstract themselves from their relations to place, community, and family in order to be optimally successful in attaining the best positions available in the economy.

Heinz Kohut's self psychology reveals that this ideal not only misunderstands what it means to be a self but helps create social practices that undermine the development and sustenance of self-structure. I believe that Kohut achieved the deepest understanding of the human psyche that has yet been produced and, therefore, it is of the utmost importance that our society comes to understand his theory in order to deal with its massive problems of mental health and social pathology. The purpose of this book is to comprehensively elucidate Kohut's concept of the self, use this concept to expose how misguided the contemporary ideal of self is, show how this misunderstanding of the self lies behind many of contemporary society's most pressing problems, and, finally, to construct a model for an ideal self-psychological community in order to point the way out of our fragmenting society into one that can genuinely support self-structure.

Kohut produced his theory of the self a half century ago, but due to misunderstandings of his work by commentators, his own very difficult prose, and a society organized around an ideal that is antithetical to his, Kohut's thought has not gained the ascendence that it should have. It is therefore heartening that three excellent books have recently appeared that will help overcome this deficit. The most pertinent is Charles Strozier's, Konstantine Pinteris', Kathleen Kelley's, and Deborah Cher's, *The New World of Self: Heinz Kohut's Transformation of Psychoanalysis and Psychotherapy* (2022). This work interweaves clinical material, theory, biographical vignettes, and historical details in presenting Kohut's thought. It offers especially fine understandings of how empathy can cure, why and how sexualization and narcissistic rage arise from injuries to the self, and the role of dreams in Kohut's work. It is an essential volume for every self psychologist's library, and, I hope, the libraries of all psychotherapists.

George Hagman's, Peter Zimmerman's, and Harry Paul's *Intersubjective Self Psychology: A Primer* (2020), while not explicitly about Kohut's theory, skillfully relates the innovations in therapeutic technique from intersubjective theory to Kohut's theory of the self. Although some intersubjectivists, like Robert Stolorow and George Atwood, want to eliminate the notion of the self (2020), Hagman et al. show that the purpose of intersubjective therapeutic practices and perspectives is the restoration of self-structure. That is, Kohut's concept of self is seen as the fulcrum for clinical work. This book is full of clinical cases showing how working with leading and trailing edges of both the therapist and patient can lead to a restoration of self-structure.

Finally, Marcia D-S. Dobson's *Metamorphoses of Psyche in Psychoanalysis and Ancient Greek Thought: From Mourning to Creativity* (2023) not only attempts to connect liminal and transitional experiences to self psychology but also presents her own self psychological analysis with Ernest Wolf. By comparing Wolf's approach to other psychotherapies she had experienced, she reveals the extraordinary healing power of a self psychological approach to psychotherapy. Her vision of the self opening to realms of reality and experience usually denied by the ego's containment of experience into rational structures presents new ways of thinking about the powers and possibilities of the human psyche.

These three books focus on clinical material and present it through case studies with far more richness and insight than I, a non-clinician, could possibly do. As a philosopher, what I can add to these books is a rigorous examination of Kohut's key notions—especially those that focus on his vision of the self—in order to bring conceptual and critical clarity to these ideas and to reveal their utmost importance for contemporary society. Rather than presenting case studies, I will closely examine Kohut's texts for what he says about his key concepts. I believe that this close textual examination is unique in the literature concerning Kohut's work. I intend to work through the vagueness and incompleteness of Kohut's ideas to give a full picture of his structural, functional, and dynamic accounts of the self. I will then use this robustly developed concept of the self not only to critique how modern Western society is constructing individuals but also to show how modernity's misguided notion of the self is an important factor lying behind many of the social, political, and personal woes of the contemporary world.

Finally, I want to offer a vision of what an ideal self psychological world would look like and how we need to transform our social practices in the home, workplace, and technosphere to bring it about. I agree with John Dewey that the purpose of philosophy is to perform "a kind of intellectual disrobing" that seeks to expose our social prejudices and "critically to see what they are made of and what wearing them does to us" (1973, 276).

That is, the purpose of this book is to bring Kohut's revolutionary notion of the self out of its foundational place in the clinic into the wider world to help right the ship of a conceptually misguided culture. There are many reasons why societies collapse. Sometimes they are conquered by others, sometimes they fail to provide for the basic material needs of life, but sometimes they construct concepts that negate essential truths about who we are and what we most need. I believe that Kohut's understanding of what selves most crucially need in terms of selfobject nourishment allows us to see how misguided the modern notion of the independent, autonomous self is and why it causes so much unhappiness today in the land of plenty.

I find myself in a unique position to write this book as I am a philosopher trained in skills that deal with abstract concepts and their interrelations. I have studied most of the significant visions of what it means to be human developed by Western philosophers, with my favorites being Plato, Aristotle, Hegel, Emerson, and the existentialists. When I had a psychological breakdown in the late 1970's, I discovered the power of psychoanalytic therapy to engage the depths of the psyche in a way that philosophy could not. I decided that I wanted to devote my life's work to the integration of these two great discourses around issues of philosophical anthropology (what it means to be human) and ethics. In addition to teaching a course, *Philosophy and Psychoanalysis*, for two decades and having written four books and many articles inter-relating psychoanalysis and philosophy, I have, with my spouse and fellow colleague in Classics, Marcia Dobson, invented and taught an unprecedented undergraduate course in psychoanalysis at the Chicago Psychoanalytic Institute in which a number of analysts appear to talk about both their cases and their theories of how the human mind works.[1] In this course I have learned from some of Kohut's most important colleagues—Ernest Wolf, Marian Tolpin, Arnold Goldberg, and David Terman.

In short, I find myself in an exceptional position to carefully probe Kohut's key concepts in relation to both philosophic and psychoana-lytic traditions and to elucidate their importance for modern society.

Note

1 *Psychoanalytic Inquiry* devoted an entire issue (Vol. *39*(6)) to this course, including articles on why it is important to teach psychoanalysis to under-graduates, sketches of the classes taught by the analysts and the students' reaction to them, and a sample of the papers students have written about what they learned.

References

Dewey, J. (1973). *The Philosophy of John Dewey*. Ed. J. McDermott. Chicago: University of Chicago Press.

Dobson, M. (2023). *Metamorphoses of Psyche in Psychoanalysis and Ancient Greek Thought: From Mourning to Creativity*. New York: Routledge.

Hagman, G., Zimmerman, P., Paul, H. (2020). *Intersubjective Self Psychology: A Primer*. New York: Routledge.

Strozier, C., Pinteris, K., Kelley, K., Cher, D. (2022). *The New World of Self: Heinz Kohut's Transformation of Psychoanalysis and Psychotherapy*. Oxford: Oxford University Press.

Acknowledgments

I first want to thank George Hagman for initiating and editing the Routledge series on *New Directions in Self Psychology*. This book would not have been written without the possibility of its being part of this series and without the encouragement of George. I next need to thank Charles Strozier both for giving me important feedback on my manuscript and for teaching me so much about Kohut. His autobiography of Kohut, his collection of Kohut's essays in *Self Psychology and the Humanities*, and his new book: *The New World of Self: Heinz Kohut's Transformation of Psychoanalysis and Psychotherapy* have taught me more about Kohut than any source other than Kohut's writings themselves. Peter Zimmerman read the manuscript and was very encouraging for proceeding with it. Raanan Kulka, a friend as always, allowed me to think that the manuscript was important and moving. Macie Aronski, a philosophy major, researched statistics for me on the Internet and gave me fine feedback on an initial version of the manuscript. She helped me see it through the eyes of the young. In general, Colorado College students keep my mind alive and challenged and I thank all who have populated my classes for the past half century for their vibrancy, intelligence, and hope that life is, indeed, meaningful. I also need to thank the editorial team at Routledge for their guidance and help.

Most of all I need to thank my colleague and spouse, Marcia Dobson, for her careful reading of the manuscript and invaluable help in making it better. Her love and care for me over 40 years of marriage have sustained me, and her depth of knowledge about psychoanalysis and the human soul have nourished me beyond measure.

A note on the image on the front cover. It is Maria Battista's stunning sculpture of Narcissus.

Maria Battista is an artist living in Colorado Springs. Her website is: mariabattista.com

Introduction

Heinz Kohut's self psychology has not only revolutionized psychoanalytic theory and practice over the past half century but also constitutes one of the most important sets of concepts ever developed for how best to understand and inhabit our humanity—concepts as crucial as those formulated by such foundational thinkers as Plato, Aristotle, Kant, and Freud. Kohut was able to grasp the nature of the self in more depth and complexity than previous thinkers because he was a psychoanalyst who immersed himself in trying to understand the unconscious dynamics of the human psyche. It was in his treatment of persons suffering from narcissistic disorders that he was able to grasp what self-structure is, how it comes into being, how it can be injured or destroyed, and what it needs to flourish. That is, we had to await the development of psychoanalysis before Kohut could gain his original and life-changing insights into the nature of the self.

As brilliant and important as Kohut's understanding of the self is, his conceptualization of it is not as clear and robust as it needs to be to take center stage in the West's pantheon of great theories. Charles Strozier et al. say, "his thoughts … about the self … remain murky and have baffled even the best observers" (2022, 45). Further, while his theory presents a radically different understanding of the self than modernity's notion of the self as being an autonomous self-sufficient individual, Kohut does not develop a critique of this regnant ideal nor show how it lies behind social practices that undermine the ability of persons to develop and sustain genuine self-structure. Nor does he show how this misunderstanding of the self is related to many of the personal and social ills that afflict contemporary society. Finally, to be

DOI: 10.4324/9781003303657-1

fully significant, Kohut's theory needs to envision what kind of society might best enable persons to develop strong vitalized selves.

This book is an attempt to remedy these insufficiencies. Part I clarifies and expands Kohut's concept of the self such that it becomes a more coherent, compelling notion. I will carefully analyze the self from structural, dynamic, and functional perspectives, offer a metapsychology that clearly distinguishes the self from the ego, identify the self's energy as a de-sexualized eros, and explain in depth the self psychological understanding of psychopathology. As I develop and expand Kohut's notion of the self, I will also offer responses to his chief critics, including Stolorow, Cushman, Bromberg, Benjamin, and Lacanian post-modernism.

Part II uses Kohut's concept of self as a basis for critiquing how modern economic culture is constructing human beings. It explains why the ideal of the autonomous, mobile individual arose with the emergence of a market society and shows why this ideal deeply misunderstands the needs of the Kohutian self. It will further show why this misunderstanding is implicated in many of the socio/political/economic problems infecting contemporary society, including the plague of loneliness, deaths of despair, multifold addictions, sexual and gun violence, vicious bigotry, and even environmental degradation.

Part III attempts to imagine what an ideal society would look like if it were based on Kohut's notion of the self. In this endeavor I will play off Plato's *Republic*, the book that stands as one of the foundational cornerstones of Western culture. The *Republic* constructs a vision of the ideal human being as one in which a rational ego controls and directs the emotions and desires. He says that this psychic organization can come into being only if a person develops crucial virtues—wisdom, courage, temperance, and justice—and receives an education that fosters such a soul. Since the state is responsible for both educational institutions and the social practices that are needed in the production of good persons, the *Republic* develops in detail what the nature of this state must be, along with specifying the content of its educational practices. Throughout the book Plato makes it clear that the good state cannot come into being without good citizens and good citizens cannot come into being without a good state. While this might look like an impossible chicken/egg problem, there is a synchronistic development here in which better persons can over time demand a better state, and a better state can introduce practices and institutions to help generate better persons.

I think that Plato expresses a truth in seeing the interplay between the organization of the soul and the socio/political/economic practices of the state. It is the social practices of a culture that are largely responsible for how its members construct their humanity. What I want to do in the last part of this book is to inquire into what kind of world would be optimal for the development and sustenance of nuclear selves, so that more human beings could reap the deep sense of flourishing that comes with the presence of a self at the core of experience. That is, I want to re-write Plato's *Republic* from the viewpoint of self psychology and imaginatively construct what an ideal self psychological world would be rather than an ideal rational world.

Kohut's work excites me because I think he got four crucial ideas right about the self, ideas that no one had completely put together into an understanding of the self before he did. *First*, Kohut discovered that the self is not some kind of inborn entity but a structure that comes into being through a developmental process, one which he describes with more clarity and rigor than any other theorist. He brilliantly discloses how and under what conditions the perfection and grandiosity of primary narcissism can be transformed into the ideals and ambitions of a nascent self. That is, selves do not come ready-made in our psyches but must be developed through a process that can produce a vitalized coherent core to our experience if it goes well, but various psychopathologies if it doesn't. In making the claim that the self is a psycho/social achievement rather than an ontological entity or merely the result of social conditioning, Kohut created the first genuinely psychological theory of the self. In seeing the self as an evolution of narcissistic libido, he further taught us that we are inherently narcissistic and need to accept this as an essential part of our human nature. He did for narcissism what Freud had done for our sexuality. He taught us that we need to love our selves and be forever concerned about our self-esteem. In so doing, he freed us from longstanding prejudice against self-love in favor of a selfless altruism. We are by nature narcissistic and never outgrow it; however, it makes all the difference whether we can transform infantile narcissism into more mature forms. I will detail Kohut's theory of how narcissistic libido transforms into a self in the first chapter.

Second, Kohut discovered that our selves are not what they have been presumed to be for almost all of Western history: our conscious egos. While the ego and the self both carry the sense of being who "I" am, Kohut found that their functions, needs, development, and values are extraordinarily different. The ego's fundamental functions are, as Freud said, to negotiate the organism's relationship to its environments and keep order within the psychic household (1923). According to Kohut, the self is different—it is that psychological structure which, when healthy, provides a person with a profound sense of meaningfulness and zestful energy for engaging in life, often with little concern for whether its values will lead to optimal environmental negotiations. The self's values can differ greatly from the values that socially define success for a culture. As Western philosophers discovered, the ego needs education, discipline, and knowledge to develop its powers. Kohut found that the self, on the other hand, needs empathic responsiveness from others to develop its core sense of worth and vitality.

The reason Kohut could discover the self as a largely unconscious structure that can be present or absent from ego consciousness is that he was working in the psychoanalytic tradition. That is, neither he, nor anyone else, could have discovered and described the self before the psychoanalytic tradition came into existence with Freud's work at the beginning of the 20th century. It was because Kohut was trying to understand patients with significant narcissistic disorders that he was able to discover the self by finding what was missing from these patients and what functions they desperately needed him to play. Just as Freud came to understand the dynamics of psychological life by dealing mostly with women who suffered from hysteria, so Kohut discovered the dynamics surrounding the development and sustenance of a self by working with patients who had failed to develop adequate selves.

While Kohut expressly makes the revolutionary claim that the self and the ego are different (1971, xiii), he never develops a new metapsychology to fully explain their differences, functions, and interrelations. One of the purposes of this book is to provide a new self psychological metapsychology without which we cannot fully understand what Kohut means by the self. I will develop this new metapsychology in Chapter 4 and use it to show how a misidentification of the self with the ego is implicated in many of the problems of modern life.

The *third* idea about the self which Kohut got right is that it is structured around ideals and ambitions that relate to idiosyncratic traits and predispositions. This vision of the self captures a number of important ideas from the most profound philosophers writing about the nature of the self. It reverberates with Plato's philosophical truth that humans need to be motivated by ideals rather than just desires if they are going to live meaningful lives, a claim that has resonated throughout almost all the Western philosophical tradition and is an anchoring idea in Confucius' thought. However, Kohut differs from these philosophers in distinguishing between general ideals derived from reason or society and those that originate organically in our singular beings—ideals that spring from the soil of our particular traits/predispositions. When we are actualizing our self's ideals, we feel vitalized and believe that what we are doing is meaningful; when we are following ideals imposed by external sources, we feel obligated. In differentiating self-ideals from social-ideals Kohut aligns his theory with the existentialists and Emerson, who claim that acting from our singular selves rather than social codes is the ultimate source of personal vitality. However, Kohut distinguishes himself from these great philosophers of the self by disclosing our need for recognition and confirmation from others. The existentialists proclaim the heroic lonely individual asserting his singularity against the monstrous generalizing forces of society; Kohut's vision is of the unique individual remaining in connection with others.

Kohut also captures Hegel's crucial idea that the self is inherently dialectical: a tension between who one actually is and an ideal of what one might become. For Kohut the dialectical tension occurs between my narcissistic grandiosity and my ideals. In my grandiose self-esteem, I glory in who I am and what I have accomplished; but my ideals represent the self that I long to be but am not yet. I am both who I am and who I might be. Hence, Kohut's concept of the self is inherently dynamic, for the self must always be in the process of achieving ideals that stand beyond what we have already become. The bipolar self is a process, not a thing—a teleological questing into the future rather than an entrapment in some repetitive structure of identity.

While Kohut is without parallel in his conceptualization of how infantile perfection and grandiosity transform into the qualities of a self, he almost never writes about the "narcissistic libido" that provides the quantitative side of the self—the energy that binds the poles together and which issues into the vitality that the self grants the psyche. I will attempt to mend this gap in Kohut's theory by connecting narcissistic libido to a concept of de-sexualized *eros*—one I get from both Plato and the later Freud. I think that once we find that the self's energy is *eros* (embodied love), a great deal of what Kohut says about the self will make more sense and be more alluring. Structure tends to be boring; erotic love is thrilling. I develop a concept of the self's energy as eros in Chapter 3.

The *fourth* revolutionary idea Kohut discovered about the self is that it is inherently relational. Self-structure is so intrinsically interconnected with others that they literally constitute an intrinsic part of our selves. Since one of the primary ways Kohut defines the self is as a set of functions, others literally become part of the self when they are performing these functions. That is, the self is both a psychic structure within a person but also a field of relationships extending into others. They are not just objects, but *"selfobjects."* We need selfobjects desperately when we are developing a self in childhood, but never outgrow our need for others to support and sustain the self—to literally be part of our selves.

This understanding of the self as inherently fused with selfobjects has helped revolutionize psychoanalytic practice. The notion that the therapist is a selfobject for the patient moves the therapist/patient relation from a "one-person" interaction in which an omniscient distanced therapist examines a patient and offers objectively valid interpretations to a two-person interaction in which the subjectivities of both persons are taken into account and healing takes place at the intersection of those two subjectivities. Even more important, Kohut's claim that empathy is both the therapist's fundamental tool for understanding what a patient is feeling and that which primarily fosters psychological health has been adopted by therapists of all stripes.

Not only has Kohut's notion of the selfobject transformed clinical experience, but it can also be used to justify to modern persons why it is good to become an ethical person (Riker, 2010), a justification that is sorely needed in a world in which it seems that many are prone to cheat and commit other unethical acts. Once Kohut re-defines the self, he also re-defines self-interest. Since it is in our deepest self-interest to have friends who can be selfobjects for us, we need to be able to be selfobjects for them, for it is mainly in reciprocity that adults are able to live within a matrix of selfobjects. It is not hard to show that the kind of person best able to be a selfobject for others is someone who has developed the moral virtues and expanded capacities for empathy and care. That is, it turns out that the kind of person who can best be a selfobject for others is an ethical person. It is good to be good! Chapter 2 focuses on the self's functions, selfobjects, and the importance of this theory for ethics.

As important and revolutionary as Kohut's concept of the self is, it has been criticized by some important clinicians and not been adopted by society at large. Within the clinical world, Robert Stolorow and colleagues have claimed that Kohut's "self" is a reified term that takes us away from lived experience and causes us to think of ourselves as isolated Cartesian egos (2019). Stolorow wants analysts to focus on intersubjectivity and contextuality rather than some "metaphysical" entity termed "the self." Phillip Cushman declares that Kohut's concept of the self fosters the "masterful, bounded, and empty" human beings who roam the capitalist streets of modern society (1995). Jessica Benjamin finds that using others as selfobjects can generate a tendency to not recognize them as independent subjects (2018). Kohut's theory has also been challenged by Philip Bromberg, whose work claims that there is not one central self but many self-states revolving around an ego (1998).

While I will fully develop responses to these critiques in subsequent chapters, let me say that they all involve misconceptions of Kohut's notion of the self. It is not a thing as Stolorow claims, but a structured process that is profoundly inter-relational. It does not foster capitalistic emptiness as Cushman claims, for in its insistence on singular ideals, it stands as a ballast against generalized socioeconomic ideals. Kohut never implies that we see others *only* as selfobjects; and without some conception of the central nuclear self, we cannot make sense of the crucial ethical notions of integrity and "being true to one's self."

However, there are wider, deeper reasons for why society at large has not adopted Kohut's understanding of the self. For one, there is the decline in the acceptance of psychoanalysis as a science that offers the premier way to deal with psychopathology. Rather than long-term engagement with an in-depth process for exploring one's unconscious motivations and life-history, quick-fix–loving Americans prefer to take a drug or make some cognitive/behavioral shifts that are under their conscious control. Jonathan Lear says that psychoanalysis is being dismissed partly because insurance companies do not want to pay for long-term treatment, partly because analysts in the 1940's/50's made inflated claims about psychoanalysis' effectiveness, but mainly because Americans reject the idea "of humans having depth—as being complex psychological organisms who generate layers of meaning which lie beneath the surface of their understanding" (2000, 27). Insofar as Kohut is in the psychoanalytic tradition, his work gets dismissed.

Another reason for why Kohut's work has not entered society at large is that it is at odds with the reigning postmodernist mindset in which anything that appears to be an objective ground of meaning is cast into a graveyard of dead ideas. Postmodernists tend to dislike set structures, especially those that carry rigid forms of identity or authority. They prefer de-constructing to constructing. They value fluidity, difference, de-centering of power and authority, and seek the end of grand narratives that have been used to organize our thinking about the world and ourselves. The grandest of these grand narratives, according to arch-postmodernist Lyotard, is "the self" (1979). Even if Kohut's concept of self is the most fluid, permeable, and de-centered (in terms of its existence both in a person and that person's selfobjects) ever proposed, just the use of the noun "self" is enough for many postmodern thinkers to never read Kohut.

Postmodernists prefer to talk about "the subject" rather than "the self" because subjectivity is phenomenologically available and can be explored for the way it structures experience. As such, it is extremely useful in socio/political discourse, for we can detect different ways of structuring subjectivity, including ways that embody cultural prejudices and contextualized perspectives, such as the patriarchal or racialized subject. Making the subject rather than the self the central notion for understanding why humans are the way they are is especially important in deconstructing certain forms of subjectivity, such as those that arbitrarily assume privilege and power, and constructing new ideals, such as "the post-colonial subject." While we can articulate what colonial and post-colonial subjects are, it makes little sense to talk about selves in this way. "Subject" can also be paired with "object" and "objectification"—a process in which subjects are reduced to objects and, hence, de-humanized. In short, the matrix of concepts connected to "being a subject" are key players in the discourse concerning power and justice; something that the complex of concepts around "being a self" are not. As socio/political discourse attempting to deconstruct arbitrary forms of power, such as white privilege or patriarchy, is ascendant in the contemporary world, discourse about a "nuclear self" seems not only archaic but dangerously obfuscating. I will show why this critique is misguided in Chapter 4 when I distinguish between the self and the ego and show that we need a psychological conceptualization of who we are rather than one that reduces humans to their socio/economic/political identities.

A third reason why the concept of self has declined in significance is the rise of phenomenology as the preferred way to examine human experience. Phenomenology seeks to describe our lived experience without theorizing about structures or entities lying behind or beneath experience. Just as the impressionists strove to paint light and life as we experience them rather than trying to invoke positive or negative spiritual forces underlying the world, so phenomenologists attempt to depict what appears, not what lies behind the appearance. As Heidegger says, phenomenology and ontology are one—that which is is that which appears (1927). Rather than theorizing about some strange subaltern structure—"the self," Stolorow, Atwood, and many current analysts are content with the phenomenologically available "sense of self" that is experienced by their patients and themselves (2019). If patients experience a stronger "sense of self," then the therapy is going well; if it is weak, highly fluctuating, absent, etc., this indicates psychological disturbance. What seems to be eliminated as unnecessary is a theory about some metapsychological self that lies beneath the surface of these experiences. Again, I will show that without some kind of theory about psychological structure, we will not be able to make much sense of what phenomenologically appears.

The above are reasons enough for seeing why Kohut's work has not made the impact that it should have, but Kohut's dense, jargon-laden writing has also been responsible for his lack of impact. A number of his crucial ideas and concepts are left as murky as a southern swamp. For instance, Kohut says that the self is a psychic content and not an agency, but never explains what he means by making this important distinction. He often writes as though the self is the whole person but also writes as though it is a particular psychic structure. He writes that the nuclear self has two poles (ideals and ambitions), but rarely says what it is that has these two poles; that is, we never learn what the energy of the nuclear self is that holds the poles together. He also says that we "love our ideals" and feel "pushed by our ambitions," but never specifies who the we is that is feeling the love and the push. Is it the ego that is loving the self's ideals, the whole person, or the self's loving its own ideals? Is it the ego that is feeling pressured by the narcissistic ambitions of the self, the self's response to its own ambitions, or the whole person? He describes the self differently in different places: as a discrete structure, a set of functions, a process, a subject, or a diffuse presence infusing subjectivity. What really is it?

Kohut often writes as though the self and the ego are different psychic agencies but never clarifies their difference; yet this difference is crucial if he is to maintain his radical differentiation from Freud, and crucial if we are to understand his new psychological dynamics. He also writes that narcissistic love and object love have two different developmental trajectories, but since the narcissistic self is fully intertwined with selfobject others with whom we supposedly have loving relations, this cannot be so. Might self-love and object-love be so interfused that their trajectories cannot be easily separated?

This book will respond to these criticisms and questions by developing, creatively expanding, and explaining in depth Kohut's concept of the self. Once we fully understand the self, we will be able to see why it is not the kind of privileged static ground that postmodernists dislike, and why it is a decisive concept in understanding how to construct subjects that are open-minded, capable of interacting with diversity, and capable of treating others humanely with empathy rather than objectifying them. We will also see why it is essential to go beyond phenomenology to theorize about structures that lie beneath the surface of experience, for without such theories we cannot fully understand who we really are or why we are experiencing things in the ways that we do. In fact, without a theory of the self, I do not think that the fundamental tenets of phenomenological intersubjectivity make much sense.

However, there is a final, and perhaps most important, reason for why Kohut's concept of the self has not entered the culture: it is a revolutionary concept, one that forcefully challenges contemporary society's notion of self as an autonomous self-sufficient individual. Insofar as this concept has been generated by such powerful players as capitalist economics, existentialist philosophy, democratic politics, and Emersonian individualism, it tends to crush all concepts that oppose its understanding of what it means to be a self. Kohut's concept of self is a David in battle with an immense Goliath.

The capitalist input into the modern concept of self instructs us to attain economic self-sufficiency by becoming highly productive and rationally self-interested in our market exchanges. We are not to care about other values, such as community, family, the environment, etc., in making economic decisions, but consider only whether we are selling our goods and services at the highest level and buying at the lowest. That is, this concept of the autonomous rational economic person is that of the abstract individual—the person who abstracts themselves from all contexts other than those of economics. Since much of our lives are spent working, purchasing goods and services, and then enjoying what we have gleaned from our market engagements, this economic notion of the rational, abstract individual governs much of how persons are constructed in the modern world.

The contemporary concept of the autonomous individual also has philosophical roots in transcendentalism and existentialism. Emerson commanded us to be fully self-reliant, while Thoreau put on his old leather boots and walked individuality to a place of radical independence from others. Nietzsche, in the guise of Zarathustra, stood on a lonely mountain top with his eagle and serpent and proclaimed that we need to negate all the social inputs that have formed us and then creatively generate values out of our disconnected particular beings. Heidegger declared that to become authentic individuals we need to live from the depths of our encounters with our mortality and existential singularity. And the rise of democratic politics proclaims that it is the right of each and every individual to pursue their own vision of life, liberty, and happiness.

All these sides to the modern individual de-emphasize connectedness with others as essential to human existence and extol individual freedom as the crucial aim of life. Freedom is variously thought about in terms of having money—as it is wealth that frees us to satisfy any desire that might arise; having minimum baggage—witness Thoreau and many of today's young who seem to desperately fear commitments; and generating one's own values independently of social pressures or the expectations of others. (I will elaborate on the construction of modern individuals in Chapter 6.)

This modern notion of the ultra-free individual is a heady, tempting brew of concepts for how to construct one's self. It presents the tempting illusions that we can heroically master our inner worlds and rationally control the circumstances of our outer worlds. The sense of power, control, freedom, and economic success that pervade the modern concept of self make it very difficult to relinquish. However, the identification of the self with the ideal of self-sufficient ego autonomy is highly problematic, for it has led to many social practices that in fact undermine the development and sustenance of Kohutian intersubjective selves, thereby leading to a society of persons with very strong egos and quite depleted selves. Persons with depleted or absent selves then display the various forms of pathological narcissistic behavior that are so prevalent in society today and which are undermining its most important institutions and practices. One need look no further than the insurrection of January 6 to see how dangerous individuals who substitute ideology for a depleted self can be. We need Kohut's concept of self to fully analyze how the misguided modern notion of self lies behind many of our socio/economic/political problems. We need it as the basis for conceiving new ways to construct human beings and a more humane society.

Kohut's concept of self also needs to be restored as a central concept in psychoanalytic therapy. While intersubjectivity and relational theory have done a great deal to explore the clinical dyad and the forms of clinical interaction that are most beneficial, the aim of the therapy to create a greater "sense of self" (Stolorow and Atwood, 2019) makes little sense unless there is an actual psychological structure—the self—that generates this experience. That is, if therapy generates a stronger "sense of self" when in fact there is no self, then it is generating an illusion. We can experience a "strong sense of self" when in reality there is not a strong self at all. The feeling of "a sense of self" can be a defensive delusion (one that I had for many years). The problem with a person's saying that they have a strong sense of self is that there is no way to check whether it is a delusion or an accurate report of a felt internal structure. As Wittgenstein says, subjectively checking up on an internal impression to see if it is accurate is like buying a second copy of the morning newspaper to see if the first one is correct (1958). The complex, multi-dimensional evidence for saying that one has developed a coherent, vitalized self needs to be grounded in a theory about what constitutes a self. It cannot be equated simply with the phenomenological feeling of "having a sense of self." In order to understand what went wrong with a person's life, what deficits afflict them, and how to repair those deficits, therapists need a robust theory of the self, how it develops, what it needs, and how it can be best repaired. Developing this concept is one of the chief aims of this book.

～ ～ ～

Humans suffer not only from illnesses, psychological traumas, and environmental devastations; we also suffer when the concepts through which we live our lives do not allow us to live fully. We are a strange animal insofar as we do not live simply by our desires or needs but by our concepts, by our visions of what constitutes a worthy way to live our distinctive human lives. This book is an attempt to overcome the conceptual suffering that modern persons endure by exposing the misconception of the self under which we labor and replacing it with Kohut's brilliant notion of the intersubjective, singular self.

References

Benjamin, J. (2018). *Beyond Doer and Done To: Recognition Theory, Intersubjectivity, and the Third*. New York: Routledge.

Bromberg, P. (1998). *Standing in the Spaces: Essays on Clinical Process, Trauma, and Dissociation*. Hillsdale, NJ: Analytic Press.

Cushman, P. (1995). *Constructing the Self, Constructing America: A Cultural History of Psychotherapy*. New York: Da Capo.

Freud, S. (1923). *The Ego and the Id*. In *Standard Edition of the Collected Works*. Tr. & Ed. James Strachey, et al. SE 19: 1–66. London: Hogarth Press. Hereafter: SE.

Heidegger, M. (1927/1996). *Being and Time*. Tr. J. Stambaugh. Albany, NY: SUNY Press.

Kohut, H. (1971). *The Analysis of the Self*. New York: International Universities Press.

———. (1977). *Restoration of the Self*. New York: International Universities Press.

Lear, J. (2000). *Open-mindedness: Working out the Logic of the Soul*. Cambridge, MA: Harvard University Press.

Lyotard, J-F. (1979). *The Postmodern Condition*. Trs. G. Bennington & B. Massumi. Minneapolis, MN: University of Minnesota Press.

Plato. (1961). *The Collected Dialogues of Plato*. Eds. E. Hamilton & H. Cairns. New York: Pantheon Books.

Riker, J. (2010). *Why it is Good to be Good: Ethics, Kohut's Self Psychology, and Modern Society*. Lanham, MD: Jason Aronson.

Stolorow, R. and Atwood, G. (2019). *The Power of Phenomenology: Psychoanalytic and Philosophical Perspectives*. New York: Routledge.

Strozier, C., Pinteris, K., Kelley, K., & Cher, D. (2022). *The New World of Self: Heinz Kohut's Transformation of Psychoanalysis and Psychotherapy*. Oxford: Oxford University Press.

Wittgenstein, L. (1958). *Philosophical Investigations*. Tr. G. Anscombe. New York: Macmillan.

Part I

Kohut and Self Psychology

Chapter 1

The Structure of the Self as a Transformation of Narcissistic Libido

Kohut's first and most important claim about the self is that it is a transformation of narcissism, which he defines as "the libidinal investment in the self" (1966) or as "ego libido" (1971). Hence, to understand his concept of the self we need to grasp what he means by "narcissistic libido," as it is this that will transform into a self. I will explore the general concept of *libido* in Chapter 3; in this chapter, I want to consider what kind of libido is *narcissistic*, how it can transform into a self, and how it can keep transforming into a mature narcissistic state.

The first crucial change from our ordinary ways of thinking about narcissism that Kohut makes is to affirm it as an essential part of our human make-up, thereby criticizing the general prejudice that advocates altruism and self-denial (1966, 1971). Rather than condemning narcissistic self-love as immoral, he shows how and why it is that we all are narcissistic. The question is not whether narcissism is good or bad, but whether it matures from infantile to mature forms.

The touchstone for Kohut's work on narcissistic libido is, of course, Freud's monumental essay "On Narcissism—an Introduction" (1914) in which he defines narcissism as libido directed towards the ego rather than objects. Freud further devises a hydraulic schema in which libido can flow either to objects or to the ego, but if it goes towards one, it depletes itself towards the other. If too much of libido remains cathected in the ego, according to Freud, we have a tendency towards psychosis (paraphrenia), as we live only in the omnipotent fantasies of our own egos without a relation to the world. If too much libido goes out to objects, we can be deficient in looking out for ourselves—deficient in self-preservation.

DOI: 10.4324/9781003303657-3

Kohut agrees with Freud that all humans begin life in a state of archaic narcissistic libido but rejects Freud's libidinal hydraulics in which ego libido and object libido are opposed. Kohut found that since others could perform self-functions, directing love towards them could actually be part of narcissism—a love of one's self as it is located in another. Rather than defining narcissistic libido by its investment in the ego or self—a highly problematic definition as there is as yet no ego or self at the beginning of life, Kohut defines narcissistic libido by its qualities: *"Narcissism, within my general outlook, is defined not by the target of the instinctual investment (i.e., whether it is the subject himself or other people) but by the nature or quality of the instinctual charge"* (1971, 26).

Hence, if we want to understand the transformation of narcissism into the self, we need to concentrate on the qualities of narcissistic libido. Kohut, like Freud, found that the qualities that characterize narcissistic libido are the feelings of being perfect and grandiose. To be more precise, what Kohut found in interpreting narcissistic transferences is that all humans have primal narcissistic needs to relate to perfection and to be empathically mirrored, recognized, and admired as special (1966, 1971). These narcissistic needs are present at birth and remain with us as primal motivating forces for our entire lives. To not deal with narcissistic pressures in satisfactory ways leads to pathologized psychic functioning.

Rather than seeing these primal narcissistic needs as drives or instincts, I prefer to see them as "pressures." We feel pressured to relate to perfection—either in ourselves, an ideal other, our ideals, or an idealized metaphysical being such as God—and feel pressured to be recognized, affirmed, and delighted in as special.

"Pressure" is a more adequate term than "drive" or "instinct," because we don't phenomenologically experience a drive or instinct, but certainly experience "being pressured"—all the time. We are under pressure from all kinds of sources—our bodies, our jobs, our friends, our pets, the world in general. Life is lived under pressure (Lear, 2003). Pressures need not be painful; indeed, they are necessary for us to feel alive and engaged with the world, especially when we feel pressure from our ideals to actualize them—a pressure Kohut says feels like a "pull" rather than the pressure from the ambitions which feels like a "push" (1966, 1971). In general pressures give us an impetus to act, to do something to deal with them. I believe that "pressure" is the kind of "experience-near" concept that Kohut favored rather than the "experience-distant" notion of a Freudian drive.

Although the narcissistic pressures continue for our lifetimes, we can mature in how we deal with them. I think it was Kohut's most important theoretical discovery to articulate what these primal narcissistic needs are, show how they can be transformed into self-structure, and then further develop into such mature characteristics as to constitute an optimal way to be a human being (1966, 1971). I believe that Kohut's uncovering of a developmental sequence for narcissism is original and of the utmost importance for understanding who we are as human beings.

Kohut makes the surprising claim that the self first originates in the mother's expectation that her infant baby has a self and treats it as such. That is, the first instantiation of the self is a 'virtual self" in the mind of the mother (Kohut, 1977; Strozier et al., 2022). From the very beginning of life, others are intrinsically involved in the process of creating self-structure by expecting it to come into being. Within the background of the mother's treating the child as though it has a self, the self begins to come into being through the transformation of the child's sense of narcissistic perfection into ideals and the transformation of infantile grandiosity into a set of ambitions for engaging the world.[1]

1.1 The Transformation of Perfection

In relation to our narcissistic need to relate to perfection, the Kohutian narrative goes something like this. We begin life in a state of feeling ourselves to be perfect and this perfection involves a sense of full control over our worlds, especially our caretakers. At some point, our caretakers will traumatically fail us—by not being present, by misreading our needs, etc., and we now realize that we are not only not perfect but are, indeed, the most helpless creatures in existence, unable to do anything for ourselves. To alleviate our anxiety and sense of helplessness, we project some of our perfection into our primary caretakers, turning them into divine figures whose primary task is to care for us. The infant now can tolerate its helplessness, for it knows it will be helped and cared for in ways it cannot fully understand but which it trusts are best for it. Hence, the first transformation of our relation to perfection is the idealization of others. This idealization of young children for their parents is a universal phenomenon, and Kohut's understanding of it as a transformation of our primary narcissism is a compelling story of why and how it occurs. However, Kohut's most original idea is that in loving these idealized others we are actually loving ourselves because the perfection we experience them as being is none other than our own narcissistic need for perfection projected onto them. When we see our caretakers as "perfect" (in Latin, "complete"), we can fully trust that they will attend to our narcissistic needs. They are our original selfobjects.

This ability to project our narcissistic sense of perfection onto others and idealize them is so crucial that one can hardly live a satisfying human life without it. As we grow up, we typically continue to project our narcissistic perfection onto friends, lovers, teachers, institutions, favorite artists or teams, places, etc., and they glow with meaning for us. To survive, to feel safe, to feel vitalized, we need to live in a partially idealized world. While there will be a further transformation of perfection from the idealization of others to having one's own ideals, living in a partially idealized world grants a sense of well-being, a sense that the world is good and worth relating to. For instance, I idealize Colorado College, and this helps my life at the college to be a deeply satisfying one.

The second transformation of our relation to perfection is its re-integration into ourselves as ideals. As our caretakers non-traumatically reveal that they are not perfect by, for instance, failing to catch us in a lie, we incrementally re-invest ourselves with perfection. However, we cannot identify ourselves with perfection the way we did as infants, because our growing maturity and the world won't allow that. We already have a sense of our limitations; hence, we re-integrate the sense of perfection not as who I am but as ideals which represent the perfection I would feel if I could realize them. In short, we have transformed our relation to perfection from "I am perfect" to "You are perfect and I am part of you" to "I have ideals that are perfect" (Siegel, 1996). When I act to realize my perfect ideals, I restore some of my original narcissistic bliss and attain a deep satisfaction with myself.

This is Kohut's explanation for why our most profound satisfactions come not in desire gratification but in striving to realize ideals we set for ourselves. He says that we experience "joy" when we realize our self's ideals, but only pleasure when we satisfy desires. It is our ability to idealize the world and strive to realize our ideals that might, more than anything else, demarcate what it means to be human. Kohut even defines a hero as someone who stays true to their ideals, regardless of adversarial conditions. We admire our heroes because they reveal the strength and courage it takes to live so deeply connected to the self's ideals that they will die for them (1985).

It must be noted that this transformation of perfection ought not to be understood as a conscious construction of ideals but rather as attaining the impetus to act according to ideals along with the emergence of what might best be called "proto-ideals." By proto-ideals I mean that there is some kind of notion of who we want to become, but it is not consciously articulated into a clear concept. It is just a sense that we want to grow up to be more than we are. As important, if not more important than the formation of these proto-ideals, is developing the motivation to act not just from desire but from a yearning to actualize ideals. The content of ideals can transform over time; but the strength and depth of our ability to be motivated by ideals seems to remain a constant feature of the self. I find it of immense importance that our ability to be motivated by ideals is our transformed narcissism—that what stands over us as an obstacle to returning to infantile narcissism is nothing other than this very same narcissism now transformed into ideals.

Our first ideals tend to be "I want to grow up to be just like mommy or daddy," but as we mature, there ought to be an unconscious or semi-conscious sense of formulating an ideal that fits us as singular individuals—that fits our idiosyncratic traits and predispositions. As we mature, so must our ideals. Ideals stand over us as that which we are not yet, as that which we long to become. That is, an essential part of our selves is what we potentially can be, and this means that our selves are inherently dynamic. We are both who we are and not yet who we are.[2]

It is crucial for persons to be able to discern the difference between self-ideals and socially prescribed ideals—between being able to be true to yourself and being a variable of the social codes. When we are realizing a self-ideal, we feel fully engaged and intensely alive; when we are acting to realize a social ideal, we feel somewhat put upon because we are doing what "we ought to do" rather than what we love. The motivation to follow social ideals often comes from fear of what will happen if one doesn't, as well as a desire to please others. We can, as Bernard Brandchaft has so eloquently shown, lose our selves by pathologically accommodating to ideals imposed on us by our caretakers and society (2007). However, self-ideals and social ideals are often hard to separate and can fuse together, as, for instance, when one uses their social persona to help realize the ideals of the self. We will understand more fully why the self's ideals are not based upon conscious decision making but on our spontaneous eruptive loves when we discover that the self's energy is *eros* in Chapter 3.

We find our self's ideals not by introspecting into our consciously held values, as most of these derive from social pressures, but by exploring situations in which we become most alive, in which we feel most like our selves. The self's ideals can spontaneously and unexpectedly appear, as they did for me when I took my first philosophy class or when I went on my first hike. When the self's unconscious ideals emerge into conscious awareness, we need to make commitments to explore what they mean. It is these commitments based on the ideals arising from the self that gives our lives a deep sense of meaningfulness.

1.2 The Pole of Ambitions

The second sector of our original narcissism that needs to transform into self-structure is grandiosity. "Grandiosity" is a complex concept that combines three different but interwoven traits: the feelings of greatness, omnipotence (power), and specialness. The sense of greatness is the feeling that one is magnificent—the center of the world. Omnipotence has to do with a sense of agency—of having power; while specialness has to do with feeling that one is unique and stands out in the eyes of significant others. Kohut says that the maturation of narcissistic grandiosity culminates in the self's pole of ambitions. An ambition is concentrated energy intent on accomplishing a specific task in the world, which, when done, makes us feel both great and special. Our ambitions lie behind our quests to shine forth and be admired. Underlying all the aspects of this pole of the self is one's sense of self-esteem. If it is strong and positive, we feel vitalized, have confidence that our agency will be successful, and carry a deep sense that we are special.

Self-esteem—the foundation for our sense of personal vitality and efficacy—is derived from two major sources. The first is the esteem we get by being empathically mirrored and recognized as someone special. One of Kohut's favorite images is "the gleam in the mother's eyes," for little else confirms our sense of worth more than a sparkling gleam coming to us from a beloved's eyes. Our initial narcissistic feeling of being the most wonderful thing in the world needs confirmation, and nothing seems to confirm our specialness and greatness more than a beloved's face beaming at us. There is an essential narcissistic need to feel special, and it is empathic mirroring which more than anything else makes us feel this way. When we sense that someone empathically knows and understands us, we feel deeply affirmed in being just the person that we are.

However, as we mature, we also need to accrue self-esteem by accomplishing—from feeding ourselves, to crawling, toddling, toilet training, and so on to having successes in the wider world. This is the transition from "I am great just because I am" to "I am great because of what I have accomplished." Kohut sees the path to this kind of self-esteem as a series of optimally frustrating situations— experiences that we cannot easily solve given our abilities but can if we extend those abilities. At one time we could not feed ourselves and needed the breast or a hand-held bottle, but then, over time, we learned to hold the bottle ourselves. Kohut terms this taking over of a function once played by others, "transmuting internalization." Although this is akin to Freud's theory of building the ego through identifications, it emphasizes that a creative self is already at work, for whatever is being internalized is also being transmuted—it is being transformed into our personal idiom rather than merely being adopted wholesale.

If a child can negotiate the optimally frustrating tasks that life presents without being traumatically shamed or punished for failures, then a love of engaging the world and taking on its tasks develops. We look forward to the challenges of school and sporting competition rather than shying away from them for fear of failure and being shamed. We get upset and bored when school courses are too easy or the athletic competition is beneath our ability. If upbringing goes well, we come to love challenges, love the recognition that comes with success, and allow ourselves to be buoyed by such recognition.

If we receive abundant empathic mirroring, successfully negotiate optimally frustrating experiences, and transmutingly internalize functional abilities, we develop the pole of ambitions, the sector of the self that harbors dynamic energy for engaging with the world. If this pole of the self is strong, we get up in the morning brimming with energy, hopes, and self-assurance for successfully engaging in the tasks the world throws at us that day. When the pole of ambitions is injured or ill-formed, we can shy away from the world, feel depressed, feel afraid and uncertain of our abilities to succeed. We tend to retreat to safe, non-threatening places.

The pole of ambitions is the narcissistic side of the self that wants to stand out and be recognized as special, as great. The importance of this side of narcissism is evident throughout Western literature. In Homer's *Iliad*, heroes are motivated primarily to seek fame and honor. The event around which the action revolves is Achilles' losing honor when Agamemnon takes away his concubine, Briseis. Achilles must withdraw from the fighting until his honor is restored, even if it means devastation and suffering for the Greeks. This is a world in which the narcissistic need to feel special, great, and powerful dominates all other motivations, the characters, and the action. Homeric heroes know that without poets to sing about their deeds, they literally do not exist. The great Greek historian, Thucydides, proclaims that the three basic motivating forces for humans are, fear, honor, and self-interest—two of the three being connected to the pole of ambitions. Heidegger even says that something only attains "Being" when it stands out, when it shines forth, when it appears. "Being essentially unfolds *as* appearing" (1953/2000, 107). When Marcia (my spouse) and I are dancing and we notice that some others are watching us, our energy picks up, our posture becomes more erect, and we flow across the floor with more verve. From childhood through old age, humans love being recognized and love standing out. It is just how we are built.

The pole of ambitions typically includes a fantasy of narcissistic greatness which, as we mature, needs to be adjusted to the reality of who we in fact are. If it does not mature, we can be haunted by grandiose fantasies that cause us to compulsively daydream about achieving stupendous fame and recognition. Just as we were the center of the world in our infancy, we can long to be center of the world again—to stand out as truly exceptional—president of the United States, movie star, rock star, etc. Such infantile narcissistic fantasies can so preoccupy us that we get little satisfaction from our actual accomplishments. I had a favorite student who went on to become a cherished secondary school teacher but who reaped little pleasure from this achievement because he was ensnared in his fantasy of being a great college professor. I also know some college professors teaching at fine institutions who are not happy because they are not at Harvard, Yale, Princeton, Stanford, or the University of Chicago.

There are two chief ways to help combat the pressure of grandiose fantasies. The first is to relinquish "the world" as one's primary social environment and adopt the small communities to which we belong as our primary world. Most of us can be special in our love relationships, our families, and our particular places of work. I am a well-known and admired professor within the department of philosophy at a small liberal arts college, and so long as my horizons are my classes, my status in the philosophy department, and my status in the Humanities, I can feel quite special. Most students who attend the college never have a course from me and those in the sciences might have not even heard of me. Many of my science colleagues do not know who I am. No matter, they are not part of my personal world. We can think of the realms we occupy as a set of concentric circles, with the central circle being my closest friend or friends—my intimates, the next circle being good friends, the next circle being filled with acquaintances and more distant friends, and so on until we reach the world at large. The more the first couple of circles are filled with empathic, admiring persons, the more we can retain the feeling of being special.

The second way to move from fantasy to reality is to engage in what Aristotle calls "choice." For Aristotle, genuine choice involves deliberating about the means to bring about the goal we seek. A college first-year wants to be a physician and knows she must take a pre-med set of courses and knows that for some of them she needs calculus, and so she pre-registers for calculus. One can fantasize about being a glorious physician but must take concrete incremental steps to become one in reality. These steps involve getting knowledge about the world, knowledge about one's skills, talents, and temperament, and then realistically taking steps to attain the goal for which one is ambitious. Fantasies are always connected to wishing, while choice is related to rational deliberation. We wish to be famous or rich or a great athlete or rock star but have no idea of what concrete steps to take to get there, for fame and fortune often rely on luck. Mature ambitions are located in a pragmatic intersection with reality rather than the wishing of infantile grandiosity.

Since the pole of ambitions is grounded in our unconscious sense of self-esteem, it is that part of the self that is the most vulnerable to slights, failures, setbacks, illnesses, low points, and so on. One of the crucial signs that one's self has been injured is highly labile self-esteem, a condition in which one feels depressed and crushed when one fails, is criticized, or is slighted in some way and a scary feeling of grandiose omnipotence when one is successful or triumphant. A crucial sign that one has a healthy intact self is a steady sense of self-worth that is not overly stimulated by triumphs nor too devastated by failures.

Since self-esteem is largely unconscious, it is difficult to determine how strong or labile it is by how we consciously feel about ourselves. One of the most significant ways I have had of checking my level of self-esteem is by attending to dreams, especially elevator dreams. As self-esteem is about how elevated we feel about ourselves, elevator dreams are a remarkable way to symbolize our states of self-esteem. I have dreamed about being in elevators that soared through roofs (overly stimulated grandiosity) and crashed in basements (plummeting self-esteem). I have had scary dreams of elevators leaving the shaft and going sideways rather than up and down (self-esteem being trapped on a floor and going nowhere right). And sometimes I have had dreams of elevators working the way they should!

It is because life always has its ups and downs, its "slings and arrows of outrageous fortune," that we need a constant bolstering of the self through empathic mirroring. The esteem that comes from mirroring seems to be deeper and more sustaining than that which comes from accomplishment, as can be seen from the fact that many persons who attain greatness—CEO's, famous actors/actresses, great successes in all fields—can succumb to depression and a sense of worthlessness despite their outstanding accomplishments. In such cases it appears that the compulsion to succeed is an attempt to fill the void of insufficient early empathic mirroring.

Empathic mirroring is so important that Kohut compares our psychological need for others to our biological need for oxygen (1984). Just as blood gets drained of its supply of oxygen as it nourishes the cells of the body and must return to the lungs to get replenished, so our psyches need to return to our selfobject others to help sustain our self-esteem and keep us vitalized. The self's pole of ideals seems steadier and less in need of selfobject affirmation; it is the pole of ambitions that pushes us to shine and be recognized, the part of the self that wants to be special, that is most in need of a constant supply of affirmation through empathic mirroring.

1.3 The Tension Gradient

In his early writings (1966, 1971), Kohut says that we feel most like our selves when we use our ambitious energy to actualize our ideals, so long as both are connected to our idiosyncratic traits. In *The Restoration of the Self* (1977) Kohut tries to formulate the connection between the ideals and ambitions of the self by saying that there is a "tension gradient" or "tension arc" between them.

> Just as there is a *gradient* of tension between two differently charged (+, −) electrical *poles* that are spatially separated, inviting the formation of an electrical *arc* in which the electricity may be said to flow from the higher to the lower level, so also with the self. The term "tension gradient" thus refers to the relationship in which the constituents of the self stand to each other, a relationship that is specific for the individual self even in the absence of any specific activity between the two poles of the self; it indicates the presence of an action-promoting condition that arises "between" a person's ambitions and ideals. With the term "tension arc," however, I am referring to the abiding flow of actual psychological activity that establishes itself between the two poles of the self, i.e., a person's basic pursuits towards which he is "driven" by his ambitions and "led" by his ideals.
>
> (1977, 180)

Kohut follows this passage with a quote from Goethe's *Faust*: "'Who always striving efforts makes, for him there is salvation'" (1977, 182).

Faust is the archetypal work extolling striving as the essence of human life and in quoting Goethe, Kohut is affirming this insight. In short, the essence of the self is neither its ideals nor its ambitious energy for engaging the world, but the striving of ambitious energy towards realizing ideals. This striving constitutes "a relationship that is specific for the individual self" and is responsible for the "action-promoting tendency" of the self (1977, 180). He further states that it is neither our ideals nor our ambitions that give a person the sense that they are the same self through time, but "the abiding specific *relationship* in which the constituents of the self stand to each other" (1977, 179–180). The self is a striving to become a self.

While ideals and ambitions constitute essential aspects of the self, it is the fused union of them we feel in striving that defines us more than any other element. "The sense of abiding sameness along the time axis—a distinguishing feature of the healthy self—is laid down early as the result of the abiding action-promoting tension gradient between the two major constituents of the nuclear self" (1977, 183). To have a self is to have a singular tension at the core of who we are—a tension that longs to keep striving throughout our lives. We might change our ideals and ambitions over time, but the tension that holds them together seems to keep the same quality of vitality to it.

In sum, the self is neither our ambitiousness nor our ideals, but a dynamic tension that exists between them. It is this "tension" that is who we most feel our selves to be. When we wake up in the morning and just "feel like ourselves" what we are feeling is the tension gradient—the amount of zest we feel for living a meaningful life.

I might express this gradient tension in the following way. Part of me says "I have ideals that are perfect and great, but I am not yet my ideals." Another part says, "I am great in and of myself just for what I am and what I have accomplished." There is a dialectical contradiction between them, as one side says, "I am not good enough as I am" and the other says "I am quite good enough as I am." The truth of the self is held in the tension of these two opposing sides, both of which are true. It is this dynamic tension between the potential I could be and the actual that I am that makes us feel vitalized, meaningful, and coherent. Without ideals to strive for, life falls into a dull repetitiveness; without a robust sense of self-esteem for who we are, we fall into depression.

As much as I think that Kohut has found a deep truth about the self in his notion of the tension gradient, I find it to be an awkward and somewhat unpleasant concept. Kohut's likening it to electrical poles makes it seem mechanical, and, heaven forbid, "experience distant." I never experience the presence of my self as a tension gradient! What I hope to do in Chapter 3 is to show that if we combine the concept of libido that Kohut uses to define the primal energy of the self in his early writings with the image of the tension arc in *Restoration*, we get a notion of a primal energy that looks very much like the *eros* Plato describes in his *Symposium* and to which Freud alludes in his later works.

1.4 The Nuclear Self

When the two poles of the self are woven together through a tension arc, such that our ambitiousness is used to realize our ideals and both relate to our idiosyncratic talents, predispositions, and traits, then a *nuclear self* comes into being.

> I obtained the impression that during early psychic development a process takes place in which some archaic mental contents that had been experienced as belonging to the self become obliterated or are assigned to the realm of the nonself while others are retained with the self or are added to it. As a result of this process a core self—the nuclear self—is established. This structure is the basis for our sense of being an independent center of initiative and perception, integrated with our most central ambitions and ideals and with our experience that our body and mind form a unit in space and a continuum in time. This cohesive and enduring psychic configuration, in connection with a correlated set of talents and skills that it attracts to itself or that develops in response to the demands of the ambitions and ideals of the nuclear self, forms the central sector of the personality.
>
> (1977, 177–178)

For Kohut the self is "nuclear" in that it acts like the nucleus of an atom insofar as all other psychic elements revolve around it. It is the crucial psychic structure that determines the well-being of the whole psyche. If

it is healthy and intact, then the psyche functions well without significant distortions or constrictions. If it is injured or traumatized, then
there will be distortions, debilitating fantasies, and constrictions to
our experiences, especially ones that deal with our relation to perfection and grandiosity. The nuclear self is not the same as the ego
(Chapter 4), the whole of subjectivity, or the whole personality,
although its presence is felt throughout subjective experience. The self
does not itself act, perceive, or consciously think and plan—persons
or subjects do those things. Intact self-structure allows persons to do
those things well.

Kohut says that the nuclear self revolves around a "nuclear
program"—a fusion of ideals/ambitions/traits that constitutes what
we need to achieve in life in order to actualize our selves.

> While the environment has contributed to its formation, from a
> certain time on the self is a coiled spring, a wound clock, not any
> more a vending machine on which one pushes a button and some-
> thing comes out. In other words, it is a structure that, though it has
> its limitations, is firmly formed and, from that moment on, has free
> will ... [T]he self, once formed, must live out a particular life curve,
> must express its own basic pattern ... its particular destiny.
>
> (1996, 390–391)

Kohut frequently uses the image of a coiled spring in a wound clock to
express his concept of the self's having a nuclear program that needs to
unfold. In this claim, Kohut goes against an idea that has been pervasive in modern life: that we are free to be anything we choose to be, or,
in more technical terms, the ego is free to choose whatever kind of life
it wants. Kohut is revolutionary in saying that this modern prejudice is
misguided. We have a destiny, and our discovering our destiny and
then trying to actualize it is the only way to achieve full happiness. We
have free will to realize our selves, not free will to choose to be anything we desire. When we act out of our selves, we feel free—free to be
our selves; all other motivations are to some extent unchosen. To be
free is to accept one's destiny and enact it. This is the freedom to actualize one's self rather than freedom to choose whatever you want to do.

I do not think that this means that the ideals and ambitions in the
nuclear self cannot develop, complexify, and expand, for ideals can

contain a multitude of possibilities that can only be known and explored in sequence. It is also true that our environments change as do our bodies. What were once possibilities within my self-activity of ballroom dancing are no longer available, as my body enters its ninth decade of existence. But new possibilities open up—possibilities for how to be a graceful, elegant dancer within the boundaries of an aging body. What is important here is to see that ideals don't just disappear and get replaced by utterly different ones; ideals unfold and develop like the blossoming of a flower. And like all organic unfoldings, there will be the death of possibilities and mourning.

Yet, we can ask, what kind of thing is this nuclear self? Kohut describes it variously as a structure, a configuration, a content (but not an agency (1971)). Let's unravel these important terms: structure, configuration, content. I follow Wolf in thinking of structure "simply as stability over time" (1988, 27); Goldberg in thinking of the self's structure as a set of enduring functions; and Strozier defining structure as "an evolving pattern of lived experience" (2022, 100). That is, the structure of the self is simply a set of stable predispositions that characterize our experience over time and whose presence can be counted on to perform certain basic functions. We can say that someone has a self when they are able to feel as though they are the same person as they journey through space and time, feel themselves to be independent centers of perception and initiative, have a steady sense of self-worth, and can regulate their affects (along with other functions to be elaborated in Chapter 2); on the other hand, we can say that persons lack intact selves to the extent that they cannot perform these functions. Perhaps more than anything else, the presence of a nuclear self allows one to feel unique, real, and singular. While the nuclear self is formed in and through selfobject interactions, this is not the same as being socialized into the values, practices, and modalities of a culture (see Chapter 4). All the other parts of our personality are highly subject to capture and colonization by social forces that successfully turn us into variables of our societies. It is the nuclear self that provides some ballast against these forces—that offers us the possibility of individuating and feeling like unique, singular beings.

The self is a "configuration" insofar as it is an arrangement of ambitions, ideals, and singular traits held together in a dynamic tension. In short, the self is not a simple identity—a thing at the core of our existence, but a dynamic interplay of constituent parts each of which can change over time and whose relation can also change over time. The self is, in the words of Kierkegaard, not a thing but "a relation"—a relation that is unfinished; an interplay between potentiality and actuality; a longing to be complete but always unfinished (1849/1989).

The most mysterious thing Kohut says about the self is that "it is a content, not an agency like the ego, superego, and id" (1971, xiv). He never explains what he means by this rather poignant but enigmatic claim. In his review of *The Analysis of the Self*, Hans Loewald says,

> While self, unlike id, ego, and superego, is not a constituent or agency of the mind, it also cannot, I believe, be conceptualized as a content of the human mind or mental apparatus ... If self is something like Freud's *Gesamt-Ich* (the total ego where the distinction between id, ego, and superego remains unspecified), then, far from being a content or a structure within the mind, self would be the mind as cathected in its totality.
>
> (1971/2000, 351)

In other words, the only sense Loewald can make of the self's being a content but not an agency is that it is something equivalent to the whole mind itself. But this certainly cannot be the case, as we always have our minds, but not our selves. Sometimes our selves infuse our minds, at other times they don't, as when people "opportunistically adjust their convictions under the influence of external pressures," such that "the nuclear self ceases to participate in the overt attitudes and actions and becomes progressively isolated and is finally repressed or disavowed" (1985, 11). Further, Kohut usually speaks of the self as a particular psychological structure with functions, not as the whole mind itself. But if it is a particular psychological structure with functions, then why is it not an agency like the id, ego, and superego?

We might get some help in interpreting his claim that the self is not an agency but a content by looking at a passage in "On Courage" (an essay he wrote in the early 1970's, shortly after *Analysis*): "The nuclear self is that unconscious, preconscious, and conscious sector in the id, ego, and superego which contains not only the individual's most enduring values and ideals but also his most deeply anchored goals, purposes, and ambitions" (1985, 10–11). Here Kohut calls the self a "sector" of the mind and defines "sector" as a psychic structure that "has surface and depth and a history; it has not only a present-day meaning but also has roots in the actions of the childhood parent" (1996, 75). I think that Kohut is thinking about psychic agencies such as the id, ego, and superego as having definite, circumscribed functions, whereas the self is a kind of supervenient configuration that has the power of infusing each of the psychic agencies with its presence and at every level of psychic functioning—conscious, preconscious, and unconscious. It is a kind of ineffable presence that influences every process of the psyche, even when it is injured. It is the presence of an intact self which makes experiencing feel as though it is mine and that I am present in my experiences. No matter which psychic agency is actively motivating us, the self can infuse it with a sense that it is me who is acting, perceiving, thinking, etc. rather than some kind ego-calculating automaton, bio-chemical body, or socially-coded generality.

We might think of the self as a "liminal presence," a kind of being that can appear and be felt, but which has no clear boundaries, no clear perceptual or conceptual organization, but whose presence vitalizes experience (Dobson, 2023). Ego experience is highly structured; id desires and emotions are recognizable; superego ideals pressuring us are conceptually identifiable; but the self is more of a liminal presence, more like a ghost—a structure that haunts the psyche with its presence or absence but which can never be fully captured or known. I think this is what Kohut means by saying that it is not an agency but a content of the psyche. It exists; we can feel its presence in a "sense of self;" it gives signs of its presence in terms of enhanced vitality; and we can feel its absence when it is not informing our lives.

As a liminal presence, the self can fully infuse experience with a sense of erotic aliveness, be present as a grounding, stable presence, even though we are not engaged in self-activities, or be to a large degree absent from experience. When the self is present, we feel our experiencing to be vitalized, meaningful, and grounded in the core of who we are. When the self is absent or inactive, we can feel shallow—as though we are living on the surface of life without depth or a rooted core. We find ourselves being pulled this way and that by distractions, often feeling somewhat unreal and ungrounded. The self can disappear when we find ourselves in a self-negating relationship, job, or experience. These experiences of the absence of the self reveal the important—crucial—fact that the self can be present or absent or only partially present in our lives. We might have highly successful lives directed by a well-functioning ego with the help of a somewhat benign superego and with enough pleasures from the satisfaction of id desires to feel that we are living well—indeed, living the American dream. Yet, if the self does not infuse our experiences or activities, something will feel as though it is missing, something that gives meaning and vitality to life. These kinds of experience do not necessarily mean that one harbors a traumatized self but that other motivating sectors have taken such a predominant role that the voice of the self goes unheard. This is not uncommon. Kohut says that many adults

> quickly and opportunistically adjust their convictions under the influence of external pressures. Such behavior does not involve an alteration of the nuclear self but represents merely an adaptation on the psychological surface. In such individuals the nuclear self ceases to participate in the overt attitudes and actions and becomes progressively isolated and is finally repressed or disavowed. The psychological outcome, *which is unfortunately more or less characteristic of the psychological makeup of the majority of adults*, is not an individual striving toward a creative solution of his conflicts concerning the redefinition of his basic ambitions and values but a person who, despite his smoothly adaptive surface behavior, experiences a sense of inner shallowness and who gives to others an impression of artificiality.
>
> (1985, 14, italics mine)

Finally, let me say that we will not be able to understand the self as a content or liminal presence until we augment this concept of the self with what we discover in Chapter 3—that the energy of the self is *eros*.

1.5 Mature Narcissism

If all goes well, a nascent self will develop during childhood. This does not mean that its developmental trajectory is complete, for the self's ideals, ambitions, and skills will expand as the person matures. While this development is unique for each individual, Kohut also claims that narcissistic maturation should involve the development of five characteristics for all persons: creativity, empathy, humor, acceptance of transience, and wisdom (1966/1978; 1971). Most of Western philosophy has defined maturity in terms of ego functions—the abilities to successfully act in the world and attain a high degree of rationality. Having a mature self at the heart of one's psyche is different and generates a different kind of person—one who can laugh at themselves and life, empathically interrelate with others, creatively generate their lives, accept the deepest narcissistic blow of all—death, and then transform their values and ambitions into ones that have a wider purpose than simply the realization of one's personal values.

Each of these traits organically emerges from the processes that generate and sustain self-structure. The crucial psychological environment in which the self is formed and self-esteem established is empathy. The only ordinary way to assure that one lives in an empathic surround is to be empathic with others. Persons who receive empathic responsiveness are likely to return it in a dance of mutual reciprocity (see Chapter 2). In this wondrous way of mutual empathy, we enhance our narcissism as we enhance the lives of others.

Kohut thinks that mature narcissists need to be endlessly creative because they harbor the pole of ideals and are always seeking to extend themselves into further realms of perfection. While artists are the paradigm for being creative persons, all persons need to be creative in some ways to sustain themselves, for the gradient tension between the two poles demands that we be striving for forms of perfection not yet achieved. As George Hagman (the analyst who has most extensively explored creativity from a self psychological framework) says, "art occurs when people act upon their own subjectivity and perfect it. They do this by externalizing subjectivity ... and then working to perfect the subjective expression" (2010, 23). For both Hegel and Marx, subjectivity must be externalized to feel real; creative ideas that go unrealized are mere abstractions. The impetus to create—a work of art, a new arrangement to a room, a new way to dress ourselves, a new dance step, etc. is motivated by our basic narcissistic need to relate to perfection and express this relation in an embodied form.

The other three characteristics of mature narcissism—humor, acceptance of transience, and wisdom—need to develop for us to deal with the contradiction between how we narcissistically experience ourselves as the most important beings in the universe and the knowledge of how unimportant we really are. Our lives have been devoted to the strivings of the self and yet we know how all our strivings will eventually be swallowed up in death. "Man's capacity to acknowledge the finiteness of his existence, and to act in accordance with this painful discovery, may well be his greatest psychological achievement" (1966/1978, 454). We are able to accomplish this narcissistic triumph if we can acknowledge and accept our transience, laugh at the impossibility of being human, and achieve a kind of transcendent wisdom about life.

A serious acknowledging and accepting our mortal fate is the ground for the final transformation into mature narcissism. But seriousness needs to be balanced by humor, for humor both expresses and overcomes the impossible rift between our narcissistic sense of immortal self-importance and our realistic knowledge of our mortal insignificance. The mature narcissist is then an amalgam of seriousness and humor:

> If a person is unable to be serious and employs humor excessively, or if he is unwilling to face the pains and labors of everyday living and moves along continuously with his head in the clouds, we will become suspicious of both the clown and the saint, and we will most likely be right in surmising that neither the humor nor the otherworldliness are genuine.
>
> (1966/1978, 457)

Kohut sums up his vision of a person who has achieved mature narcissism:

> Yet, if a man is capable of responding with humor to the recognition of those unalterable realities which oppose the assertions of the narcissistic self, and if he can truly attain that quiet, superior stance which enables him to contemplate his own end philosophically, we will assume that a transformation of his narcissism has indeed taken place .... Neither the possession of ideals, nor the capacity for humor, nor the acceptance of transience alone characterizes wisdom. All three have to be linked together to form a new psychological constellation which goes beyond the several emotional and cognitive attributes of which it is made up. Wisdom may thus be defined as a stable attitude of the personality

toward life and the world, an attitude that is formed through the integration of the cognitive function with humor, acceptance of transience, and a firmly cathected system of values.

(1966/1978, 457–458)

This fully mature psychological constellation is one in which the reality ego and the narcissistic self fuse together such that we can most be our selves when we are identifying with a set of universal ideals that transcend our personal ones. One might say that the idealized pole has now achieved full dominance over the pole of ambitions, for what really counts in life is not how much we shine and are recognized, but how much we can be devoted to a transcendent set of values. We have relinquished our personal narcissism and entered a way of being human that Kohut terms "cosmic narcissism" (1966/1978, 455). Raanan Kulka calls this full vision of the mature narcissist "mystic man" and sees it as a stage beyond Kohut's concept of "tragic man"— the self that must remain always incomplete. That is, there is a spiritual dimension to Kohut's concept of the self in which our final resolution of the narcissistic pressures that propel our lives is a profound overcoming of our narcissistic concerns for our personal lives through the embodiment of a more universal set of meanings and a state of inner peacefulness. (See Chapter 10 for a more complete statement of spirituality in a self psychological framework.)

We must add that this final transformation of narcissism into cosmic narcissism must be accompanied by an existential sadness. "The profoundest forms of humor and cosmic narcissism therefore do not present a picture of grandiosity and elation but that of a quiet inner triumph with an admixture of undenied melancholy" (1966/1978, 458). Without sadness this transformation might look like a form of Stoicism—a disengagement from the world and one's personal well-being. That is, it might be seen as a state in which one gives up caring about what happens to oneself or others and dwells in an abstract realm of universal principles. Such a Stoic state can produce a deep serenity and peacefulness, but at the cost of losing the world and oneself. Kohut's final transformation is not to Stoicism but to a profound caring about the world and who we are at the same time as we transcend it by identifying with cosmic values. It is a melancholic state because we fully acknowledge loss while we triumph over it.

In this final transformation humor also metamorphizes. While there might have been a temptation to sarcastic humor in less mature forms, Kohut sees sarcasm as a "lack of idealized values" and a "hypercathexis of a pleasure-seeking omnipotent self" (1966/1978, 459). The fully mature form of humor is having "a touch of irony toward the achievements of individual existence, including even their own wisdom" (1966/1978, 459). This is truly "mystic man."

1.6 Conclusion

What a remarkable account of the incredible journey of the self from its origins in the virtual hopes of the mother and primitive infantile grandiosity to its final glory in self-transcendence. Unlike many theories which proclaim that humans need to have their narcissism beat out of them, shamed out of them, or transformed into object love, Kohut presents us with a theory in which it is our narcissism that underlies everything great in us—our abilities to be moved by ideals, our abilities to relate deeply to others, and our ambitions to creatively produce life. Rather than crushing our narcissism or denying it, we can transform it, first into a self, and then into becoming a fully realized human being living creatively, empathically, with a fine sense of humor, accepting our mortal limitations, and committing ourselves to higher ideals. How much fuller a notion of what it means to be a mature human being than one that sees maturity as being able to rationally negotiate reality. This is a new and compelling vision for what human beings can and should become.

Notes

1 No commentator on Kohut follows these paths more clearly than Alan Siegel in his *Heinz Kohut and the Psychology of the Self* (1996).
2 See Frank Summers, *Self-Creation: Psychoanalytic Therapy and the Art of the Possible* (2005) for an excellent account of how self-structure must be understood as a set of possibilities not just as a formed actuality.

References

Brandchaft, B. (2007). "Systems of Pathological Accommodation and Change in Analysis." *Psychoanalytic Psychology*, 24, 667–687.

Dobson, M. (2023). *Metamorphoses of Psyche in Psychoanalysis and Ancient Greek Thought: From Mourning to Creativity*. New York: Routledge.

Heidegger, M. (1953/2000). *Introduction to Metaphysics*. Tr. G. Fried & R. Polt. New Haven, CT: Yale University Press.

Homer (1951). *Iliad*. Tr. R. Lattimore. Chicago: University of Chicago Press.

Kierkegaard, S. (1849/1989). *The Sickness unto Death*. Tr. A. Hannay. New York: Penguin.

Kohut, H. (1966/1978). "Forms and Transformations of Narcissism." In *The Search for the Self: Selected Writings of Heinz Kohut: 1950–1978*, Vol 1. Ed. Paul Ornstein. New York: International Universities Press.

———. (1971). *The Analysis of the Self*. New York: International Universities Press.

———. (1977). *The Restoration of the Self*. New York: International Universities Press.

———. (1984). *How Does Analysis Cure?* Chicago: University of Chicago Press.

———. (1985). *Self Psychology and the Humanities*. Ed. C. Strozier. New York: W. W. Norton.

———. (1996). *The Chicago Institute Lectures*. Eds. P. Tolpin & M. Tolpin. Hillsdale, NJ: Analytic Press.

Lear, J. (2003). *Happiness, Death, and the Remainder of Life*. Cambridge, MA: Harvard University Press.

Loewald, H. (1971/2000). "Book Review: Heinz Kohut, *The Analysis of the Self*." in *The Essential Loewald: Collected Papers and Monographs*. Ed. J. Lear. Hagerstown, MD: University Publishing Group. pp. 326–341.

Siegel, A. (1996). *Heinz Kohut and the Psychology of the Self*. New York: Routledge.

Strozier, C., Pinteris, K., Kelley, K., & Cher, D. (2022). *The New World of Self: Heinz Kohut's Transformation of Psychoanalysis and Psychotherapy*. Oxford: Oxford University Press.

Summers, F. (2005). *Self Creation: Psychoanalytic Therapy and the Art of the Possible*. Hillsdale, NJ: The Analytic Press.

Chapter 2

The Functions of the Self, Selfobjects, and Ethical Life

We have clarified Kohut's conception of the self in terms of its structure; however, Kohut offers another decisive way of describing the self, namely, as a set of functions. While it is the structure of the self that allows it to perform its functions, it is the psyche's ability to perform or not perform these functions that provides the most important evidence for whether a person has an intact self or not. It is the self's having a unique set of functions that allows Kohut to claim that it is a separate structure or configuration, one that is different from the ego and other psychic agencies. Most important, it is the conceptualization of self as a set of functions that allows Kohut to develop his concept of *the selfobject*—what many consider to be his most important innovation. While others cannot duplicate the self's structure of ideals/traits/ambitions, they can perform the self's functions when it is unable to; and when they do, they literally act as the self.

2.1 Functions of the Self

Kohut never systematically states what the functions are that either the self or selfobjects can play, but I think they can be broken down into three fundamental categories: (1) functions that satisfy basic narcissistic needs, thereby producing a narcissistic equilibrium; (2) functions that help regulate and direct the "drives"[1] and emotions, thereby promoting a general psychic homeostasis; and (3) functions that promote a sense of continuity through space and time.

By attending to his patients' narcissistic transferences, Kohut discovered three primordial narcissistic needs: to be affirmed and admired (narcissistic grandiosity), to relate to perfection (through idealizing others or having ideals), and to feel that one is a fellow

DOI: 10.4324/9781003303657-4

human being among others (the need for twinship). We are born with these narcissistic needs and never outgrow them, although we can develop increasingly more mature ways to satisfy them. If these needs go unmet or are faultily met, the psyche enters a state of narcissistic disequilibrium and generates defensive or compensatory structures to deal with the deficits.

Kohut found that if children get sufficient empathic mirroring, opportunities to merge with idealized others, and also form twinship relationships with caretakers, siblings, or friends, they develop self-structure and this structure seems to offer a stable way to satiate the narcissistic needs and allow a person to attain a state of "narcissistic homeostasis" or "narcissistic equilibrium" (1971). With this narcissistic stability persons can handle both a moderate degree of internal disruptiveness from fragmenting stimuli and external blows that tend to undermine self-esteem or ideals. Hence, we can reduce the narcissistic needs to one: the need to develop a self. That is, the self is an internal structure whose presence functions to keep the narcissistic needs in a homeostatic equilibrium and whose absence means that these needs must seek alternative forms of satisfaction, typically non-optimal or pathological ways.

In sum, the self's primary function is to establish a narcissistic equilibrium by satisfying our narcissistic needs to relate to perfection, grandiosity, and twinship. Our ideals give us a satisfactory way of relating to perfection and our self-esteem gives us a way to receive admiration and the feeling of goodness from within. Insofar as we find ourselves to be good and have good ideals, it is easy for us to feel that we are a human like others and belong with them, thereby satisfying the narcissistic need for twinship.

However, we need selves not only to satisfy our primary narcissistic needs, but also to perform the function of keeping our psyches in a homeostatic equilibrium. Our psyches, especially when we are young, can feel overwhelmed by strong emotions, drives, and desires. All one needs to do is to fly on a plane with a young child feeling an intense disequilibrium and screaming uncontrollably to know that young psyches can be emotionally overwhelmed to the point of trauma. One of the crucial roles of the self is to soothe and calm the inner turmoil caused by rising anxiety, excessive pain, severe discomfort, gnawing hunger, and so on. If the self is not yet in place or is unable to perform its functions, then others must perform this function of soothing and calming by holding, cooing, and doing whatever it takes to relieve the child's distress. Insofar as they are performing one of the functions of a self, they are, in these moments, *selfobjects* (more on selfobjects in the next section).

In *The Analysis of the Self*, in which Kohut still thinks of himself as refining the Freudian corpus, he says that selves are necessary for "drive-controlling, drive-channeling, and drive-neutralizing" (1971, 47). That is, selves or selfobjects have the function of taking the drivenness or compulsiveness out of the drives (desires, emotions, id pressures) so as to allow for more normal functioning. If the impulsiveness of the drives/emotions/desires is not modulated, then our psyches will be frenzied and not have enough freedom to think about how best to deal with these pressures. That is, the self seems to play a kind of gate-keeper role—the drives need to pass through it for experience to become organized rather than chaotic. When the self performs its modulating function well, the affects do not overwhelm psychic equilibrium and can be experienced without excessive repression or having the psyche flooded with anxiety-provoking demands.[2]

Kohut found that we can also fall out of psychological equilibrium when we are under-stimulated by our environments. If we develop healthy selves, they can provide internal stimuli in terms of our ideals and fantasies about our grandiosity that can keep the mind within a proper range of homeostatic equilibrium. In short, Kohut recognized that the psyche is prone to fall out of equilibrium either because of over-or under-stimulation, both from internal pressures and the external environment. The self is a kind of regulator that organizes, modulates, and even generates stimuli in such a way that the psyche feels a proper amount of aliveness, zest, or awakeness. When Henry David Thoreau says, "To be awake is to be alive" (1854, 85), he is speaking about one of the self's functions—to regulate internal and external inputs in such a way that they generate a sense of awakeness rather than a dull torpor or overwhelming chaos that cannot be processed into meanings. Selfobjects who are attuned to a child have as a fundamental function to arouse the child into alertness on some occasions (as in play) and quell stimuli on others (such as when it is time to sleep).

A third function the self plays in the dynamics of psychic life is to give persons a sense of coherence and continuity through space and time. This theme runs throughout Kohut's works, as he treats patients who seem to lose touch with who they really are, fall into hypochondriacal anxieties, or float on a sea of false personas, shifting this way and that depending on how the social winds are blowing. He interprets these patients as lacking a coherent nuclear self. It is the self that makes us feel that there is a core to who we are, a core that grants us continuity through time and coherence in space. It allows us to feel that the person we were as a child is continuous with the person we experience ourselves to be as an adult, even though we are entirely different.

In sum, Kohut has a view of psychological life that sees the psyche as in a constant danger of falling out of a homeostatic equilibrium, out of a coherent organization. Strange dreams, fantasies, and desires can erupt from the unconscious. Past traumas can suddenly throw us into anxiety. Our environments can fail to empathically respond to our needs, causing anguish and anxiety. Events cannot be easily processed in terms of what they mean. It is the primary function of the self to keep the ship on course, to not allow it to be swamped by wild waves or blown over by howling winds. As Freud showed us, the psyche is always in tension, always under pressure, always assaulted by desires from within and demands from without. The self is the inner gyroscope that keeps the psychic ship from spinning out of control.

2.2 Selfobjects

When someone or something (such as a favorite piece of music) performs one or several functions of a self, they are *selfobjects*. Ernest Wolf defines a selfobject as "the *subjective* aspect of a self-sustaining function performed by a relationship of self to objects who by their presence or activity evoke and maintain the self and the experience of selfhood" (1988, 184). David Terman writes, "A selfobject is a psychological function performed by someone or something outside the physical boundary of the individual" (2021, 380). Technically, no one or thing is a selfobject *per se*; rather they become selfobjects when they are performing self-functions and cease being selfobjects when they are no longer performing those functions. However, if someone—a parent, spouse, or best friend—is shoring up the self or performing its functions in a regularly consistent way, they can be called one's primary selfobjects. Although I might not be experiencing any significantly disruptive experience that needs soothing, I believe that Marcia's presence has a calming, security-inducing, life-enhancing effect that tends to keep my self in a state of narcissistic equilibrium. And I do the same for her. When one of us is away or absent for a considerable period, we can viscerally feel the absence of our main selfobject and feel somewhat out of sorts. It is not that we constantly play selfobject functions for one another but we know that the other can and will play those functions if needed. We are *potential* selfobjects for one another and our availability is crucial to a sense of secure well-being.

Kohut thought that selves could not come into being without others constantly playing self-functions in childhood[3] but also found that the self is so vulnerable to injury and disruption that selfobjects are needed throughout life.

> Self psychology holds that self-selfobject relationships form the essence of psychological life from birth to death, that a move from dependence (symbiosis) to independence (autonomy) in the psychological sphere is no more possible, let alone desirable, than a corresponding move from a life dependent on oxygen to a life independent of it in the biological sphere.
>
> (1984, 47)

Obviously, the comparison is somewhat of a hyperbole, as no one can biologically live without oxygen, but many people live isolated lives without selfobjects. Indeed, many individuals live highly successful socioeconomic lives—lives filled with power, status, wealth—without well-formed selves or significant selfobject relations. I think Kohut would say that their lives are not deeply fulfilling; are not lives that reach into the fullness of our humanity; they are not lives that sparkle with joy or any depth of emotional connectedness. Lives devoid of selfobject relationships must be lived through the defenses which avoid the very core of who we are and demand that we live on the periphery of experience. That there are occasional persons who seem to do very well in life without selfobjects (probably because they had a very solid foundation in childhood) cannot undo the principle that in general we need selfobject others from birth until death.

While we need selfobject support for a lifetime, the quality and intensity of our need changes over time. When we are young children, we need a vast and consistent amount of selfobject connectedness. While watching my two-year-old grandchild with her mother, I noticed that she looked up every several minutes to see if she was being watched and appreciated. Every several minutes! And she had little sense that she must reciprocally provide selfobject nourishment to her mother. As we mature, the frequency and intensity of our need for selfobjects diminishes as we develop selves and become more able to perform its functions for ourselves. We might not need selfobject responsiveness and recognition for days on end rather than every several minutes.

Mature persons with well-developed selves will not only not need constant selfobject responsiveness but also be willing and able to engage in reciprocal selfobject relations with others. That is, adults should be willing to give selfobject nourishment as well as receive it. This mature reciprocity will be the basis for developing our ethical lives, for, as we shall soon see, it is people who develop the moral virtues who are best able to enter into reciprocal selfobject relations.

There have been many important theorists of the self, including Winnicott and Jung, but it is Kohut who most profoundly articulates how the self is the precipitate of a developmental process that can, and often is, derailed; how the self is so subject to slights, injuries, and traumas as to need constant selfobject repair, and how there is no steady state to the self—that it, like the body, needs a constant supply of nourishment to stay vitalized. "Under normal circumstances, we all need a steady stream of self-confirmation" (1987, 36). That is, Kohut developed a theory of the self that captures essential qualities that we don't like to admit: fragility, vulnerability, instability. It is these traits of the self that require persons to locate and secure trustworthy selfobjects in order to participate fully in the emotional depths of life.

While selfobject others can perform any of the functions of the self when it is unable to do so, the major function played by others seems to be to shore up self-esteem. Ideals tend to be stable and not shaken by events of the world, for they represent potentialities of who we might be and hence are somewhat immune to the vicissitudes of life. Our traits and propensities are likewise somewhat stable, although we can find that what we thought was a major talent turns out to be less than we thought, as we engage the world competitively and find that our talent is negligible in comparison with others. I was, for instance, a star athlete in middle-school as my body matured faster than most other boys; then they caught up, and surpassed me in size, strength, and agility. It was not my abilities that changed, but the world. Abilities that had once allowed me to star in sports now were not good enough to make the team. I had to adjust both my ideals and my self-esteem, which could no longer receive the kind of delicious nourishment one gets from starring in sports.

It is, indeed, self-esteem that is the most vulnerable and volatile aspect of the self and certainly the most crucial. Kohut mentions the need for others to help "regulate self-esteem" more than any other function. That is, it is our need to be recognized as special—to be seen as great—that is most endangered in a world in which we are not particularly special, great, and often go unrecognized. Our self-esteem often suffers little failures or indignities on a daily basis. I spilled my coffee this morning—clumsy! I catch a student looking at his phone rather than listening to me and feel diminished. Marcia wakes up and starts immediately attending to her tasks without warmly greeting me. The slings and arrows of everyday life are real; they wear us down. And then a friend, a child, a spouse looks at us with gleaming eyes to let us know we are special to them—that we are great in their eyes, and self-esteem is restored. And dogs help, too, a lot. I believe this is why there has been such an incredible increase in the presence of dogs in American households. Their gleaming eyes help restore self-esteem and make us feel that we are—to them—the most important things in existence.

Kohut discovered that what nourished self-esteem most was empathic resonance and understanding. Successes in the world can help, for sure, but they usually cannot overcome an unconscious sense of worthlessness, no matter how much we achieve. The key curative factor in psychodynamic therapy is the therapists' ability to empathically resonate with and understand the feelings and self-states of their patients. It is the acknowledgment of our friends and others of our importance to them that is the primary counter to the slights of life. Self-esteem tends to be entropic; it fades without a constant flow from others. It is the entropic tendencies of self-esteem that more than any other factor causes Kohut to claim that selfobjects are as necessary to psychological life as oxygen is to biological life.

Selfobjects are so important, that children (and adults) will accommodate to the image of what their primary selfobjects want them to be rather than assert who they truly are, if such assertion threatens their connectedness. When self-assertion and connectedness conflict, connectedness reveals its primary importance. We can live without integrity; we cannot live without the oxygen of selfobject connectedness.

While life comes with its petit failures on an everyday basis, nothing seems to undermine self-esteem more than shame. Kohut says that

> under normal, everyday circumstances something like the opposite of shame exists; that is, there is an outflow of exhibitionism vis-à-vis the surroundings, vis-à-vis the world, and a narcissistic, exhibitionistic balance in the relationships between the individual and his surroundings is maintained ... [Shame is] a disturbance in the smooth presentation of the self to the surroundings.
>
> (1996, 244)

In short, we are always engaged in acts of self-presentation in which we seek recognition and approval, and under normal circumstances, we get it. However, very few of us graduate from childhood without having suffered a goodly amount of shame—from caretakers, siblings, and classmates at school. Shame comes not only from being actively negated for our failures, but also from moments of non-acknowledgment. We bring home the magnificent picture we drew in kindergarten and our mother hardly notices. "Oh, how nice" and then she quickly turns to her occupations of the day. We feel ashamed for presenting our gift that we thought was so great. Insofar as the schoolyard tends to be a place of narcissistic struggle with everyone trying to be more special than everyone else, putting others down by shaming them is a common way to proclaim one's own greatness. "You're stupid." "You jerk, you can't do anything right." "Weakling." "You're so ugly." The insults are endless; self-esteem is vulnerable. We run home to mommy and her gleaming eyes once again restore us—if we are lucky! If we are unlucky, early shaming, especially from those from whom we expect selfobject supplies, can solidify into an unconscious mire of negative self-esteem, generating a sense of worthlessness, throwing us into a dungeon of depressiveness, and causing us to construct narcissistic and manic defenses to counter this sense of inner worthlessness.

Perhaps the worst scenarios occur with what David Terman calls the "negative selfobject," an early caregiver who provides recognition of the child only through acts that demean the child, proclaiming the child to be evil, deformed, stupid, etc. To stay in connection with the selfobject, the child must adopt the caregiver's negative view of who they essentially are. "Rather than cause deficits or result in accommodation, these interactions directly shape the emergent self in distorted ways" (2021, 380). That is, the very structure of the self carries negative self-esteem within it. When the therapist treats persons whose caretaker(s) have been negative selfobjects, they must be careful not to immediately attempt to reverse the negative self-image as this is the very core of the self. Terman says that "the therapist must be able to empathize with the perspective that the patient brings to the therapeutic encounter: that he/she is worthless, hopeless, often that suicide is the only viable option, and/or that the therapist is either helpless or malevolently hurtful" (2021, 386).

Given the narcissistic need that everyone has to be special and given that schools and families with multiple children tend to generate a great deal of narcissistic competitiveness, dealing with shame will probably always be a fundamental task in life. It is one of the reasons why selfobject support is necessary for us to maintain a narcissistic equilibrium.[4]

While helping to regulate a positive sense of self-esteem is the primary task for selfobjects, there are several other self-functions that others can perform. One of the most common is to soothe and calm emotions and feelings when they tend to overwhelm us—especially the difficult emotions of anxiety, rage, guilt, and grief. When we get out of whack with conflicting emotional tensions, others can help calm, organize, and regulate those tensions. Sharing the loss of a loved one with friends or family can make the overwhelming pain of grief bearable. When we feel driven to take revenge on offending others, our selfobjects can ease the rage and slow us down. When we feel a compulsive sexual desire for an inappropriate object, selfobject others can help quell our sexual obsession by showing us its danger. Sometimes we lose inner strength as our ideals waver, we start to fragment, and others stop the disintegration with a firm shoulder to lean upon. Sometimes we lose track of who we are, fall into a deep despair, and others provide a restorative narrative. Sometimes we feel as though we are an alien unlike anyone else in existence—a pariah—and our friends confirm that we are human and one of them.

As Ernest Wolf points out, our need for selfobject support tends to be greatest at the transitional times of life. "At major turning points, such as the oedipal phase, early adolescence, marriage, parenthood, mid-life, or upon entering old age—the so called *life-crises*—there appears to be a heightened vulnerability of the self to being injured by inappropriate selfobject experiences" (1988, 65). I experienced self-selfobject failures at most of these junctures. My mother's overt seductiveness made it impossible to surrender my oedipal longings. My foray into adolescent love was crushed when my girlfriend dumped me for a best friend. My first marriage was a disaster which I entered out of a lowered self-esteem. The birth of my sons re-activated the trauma of my early childhood and sent me into endless headaches and a deep depression. At mid-life I knew that I had failed in marriage and was tottering on the abyss of alcohol dependency. These significant failures at crucial developmental times in my life propelled me into a depression so dark that I was finally forced to seek therapeutic help. In the psychodynamic therapies that followed, I received the kind of selfobject infusion that I needed to go on with life—to successfully re-marry, establish a vitalized professional career, and more deeply enjoy the vicissitudes of human life. I am now on the verge of old age—what Wolf and Erikson say is the final transition. Will I be able to make this transition successfully? The self is always vulnerable to loss of self-esteem; so we will see—I have a loving spouse and wonderful friends and family to help me through this transition—at least for now, but life is, indeed, precarious.

Kohut's concept of the selfobject has been criticized by some as immoral, for it advocates using others as a "means" for oneself rather than as "ends in themselves."[5] This is a misunderstanding, for Kohut never says that we should treat others as selfobjects *only*. He realizes that in the world past early childhood, we must recognize and respect selfobject others as also being independent sources of perception and action. Kant's famous statement is that to be moral one "must always treat others as ends in themselves, never as a means *only*" (1785, 46). We often, if not always, use others to perform all kinds of tasks for us, but we still need to treat them as human beings deserving respect and recognition. I have my hair cut, my car fixed, my house cleaned, etc.; but in using others to perform these tasks I do not violate their humanity unless I see them merely as functionaries for my use. Likewise, I can use others to perform selfobject functions for me without reducing them to being mere selfobjects. When Marcia soothes my wounded ego, I do not think of her as a slave or as someone whose only job in life is to be there for me; I deeply appreciate how she freely chooses to care for me without manipulation or bribery, and I know that I am there in the same way for her. Indeed, if we are dominating or controlling others as slaves, then the selfobject supplies we receive from these others can never be fully nourishing, because they are not freely given. Such manipulated care is an extortion and we know it; therefore, it cannot be experienced as genuine care.[6]

2.3 A Dialectical Concept of the Self

We are now able to appreciate Kohut's most stunning claim: that rather than being isolated atoms of psychological structure located within the psyches of autonomous persons, our selves are inherently relational—inherently part of a self-selfobject system. That is, when others play selfobject functions for me, they are not just friends helping me but are literally a part of myself. Insofar as they are performing self-functions, they are my self. Kohut understood this truth about the self in his consulting room where his narcissistically wounded patients would fall apart if he failed to adequately perform the functions of the self they needed. He literally became their selves while performing these functions.

This unity of self and selfobject makes sense given an operational definition of the self. That is, the self is that psychological configuration that performs a set of functions—regulating narcissistic tensions, soothing emotions/drives, giving a sense of personal coherence, etc. If "X" is performing these functions, then "X" is my self, whether it be located in me or another person. In this way who we are is in part constituted by our selfobject relationships. When one of our close friends or partners goes away for a while, we can feel that a part of us is lost. We become moderately dysfunctional. Our activities are not as focused; we fall into diffuse diversions; we don't sleep as soundly; we might overindulge in a calming substance such as alcohol. We are unable to fully "be ourselves" because part of our selves is missing.

Kohut's discovery that the self is inherently relational has led some contemporary thinkers to proclaim that the self is entirely composed

of its intersubjective relations—that the self is so thoroughly contextualized and intersubjective that there is no singular remainder to the
self once these intersubjective relations are erased. Indeed, a whole
movement of relational psychoanalysis has come into being—in part
from Kohut, but also from Harry Stack Sullivan, Steven Mitchell, and
Robert Stolorow. However, this shift from seeing the self as an isolated
Cartesian atom to seeing the self as only a set of intersubjective relationships is misguided, for the self is both a singular structure within
individual persons and a set of relationships with others. It is both a
particular structure (see Chapter 1) and a relational structure, a self-
selfobject system.

That is, Kohut's notion of the self is thoroughly dialectical insofar
as it holds that the self is both a singular structure and a set of selfobject relations. My erotic energy (see Chapter 3), organic ideals, and
singular ambitions are mine. They define what my self in its particularity is. When I am engaged in ambitiously realizing my ideals, I feel
most zestfully like myself. However, when I think of the self as a set of
functions, then I experience myself as relational, for these functions
can be, and often are, played by others. When Marcia greets me in the
morning with smiling eyes, my self-esteem is buoyed, my eros aroused,
and I awaken to my self.

This view of the self parallels the complementarity or wave/particle
duality principle in physics—one of the most important tenets in
physics—which states that every sub-atomic entity in the universe can
be conceived both as a particle and as a wave of energy. The characteristics of something's being a wave are different from the properties of
its being a particle. Yet, every sub-atomic entity has the characteristics
of both, depending on how we are looking at it. Likewise, the self is a
particle—a particular structure in a particular person; but it is also a
wave, for it extends out into others and is reflected back from them. We
are both individualized atoms of experience and what Rupert Sheldrake
calls "morphic fields"—systems of connectedness in which we are so
deeply fused with others that we can respond to what is happening in
them and they to what is happening in us, even if we are physically
distant from one another (2017). In another theme from physics,
Kohut wrote that when we empathically interact with another person,
the empathy changes the very object we are observing, just as in physics the way in which the observer observes changes what is observed.

2.4 The Importance of Selfobjects for Ethics and Society—Back to Aristotle

This concept of self as both singular and relational is of utmost importance, for it provides a substantial reason for wanting to become an ethical person.[7] In thinking about what it means to be an ethical person, I want to abandon its modern formulations in Kant and utilitarianism and return to the virtue ethics of Aristotle. Kant wanted ethics to be a system of moral laws that would have the same validity in human life that the laws of physics have in nature. The problem is that there are no principles that have no exceptions. Even more important, Kant thinks of ethics as a way to *constrain* our pursuits of life, rather than as a way to actualize our selves. Hence, the question arises for Kant as to why we should be moral and constrain ourselves rather than doing what appears to be in our self-interest when the two conflict. Why abide by "Do not cheat" if one can make millions of dollars by doing some insider trading on the stock market and are almost completely assured that they will not be caught? Kantians can offer no compelling reason not to cheat—no reason to adopt an ethical point of view.

The utilitarians fare no better. Why should I devote myself to producing the greatest general happiness rather than just my own? After all, Adam Smith proclaimed that we should be motivated by purely selfish interests when we engage in market transactions, for then the market will reach an equilibrium (below which prices cannot fall further). Why should my happiness count no more than anyone else's? Like Kantianism, utilitarianism can offer no compelling answer to the question of why we should want to be moral persons when being moral appears to conflict with our personal interests. That is, neither of these portraits of the ethical person—the law-abiding, "no exceptions" rigorous moralist nor the altruistic agent bent on maximizing social well-being—is compelling for modern, individualistic, post-religious persons.

But there is a different concept of the ethical person—that of Aristotle and most ancient ethics, including Stoicism, Platonism, Confucianism, Taoism, and Buddhism. In these traditions, the ethical person develops moral character traits and acts according to these predispositions rather than a set of rules or principles. For all of them, good acts are done by good people and the key to living well is developing the kind of character that leads to both personal happiness and communal well-being. The virtuous person—one who is courageous, generous, self-controlled, just, and wise—is the kind of person who is able both to live well and help others live well.

In the ancient world, a trait was deemed a virtue, not because it was esteemed, but because it allowed the thing which had the virtue to function well. Hence, sharpness is the virtue of a knife; sight is the virtue that allows the eye to see. For Aristotle, the moral virtues help us to function as human beings able to rationally choose our lives because they moderate the passions, giving us space in which to deliberate about what best to do. They are the mean between the extremes relative to the person and the situation. For example, in response to situations of danger which arouse the emotion of fear, we can respond in ways that are cowardly, courageous, or foolhardy. Courage is the mean between the two extremes that allows us to feel fear without being either over-or underwhelmed by it, and this gives us the cognitive space to think about what best to do. Neither the cowardly nor the foolhardy think about what to do—the coward instantly runs away while the foolhardy person doesn't sense that there is any danger and thus there is no reason to think. It is the courageous person who, by moderating their fear, can develop a rational response about what to do in situations of danger. This pattern will hold true for all the moral virtues. Insofar as we moderate our passions, we can rationally direct our lives rather than having to react immediately. The moral virtues give us the possibility of delayed response, and this gap between stimulus and response is what allows us to bring our human powers of cognition into play.

Interestingly, the moral virtues have some of the same functions for Aristotle as the self does for Kohut. Both have the task of modulating the emotions and desires. Aristotle even says that one of the moral virtues is pride—what Kohut calls self-esteem. The extremes that we can fall into in relation to self-worth are vanity (boastfulness) and humility—both are dishonest accounts of who we are, for one is overblown and the other does not acknowledge our actual accomplishments.

If the moral virtues and the self have the same functions, are they the same? I don't think so, for the self is a structure of subjectivity while character traits are habits of responsiveness. However, I think that if one develops a self, then one must concomitantly develop moral virtues. Insofar as the self needs to modulate the drives and emotions, the person must develop habits of moderation. Without these predispositions, the self will not be able to perform its task. We can understand this in a Kohutian way by saying that when a child uses an idealized selfobject to soothe its emotions and concerns, it needs to transmutingly internalize the character traits of the idealized selfobject. That is, what transpires in transmuting internalization is the introjection of the predisposition to act in ways that modulate the emotions. I believe this paralleling of the functions of the moral virtues and those of the self allows us to see how persons with injured selves can still function well in relation to the emotions and desires if they have developed the Aristotelian character traits. And, indeed, we can think of the moral virtues as constituting a kind of self-structure, for they are performing a self-function. When we make this equation, we can read Aristotle's ethics as a precursor to Kohut's psychology. Aristotle is very nice company to have!

What Aristotle adds to Kohut is a psycho/social account of the kind of upbringing we need in order to develop moral character traits. We become virtuous by being positively reinforced by others when we do virtuous acts and negatively reinforced when we are vicious. We also become virtuous when we mimic others who are virtuous—what Kohut terms 'transmuting internalization." We become good by mimicking others who are good. Both reinforcement and modeling are crucial if we are to develop into virtuous human beings. We cannot become just without doing just acts, such as not demanding more than our fair share when lollipops are handed out. We cannot become courageous unless we do courageous acts, such as standing firm rather than running away when a soccer ball is roaring towards us. The development of these character traits helps us control tendencies towards greediness and fearfulness. I believe Aristotle's account of how we develop habits that moderate the power of the emotions and desires is an important addition to Kohut's concept of the self as a moderating inner structure. How could self-structure do its soothing, modulating work without the concomitant development of these character traits? Aristotle and Kohut go hand in hand. I doubt that self-structure can develop unless there is a parallel development of the moral virtues.

To Aristotle's list of moral virtues we need to add *empathy*, as we have found this is crucial in relation to both one's self and others, and *care*, the central virtue in most feminist ethics—the predisposition to attend to the needs of others with whom one has special relationships.[8] We cannot have genuinely supportive relations to others or ourselves without these two predispositions—to care and to have empathic concern.

Why should we develop the virtues? Why should we become empathic and caring human beings? Because without these traits we cannot sustain our self-structure. If we truly need selfobjects to sustain our selves, then we must be willing to be selfobjects for others. Reciprocity is necessary in adult life; if we are to receive crucial selfobject nourishment from others, we must be willing to give it ourselves. The question then arises as to what kind of person is best able to be a selfobject for others, and the answer is, as Aristotle said, those who develop the virtues. If we are not generous, we will likely be stingy in our ability to give. If we are not just, we might expect too much for ourselves and have a tendency not to give others their due. If we are not courageous, we are unlikely to allow ourselves to be vulnerable in a close intersubjective relationship. If we lack a sense of caring, we will not be motivated to be a selfobject for others, and if we lack empathy, we will not be able to know what others need from us.

In sum, persons who are best able to care for themselves are persons who have become ethical human beings. This is the great conclusion of both Aristotle and Kohut and is the most compelling answer as to why one would want to become a good person: *such persons are best able to sustain their selves.*

Aristotle gives a further reason for why it is good to be a good person: it is only virtuous people who can fully engage in one the most fulfilling of all human experiences: friendship.[9] It is difficult to fully love someone we don't think is a good person, and it is difficult to be fully loveable if one is a bad person. It is hard to genuinely love a cheater, a coward, a glutton, a spendthrift, a miser. We love others more deeply when we think of them as genuinely good persons who care for others. Hence, to establish a matrix of caring selfobjects who really are a part of one's self, it is important to become a virtuous person, not only because such a person is most able to supply the selfobject needs of others but is the kind of person others would want to help sustain. And, as important, when we think of ourselves as good persons, it tends to raise our internal self-esteem. Although the enhancement in self-esteem we get by thinking of ourselves as good persons tends to remain at the level of consciousness and has difficulty disrupting unconscious negative self-esteem, it nonetheless buoys us. Anything that helps make us loveable to ourselves helps enhance and sustain the self, for the self, as we will soon discover in the next chapter, is where our loving energies reside. In a dynamic that cannot be clear until Chapter 4, the self's eros infuses the ego, which can then in turn love the self and grant it increased self-esteem, thereby re-invigorating the self. In short, loving one's self is a self-conscious experience in which we have to relate ourselves to our selves. In becoming self-conscious of ourselves as good persons, we are better able to love our selves in this internal self-relationship.

Insofar as there are parts of ourselves or tendencies in ourselves that we cannot love because we consider them evil or wrong, we tend to psychologically dissociate from them by vertically splitting them off from our conscious self-conceptions and hence become multiple rather than achieving integrity. In this kind of negative multiplicity, one side of us proclaims our goodness but another part of us knows that we are frauds.[10] This is another crucial reason for becoming a genuinely good person: it allows one to achieve integrity. These insights from self psychology correspond fully with what Aristotle says:

> In a vicious man, as in the incontinent, things disagree, and for this reason it seems possible for a man to be his own enemy; but so far as he is single and indivisible, he is the object of desire to himself. Such is the good man and the man whose friendship is based on virtue; for the depraved man is not one but many, in the same day other than himself and fickle. So that a man's friendship for himself is reduced to the friendship of the good; for because a man is in a manner like himself, single, and good for himself, so far he is a friend and object of desire to himself.
>
> (*Eudemian Ethics*, 2014, 13–20)

Integrity for self psychology is not the same as it has typically been conceived in a more rationalistic framework, such as Kant's. Integrity in rational ethical systems typically means to abide by one's principles no matter what: never lie, cheat, steal, etc., even when such acts would be to one's benefit. If one abides by these principles always, then one has integrity and is being true to themselves. However, we find that such morally upright persons can in fact be cold, cruel, and inflexible in cases that call for loving tenderness and making exceptions to the rules. This notion of integrity thinks of a person simply as who they consciously take themselves to be and uses rationality as an attempt to achieve unity in the psyche. Freud and the psychoanalytic tradition have taught us how misguided this view is, as does experience. There is case after case of upright moralists—especially staunch Christian preachers—being sexually promiscuous, cheating, and lying, all the while pretending to be pure and upstanding. They suffer drastic vertical splits.

Integrity for self psychology means having the self always at the center of experience and action. For the self to be the core of our experience, it needs to be strong, vitalized, and coherent, and, as we have seen, it cannot be this way unless it is intertwined with supporting selfobjects. It cannot attain this kind of support unless a person develops the virtues of care, empathy, and a deep concern for others. In other words, the self needs to be loving to be itself—and loving means to always have care and empathy. These traits cannot go on a holiday when we are with people we dislike or consider to be our enemies, for if they do, we lose our selves, we lose our integrity. In short, we need to remain empathic and caring with all human beings—and perhaps all sentient creatures—if we are to keep the self at the core of our experiencing. When we are not loving, we lose our integrity and lose our selves.[11]

2.5 From Selfobjects to Intersubjectivity and Relationality

The major development in self psychology since Kohut has been the blossoming of the intersubjective and relational schools of psychoanalysis. These schools amplify the implications of Kohut's concept of the selfobject in their substantial re-conceiving of the nature of the therapeutic relationship.[12] Rather than thinking of therapy along what is called a one-person model in which the therapist is understood as an objective scientific observer of the subjectivity of the patient, these new schools present a paradigm in which the subjectivities of both analyst and patient engage with one another. This makes sense if the therapist is indeed playing selfobject functions for the patient, for both are intertwined as essential sectors of the patient's psyche. However, the intersubjective and relational theories oftentimes go far beyond seeing therapists merely as selfobjects whose role is to play self-functions when their patients are unable to do so. Rather, they see therapists as needing to provide adequate emotional resonance all the time for the client—as attempting to be emotionally responsive to and actively engaging with the patient. An actively engaged therapist who is aware of their emotional responses to the emotional states of their patients is one who is likely to be experienced as more supportive and helpful than the distant aloof therapist of the past.

For Jessica Benjamin (and several other theorists), a new kind of existence, "the third," appears when two people recognize one another, acknowledge their differences, and empathically come together to mutually co-create experience in a kind of intersubjective rhythmic dance in which both subjects actively participate. For Benjamin, when we engage others in thirdness, we overcome the typical relationship of twoness—"a relational formation in which the other appears as object or objectifying, unresponsive or injuring, threatening to erase one's own subjectivity or be oneself erased" (2018, 4). The world of twoness tends to be a world in which we are either doing subjects or done-to objects. In contrast, when we allow ourselves to engage in an experience of empathic recognition of each other's subjective reality, a kind of third subject appears that expresses the interplay of the mutual subjectivities, an interplay that overcomes the subject/object dialectic.

For example, although Marcia and I both love art, we have quite different tastes. When we purchase art, we do not typically have one of us choose and then the next time the other. Rather, the art we purchase is usually loved by and expresses a being that is both of us—an intersubjective "we." It might not be the painting that I would have chosen first, nor is it one that Marcia would have chosen; but it is one that we both, as a "third," love. Each of us has our individual lives, perspectives, and preferences, but much of our shared experience exists within an intersubjective third. This "we-creature" often surprises each of us in what and how it chooses. It is a realm of growth, interaction, and creative development that exists beyond the subject/object relations that are so common in modern life. Notice how different this "we" that is birthed out of mutual recognition and empathy is from a rationally negotiated "we" that achieves the goal of each person getting to be a subject by alternating the subject/object pairings. "You got your way last time; now it is my turn."

As important as the intersubjective and relational schools have been for enriching the interactive therapeutic possibilities that are implied in the self-selfobject relationship that Kohut discovered, some of them have also tended to negate the structural framework of self psychology in their significant de-emphasis on the self and hyper-emphasis on relationality. Indeed, Robert Stolorow and George Atwood go so far as to declare that Kohut's concept of the self is a reified notion that needs to be discarded:

> The theoretical language of self psychology, with its noun, "the self," reifies the experiencing of selfhood and transforms it into a metaphysical entity with thing-like properties .... A thing remains the self-same thing that it is whether it is with you or one of us. Reifying and transforming the experience of selfhood into an entity ... strips such experience of its exquisite context-sensitivity and context-dependence—the very context-embeddedness that it was Kohut's great contribution to have articulated!
>
> (2019, 92–93)

As I hope to have shown, Kohut's concept of self is not a reified notion, for it does not conceive of the self as "a thing" but as a dynamic structured process that can be used to explain many aspects of psychological life; aspects that cannot be explained merely by thinking of psychological life as a set of relational interactions. While such approaches to psychological life are right in thinking that who and what we are emerges out of our intersubjective relationships (as Kohut said), they tend to miss that these relationships precipitate into psychological structure—precipitate into *a self*.

However, Stolorow wants to do more than attack Kohut's concept of self as a reified notion; he wants to replace the whole self-selfobject framework of self psychology with an orientation that he terms *phenomenological contextualism*. His position

> is phenomenological in that it investigates and illuminates worlds of emotional experience and the structures that organize them. It is contextual in that it holds that such structures take form, both

developmentally and in the therapeutic situation, in constitutive relational or intersubjective contexts.

(2015, 123–124)

The self is no longer recognized as a central concept; it has been replaced by "emotional experience" and "contexts." While Stolorow denies that "an emphasis on relational or intersubjective contexts of emotional experience de-focuses, or even nullifies, experiences of individualized selfhood" (2015, 59), he thinks that experiences of a sense of selfhood neither need, nor point to, something like an actual self that lies behind these experiences. That is, he wants to eliminate the structural framework of self psychology which focuses on the development of the self, how it can be injured, and how it can be restored through psychoanalytic therapy.

As I said at the end of the introduction to this book, there is something very strange and misguided about "having a sense of selfhood" without there being an actual self to give rise to this experience. Indeed, one might (as I once did) have a delusional sense of selfhood when in fact one's self either does not exist or is severely fragmented. There is no way to check whether one's "sense of self" is a delusion or an accurate report of a felt internal structure without having a theory of what a self is and how it functions. That is, we need a theory of the self in order to determine what constitutes evidence for its existence and health.

A further problem with a theory that overemphasizes contextuality is that it has difficulty articulating a theory of maturity. With Kohut we discovered that maturity involves decreasing one's neediness for selfobjects as one's self develops and becomes more able to perform its functions. That is, we have a theory that can explain why it is that the contextuality of childhood is different from that of adulthood. However, if there is no self that can grow and mature but only one's intersubjective relations with others, then we need a theory to explain why and how adult contextuality is different from that of childhood. While it is possible to elucidate phenomenological markers for how mature relationality is different, it will be difficult to explain how this difference comes about without a notion of a self that has matured.

Finally, a theory that overly emphasizes intersubjective relationality has problems articulating a theory of integrity and personal responsibility. It is not a complex of intersubjective relationships that perform acts, but singular persons. It is not our contexts that are held responsible for what we do but ourselves as independent agents, agents that have a core singularity that allows us to criticize and reject pressures from the world that would cause us to commit crimes. As described in Chapter 1, Kohut gives a new way of understanding integrity as having a psyche revolving around a coherent self; intersubjectivity theory has, as far as I know, no equivalent way of articulating what it means to be a person with integrity.

In short, my major concern with the ascendance of intersubjectivity and contextualism is that we lose a theory about the psychological processes and structures that give us the possibility of being singular, unique creatures whose experience is essentially our own—beings who can be "unique centers of initiative and perception." The truth of who we are as humans is dialectical: we are both thoroughly immersed in and emerge out of contexts and yet are also individual subjects who can transcend our contextualizations. An overemphasis on our singular independent natures (the Nietzschean free spirit) produces a concept of abstract individuality (the person abstracted from all contextuality); while an overemphasis on contextuality and relationality produces an abstract sociality in that there are no individuals who make it up—just a massive matrix of relationships and socially coded behavior.[13]

2.6 Intersubjective Self Psychology

It is of vast importance that there be a unification of intersubjectivity theory and self psychology, for intersubjectivity theory has an enriched conceptualization of the therapeutic space, while self psychology has a more profound understanding of the dynamics of the human psyche. Such a unification has already been proposed in a volume edited by George Hagman, Harry Paul, and Peter B. Zimmerman: *Intersubjective Self Psychology: A Primer* (2019). This volume accepts from intersubjectivity theory the deepened notion of the curative dynamics of the clinical space in which psychological material from the patient, analyst, and their intersubjective intersection is acknowledged and processed, but retains from self psychology that the aim of therapy is to promote the repair of injured selves.

Intersubjective self psychology focuses on the forward and trailing edges emanating from the selves of both the patient and analyst and their interaction in the intersubjective field. Leading edge transferences from patients represent hopes that their traumatized selves might be repaired and once again have a positive developmental trajectory. Leading edges in analysts relate to their hopes that they can be effective, meaningful therapists for their patients. Trailing edge transferences have to do with the dread in both patient and analyst that the therapy might re-evoke past traumas along with their fragmenting effects. By attending to these transferences in both patient and analyst, a relationship is formed in which the selves of both can flourish. In short, the conceptual metapsychological framework of self psychology is melded with an intersubjective understanding of the therapeutic space. I believe that fusing Kohut's grasp of the self and its centrality in psychological dynamics with the enriched grasp of the processes by which intersubjective therapy can foster self-growth is the future of psychoanalysis.

Notes

1 Kohut will in his last works relinquish drive theory, but in *The Analysis of the Self* and even *The Restoration of the Self* he continues to write about the drives as psychic motivations.
2 It would be interesting to think of Freud's "censor" in his topographic model as playing the role that the self plays for Kohut.
3 Research has clearly supported Kohut's claim. Mark Spitz as early as the 1940's found that orphaned children placed in hospitals that attended carefully to their hygienic and physical needs but did not hold them, comfort them, etc. –did not attend to their psychological needs—became sickly and often died. The more antiseptic the hospital, the greater the death rate (see Lewis, T, Amini, F., Lannon, R. (2001, 69–70)).
4 James Gilligan has extensively interviewed violent prisoners and found that their experience of shame, more than any other factor, was implicated in their becoming criminally violent. See his *Violence: Reflections on a National Epidemic* (1997).
5 See in particular Frank Summers' *A Psychoanalytic Vision* (2013) and Jessica Benjamin's *The Bonds of Love* (1988).
6 Hegel's analysis of the master/slave relationship in his *Phenomenology* is the basis for this claim that one cannot receive recognition from another whom one has objectified.
7 I have written about the ethical implications of self psychology in a number of places, but most extensively in *Why It Is Good to Be Good: Ethics, Kohut's Self Psychology, and Modern Society* (2010).
8 See Virginia Held's *The Ethics of Care* (2006).
9 See books VIII and IX of Aristotle's *Nicomachean Ethics*.

10 See Arnold Goldberg's *Being of Two Minds* (1999) for an in-depth analysis of the vertical split.

11 Several psychoanalysts—especially Donna Orange—prefer to work with the ethics of Emmanuel Levinas, who, like Aristotle, does not understand ethics as the application of rules or principles to a situation, but the direct responsiveness to the face of the other. Levinas claims that such an appearance demands of us an infinite responsibility for this other. I prefer Aristotle's ethics of character because I think we are much more likely to respond to the other out of the character we have developed rather than an ontological response from the being of our beings, which is not enough to relate to who we are as full human beings. There is too much dualistic rather than synthetic thinking in Levinas' philosophy.

12 There has erupted a battle in recent issues of *Psychoanalysis, Self, and Context* as to whether what is implied in the new schools of intersubjectivity and relationality is a natural development out of Kohut's concept of the therapist as a selfobject or represents such novel and innovative elements as to constitute a significant new movement within the psychoanalytic tradition. See volume *16*(4) and volume *17*(1).

13 I provide a much more thorough critique of Stolorow's position in two articles: "A Critical Appraisal of Stolorow's Criticism of Kohut's Concept of the Self and his Contextualization of Heidegger's Notion of Authenticity, Plus the Possibility of an Intersubjective Self Psychology," *Psychoanalysis, Self, and Context*, 16(4), fall 2021, 338–351; "Metapsychology, the Self, and the Tragic: A Reply to Stolorow and Teicholz's Responses." *Psychoanalysis, Self, and Context*, 16(4), fall 2021, 363–370.

References

Aristotle. (2014). *Aristotle's Ethics: Writings from the Complete Works*. Eds. J. Barnes & A. Kenny. Princeton, NJ: Princeton University Press.

Benjamin, J. (1988). *The Bonds of Love*. New York: Pantheon.

———. (2018). *Beyond Doer and Done To: Recognition Theory, Intersubjectivity and the Third*. New York: Routledge.

Gilligan, J. (1997). *Violence: Reflections on a National Epidemic*. New York: Vintage.

Goldberg, A. (1999). *Being of Two Minds*. Lanham, MD: The Analytic Press.

Hagman, G., Paul, H., & Zimmerman, P. (2019). *Intersubjective Self Psychology: A Primer*. New York: Routledge.

Hegel, G. (1807/1977). *Phenomenology of the Spirit*. Tr. A. Miller. Oxford: Oxford University Press.

Held, V. (2006). *The Ethics of Care: Personal, Political, Global*. Oxford: Oxford University Press.

Kant, I. (1785). *Fundamental Principles of the Metaphysics of Morals*. Tr. T. Abbott. Garden City, NY: Dover Publications (2005).

Kohut, H. (1971). *The Analysis of the Self*. New York: International Universities Press.

———. (1977). *The Restoration of the Self*. New York: International Universities Press.

———. (1984). *How Does Analysis Cure?* Chicago: University of Chicago Press.

———. (1987). *The Kohut Seminars on Self Psychology and Psychotherapy with Adolescents and Young Adults*. Ed. M. Elson. New York: W.W. Norton.

———. (1996). *The Chicago Institute Lectures*. Eds. P. Tolpin & M. Tolpin. Hillsdale, NJ: Analytic Press.

Lewis, T, Amini, F., & Lannon, R. (2001). *A General Theory of Love*. New York: Vintage Books.

Riker, J. (2010). *Why It Is Good to Be Good: Ethics, Kohut's Self Psychology, and Modern Society*. Lanham, MD: Jason Aronson.

Sheldrake, R. (2017). *Science and Spiritual Practices: Transformative Experiences and Their Effects on Our Bodies, Brains, and Health*. Berkeley, CA: Counterpoint.

Stolorow, R. (2015). "A Phenomenological-Contextual, Existential, and Ethical Perspective on Emotional Trauma." *Psychoanalytic Review*, *102*(1), 123–138.

Stolorow, R., & Atwood, G. (2019). *The Power of Phenomenology: Psychoanalytic and Philosophical Perspectives*. New York: Routledge.

Summers, F. (2013). *The Psychoanalytic Vision: The Experiencing Subject, Transcendence, and the Therapeutic Process*. New York: Routledge.

Terman, D. (2021). "The Negative Selfobject." *Psychoanalysis, Self, and Context*, *16*(4), 380–389.

Thoreau, H.D. (1854). *Walden*. In *Walden and Other Writings* (pp. 1–312). Ed. B. Atkinson. New York: Modern Library (2000).

Wolf, E. (1988). *Treating the Self*. New York: Guilford Press.

Chapter 3

The Self as Erotic Striving*

3.1 What is Libido?

The first two chapters were mainly clarifications and expansions of Kohut's key concepts, including the implications of these concepts for ethics and the construction of personal life. This chapter is different; it is a creative exploration of the fundamental force that lies behind the development of the self: narcissistic libido. While Kohut is unprecedented in his analysis of the qualities and transformations of narcissistic libido, he never actually says what libido is, but assumes it as a primal motivational presence. I will inquire into what the libido is that underlies the transformations of narcissism into a self. In embarking on this exploration, we plunge into a territory that lurks between psychology and ontology, for we are inquiring into what ultimately motivates human beings—what ultimately it means to be human. The fundamental conclusion of this inquiry is that the energy of the self is a desexualized *eros*, and this constitutes the heart of my attempt to revision Kohut's self psychology. It is, I believe, a decisive addition to the theory, one that makes it far more exciting and coherent.

Theorists from antiquity through modern science have sought to find some primal motivation that is different from ordinary emotions and desires and whose pursuit is the essence of human life. For instance, Plato in his *Symposium* holds that we are most profoundly motivated by *Eros* and its longing for Beauty. Aristotle said that we have an internal "*entelechy*" that motivates us to strive to become fully mature human beings able to rationally direct our lives and know what is ultimately real. For both these Greek philosophers the fundamental

* An earlier version of this chapter was published as an article in *Psychoanalysis, Self, and Context*, 19(1).

DOI: 10.4324/9781003303657-5

motivating force is a *developmental* urge—an urge to keep growing and developing until our deepest human potentialities can be realized.

Others, such as the Sophists, Epicurus, and the utilitarians (Bentham, Hume, Mill), found that what motivates us most is simply the attainment of pleasure and avoidance of pain. Pleasure comes mainly from the satisfaction of desires; pain from their frustration. There is nothing developmental about this primal motivating urge to attain pleasure and avoid pain; if we develop, it is because we our bodies and society force us to.

Still others, including Spinoza, Darwin, and Freud, are drive theorists who variously describe one or several basic drives, such as Spinoza's *conatus* (the drive to remain in existence), Darwin's reproductive fitness and survival, and the early Freud's survival and libido. Typically, these drives do not include a developmental impetus, although Freud describes a developmental sequence from autoeroticism to heterosexual genitality as normal. However, this development does not seem to be governed by some innate longing to develop and grow, but is simply the fact that our biology, for the most part, demands it. Freud, at least in his earlier work, fused drive theory with pleasure theory by hypothesizing that we are fundamentally motivated to achieve pleasure and that we do this mainly by discharging our drives. Rather than being a developmentalist, he holds that humans are wired to want to remain in the libidinal stage they have reached and only move beyond it to escape pain—the pain of too much excitation building up. (Freud radically changes his theory in his later work when he re-defines libido as eros and finds a force that seeks expansiveness rather than mere discharge—more on this later.)

What does Kohut say about what fundamentally motivates us? Is he a pleasure theorist, a drive theorist, or a developmentalist? In *The Analysis of the Self* and other early writings, Kohut seems to say that the process of developing ideals commences because of a significant failure of caretakers to tend to the needs of the baby and then failures of our idealized selfobjects to exhibit perfection. The reason that we do not re-identify with perfection, but re-integrate it in terms of ideals, is because the world and our own sense of reality lets us know that we are not perfect. The same scenario seems to be true for ambitions. We relinquish our infantile grandiosity mainly because failures and reality tell us we are not the greatest beings in the world, but, as with perfection, we try to hang on to as much of our early narcissistic greatness as we can. In short, the process of transforming narcissism from its primitive instantiation into a self seems to be driven not by an inner urge but by events and pressures delivered by the external world. In this way, Kohut seems to follow Freud's economics—that we relinquish a libidinal position only when we are forced to. However, once the self comes into existence, it then becomes developmental and dynamic as we strive to realize its ideals and ambitions.

In this view of Kohut, there does not seem to be an internal impetus to develop, but external conditions push the child into transmuting its perfection and grandiosity into the rudiments of a self. Does this mean that we are still in a pleasure/pain schema? Does Kohut's adoption of Freud's concept of libido mean that he is still a drive theorist? How are we to understand Kohut's writings about the self's needing to continually develop into more mature forms? Does this have to do only with the structure of the self being ideals and ambitions or is there a more fundamental internal pressure to develop into ever more expansive iterations of our selves?

The answer to these questions lies in examining what Kohut might mean by "narcissistic libido." While we determined in the first chapter that narcissistic libido is characterized by the qualities of perfection and grandiosity, we did not discover what the libido is that has these qualities. What is libido? What is this underlying force that lies behind narcissism?

Kohut, in his 1974 lectures at the Chicago Psychoanalytic Institute, asks exactly this question: "What is libido?" and goes on to say that answers to this question "can be too concrete" if they are biological or chemical, but can also be "so slippery that very little is useful" (1974/1996, 179). He continues:

> as long as we stay within the conceptual framework of libido theory an important device is available to us—one could call it a crucial conceptual gimmick of psychoanalytic theory—we can use the term, the concept of cathexis… We can recognize that there is an urge in us and that it can be stronger or weaker.
>
> (1974/1996, 181, 183)

That is, there is a "psychic energy" that is experienced as greater or lesser pressure. He develops his connection of libido and energy in

The Restoration of the Self by identifying the self with a tension gradient between the plus and minus poles of a magnet (1977, 184). But, as we discovered in Chapter 1, the notion of the self's energy as a tension gradient is hardly adequate, as it is too experientially distant and mechanical a concept to express Kohut's more humanistic psychoanalytic theory. So, we need to return to the original notion of narcissistic libido and ask what it might mean to think of the self as emerging out of this kind of libidinal energy. Does Kohut think of libido as a drive, as part of a pleasure-seeking psyche, or as a developmental impetus? What is this primal "libidinal urge" that lies behind all we do?

3.2 Narcissistic Libido as *Eros*

Since Kohut situates his exploration of narcissism within classical libido theory, we turn to Freud to see if he can help us understanding what libido is. While Freud usually equates libido with "the energy of the sexual instincts and that energy alone" (1924, 35), he several times says that all he means by libido is "love." Here are two telling quotes:

> Libido is the energy, regarded as a quantitative magnitude ... of those instincts which have to do with all that may be comprised under the word 'love.'
>
> (1921, 90)

> We use the word 'sexuality' in the same comprehensive sense as that in which the German language uses the word *lieben* ('to love').
>
> (1910, 223)

If libido is not merely a sexual drive, but love in all its comprehensive human meanings, then I think that we can see the narcissistic libido that transforms into Kohut's notion of the self as some form of love. The quantitative energy of any and every motivation is the amount of *pressure* we feel to do work to satisfy the motivation. Kohut says that the pressure to attain our ideals is "*love.*" "Our ideals are our internal leaders: we love them and are longing to reach them" (1966/1985, 105). Although Kohut says that the kind of pressure we feel to act on our ambitions is a "push," it is easy to see that behind the push is the need for self-esteem, and self-esteem is nothing other than the love for oneself. Hence, the tension arc that binds the poles of the self together must be love, not some kind of magnetic energy.

However, "love" is a vague term used for all kinds of feelings. The Greeks distinguished among many forms of love, such as the kind of love we feel for family members (*philia*), the kind of love God feels for humans (*agape*), and an embodied kind of love, *eros*. Eros is love that is felt in the body and expressed through the body and, as such, is always particularized. It is not an ethereal or generalized soul-love, but a particular love for and longing to unite with particularized objects—a love for this special person, this particular landscape unfolding before me, this particular hike that I am taking through these particular Colorado mountain meadows, this extraordinary painting by Cezanne. That is, eros expresses our singularity, our embodied existence in the world. Embodied love—eros—is the celebration of being incarnated. Just as for Freud "the ego is a bodily ego" (1923, 26), so is eros a bodily love.

Freud replaces "libido" with "*eros*" in his later works in part because he needed to find a motive for why humans sought to get well in psychoanalysis when the treatment itself involved so much pain (Lear, 2004), but also because he needed a motivation to explain why humans strove to create communities and other groupings that were not simply sexual couplings. Jonathan Lear claims that the shift from libido to eros is far more revolutionary than the addition of the death drive, which looks very much like the pleasure principle—a fundamental need to reduce tension. For Lear, moving from libido to eros is Freud's shift from a mammalian psychology of sexual reproduction to a human psychology of seeking all kinds of harmonious unions.

Freud says that "The main purpose of Eros [is] that of uniting and binding" and that eros "aims at complicating life and at the same time, of course, preserving it" (1923, 45, 40).

> I may now add that civilization is a process in the service of Eros, whose purpose is to combine single human individuals, and after that families, then races, peoples and nations, into one great unity, the unity of mankind. Why this has to happen, we do not know; the work of Eros is precisely this.
>
> (1930, 122)

In sum, it seems that Freud is saying that eros is a powerful internal pressure to seek unifications, both within the psyche and the world, and that sexual coupling is merely one form of the erotic. Eros is a life-affirming creative impetus to generate greater inner psychic harmonies and more expansive forms of external togetherness. However, when it comes to elaborating further on the essential nature of eros, Freud defers to Plato:

> What psychoanalysis calls sexuality was by no means identical with the impulsion towards a union of the two sexes or towards producing a pleasurable sensation in the genitals; it had far more resemblance to the all-inclusive and all-embracing love of Plato's *Symposium*.
>
> (1925, 218)[1]

Let's follow Freud's suggestion and turn to Plato to see if his concept of eros can help us deepen Kohut's theory of the self. I think it can, for Plato offers four characteristics of eros that, when amalgamated into Kohut's theory, make it more coherent, vibrant, and exciting: (1) erotic love seeks to connect/unite with others; (2) eros is deeply related to beauty—to the aesthetic, (3) eros is a *daimon*—a spirit that is unique for each person; and (4) eros is developmental—it always seeks more complex and mature states of unification.

(1) Since the self cannot develop in childhood without selfobjects helping to perform its functions, Kohut's theory needs to posit that there is a primal longing to connect with others who can offer selfobject nourishment. Eros is the kind of primal motivating force which lovingly seeks to bond with others and which feels nourished by receiving love from them. That is, narcissistic libido must be conceived as erotic, for it is not only a love of oneself but the kind of love that seeks unification with others. If we see narcissistic libido as eros, it can explain why infants are both autoerotic and longing to connect with selfobjects. As we grow up, we find ourselves wanting to erotically expand into wider, more profound unions with lovers, friends, subject matters, the cosmos. To be is to be connected; it is eros that seeks unions and the expansiveness of life.

(2) Eros is that primal motivation which seeks and is nourished by beauty. Socrates begins his speech in the *Symposium* by saying that the previous speaker, Agathon, is wrong in claiming that eros is a beautiful god because we only long for what we lack, and since eros seeks the beautiful, it cannot itself be beautiful. In this stunning interchange with Agathon, Socrates makes two crucial claims about eros, namely, that it arises out of lack and that beauty arouses it. The first claim is that the human soul lacks beauty because it is incomplete and disorganized, as there is no center, and a chaos of conflicting desires and emotions swirls it this way and that. Eros is the one motivation that seeks harmonic organization of the whole psyche rather than just being one more desire seeking its atomized satisfaction without regard to the whole. In short, eros is the motivation that causes us to strive to achieve coherent, harmonic, functional—beautiful—psyches. Given that Kohut assigns the function of generating psychic harmony to the self, seeing the self's energy as eros fits perfectly with his theory.

There is another gaping lack in the soul according to Socrates: the presence of death, the knowledge of our mortality. Eros is that motivation that seeks to attain immortality, first by procreating children through sex but also through all forms of creativity. The final longing of eros is for the absolute form of Beauty, for when we gaze on this eternal, unchanging form, our souls take on its character and "if any human being could become immortal it would be he" (*Symposium*, 212b). Kohut, obviously, will not try to solve the problem of mortality by gazing on an eternal, unchanging form, but he says that mature narcissists are persons who have come to terms with mortality and have become wise by transforming their ideals to more universal ones. Such persons enter a state of "cosmic narcissism." I think this is as close to Plato as one can come without travelling the road into metaphysics. We might say that the empathic, creative, laughing, wise soul of the mature narcissist is a "beautiful soul," for it has achieved a fullness of integration.

Two of the most frequent terms Kohut uses to describe a healthy self are "coherence" and "harmony." These are aesthetic terms used to describe a whole that works as one. It is in the seeking of beauty, the creating of beauty, the cherishing of beauty in which we develop our selves and psyches, thereby realizing our humanity.

The aesthetic dimension of human lives is not a nice extra, an entertainment that comes after the pragmatic work of survival and reproduction. It is the essence of who we are. As Emerson says, "The world thus exists to the soul to satisfy the desire of beauty. This element I call an ultimate end. No reason can be asked or given why the soul seeks beauty" (1836/1982, 48).

(3) A third major claim Socrates makes about eros further connects it to self psychology: eros is a *daimon*. For the ancient Greeks, *daimones* were divine spirits, but not Olympian gods.[2] They could traverse between the divine realm and human realm, and when they entered someone, they filled that person with spirit. When we erotically fall in love with someone, some place, some activity, we fill with spirited vitality, as if some god had shot us with an arrow of life. This mythic language captures iconic truths about our experience of eros. First, it seems to have no source other than itself—it is primordial. Not only are we born with an innate spirit that is most who we are, but we cannot arrange to fall in love or decide what we will love, for erotic love comes upon us in spontaneous, sudden ways. That is, everyone has a unique self and more than any other aspect of who we are, this daimonic spirit is who we are. We feel most our selves when we are erotically loving. Our eros feels like a gift from the gods; when it erupts in us, we feel that we have left the ordinary humdrum of life and entered a divine state of being.

Heraclitus, the riddling pre-Socratic philosopher, aphoristically wrote, "*Ethos Daimon.*" This is often translated as "A person's character is their daimon," but I think it really means that the essence of persons—their selves—are their daimonic spirits. If we fuse Heraclitus, Plato, and Kohut, we can say that the essence of who we are is our erotic self, our inner daimon. It is our spirit that expresses what is singular and unique about us, whereas our character traits, personality construction, etc. can all appear to be shared by many and even socially constructed. Underneath the various characteristics through which we are identified, there is a singular self, a unique *daimon*, a fundamental *eros*, the unique spirit that is the essence of who anyone is. This daimonic spirit cannot be captured by any set of descriptors but it is who we experience ourselves and others most to be. In short, the self is that in our souls which harbors our spirit—it is not just a structure of ideals/ambitions or a set of functions, it is our singular unique spirit. When a person's self is crushed, so is their spirit. Surprisingly, a number of philosophers, including Plato, Emerson, and Jung find that when we are being our most singular selves, we also express universal truths. Daimonic individuals locate and express something universal about what it means to be human.

(4) A fourth truth about eros that we learn from Plato is that it is a developmental impetus. It seeks ever expansive and complex unifications, ever richer forms of beauty. What we want to make beautiful is, of course, our souls and this is dependent on the development of our selves. Unlike Plato, who holds that there is a final completion to erotic striving—namely the experience of the Form of Beauty, Kohut thinks that there can be no final good, no final completion to the self. Insofar as our selves are structured around ideals, we must always keep striving to realize them. That is, the self is a dynamic psychological configuration— the source of our endless restlessness to go beyond ourselves. Our ideals need to keep complexifying if they are to remain ideals rather than facts about who were once were. Nietzsche proclaimed that the essence of being a free spirit—a truly individuated person—is to engage in "self-overcoming," a process in which we continually seek to go beyond any self-realization that we have attained (1883/1978).

That the self is an erotic striving that never can be fully satisfied explains why Kohut calls humans "tragic man" in distinction from Freud's "guilty man." For Freud we are inherently guilty because we harbor transgressional wishes; for Kohut, we are tragic because we harbor a nuclear self whose ideals and ambitions can never be fully realized, both because the world often opposes them but also because those values need always to transcend our actual realizations to remain ideals and ambitions. Kohut's concept of the self is not one of a set identity but of potentialities that need to unfold as life progresses. Seeing the self as erotic striving allows us to grasp how the self can be both deeply fulfilled while it is striving (for this is its essence) and also unfulfilled, for its ideals always exceed its actuality. It is the impossibility of the self's completion that lies behind Kohut's calling humans "tragic man."

We posed a question at the beginning of this chapter as to whether Kohut's psychology was ultimately one in which we are fundamentally motivated by drives, a pleasure/pain calculus, or a developmental entelechy. Kohut clearly distinguishes his self psychology from drive theory, as there is nothing in his concept of the self which locates it in a sector of the body or which exhibits driven activity. Kohut also distinguishes life as motivated by the pleasure and reality principles and that motivated by a self:

> Every individual has two courses open to him and every individual, in one way or another, follows both of them. In his ordinary day every man lives by the pleasure and reality principles: He is the man of work and love. But no man is excluded from participating in the tragic dimensions of life.... There will be periods, at least moments, in the life of every man when he becomes aware, if only dimly, of a yearning that does not relate to the attainment of the pleasureful discharge of drive-wishes but to the compelling urge to realize the deep-rooted design of his nuclear self. Man is propelled by both of these forces, and human life lacking either of them is incomplete.
>
> (1985, 38)

> The living out of the pattern of the self provides an experience that is different from pleasure, even from the most sublimated forms of pleasure. I'll use a word for it, even though I know it's a word that will arouse the suspicions of the scientist: the word is "joy."
>
> (1996, 191)

Since the motivational urge lying behind the formation of a self is neither a drive nor the attaining of pleasure, but a teleological yearning to fulfill the nuclear program of the self resulting in joy, I think it makes sense to say that the narcissistic libido that becomes transformed into a self is a developmental force, and I think that this force is best understood, as Plato did, as eros. It is eros in its longing for beauty/harmony that can explain why the three basic elements of the self—ideals, ambitions, idiosyncratic traits—come together to form a self and also why the self can function to produce a wider psychic harmony. It also explains why we seek selfobject connectedness—eros is the motivation to unite and bond with others. In short, we develop selves and seek to mature into ever more complex beings not because external, contingent circumstances are forcing us to do so, but because there is an internal erotic urge to develop an organized psyche. Kohut is a developmentalist rather than a pleasure or drive theorist. Notice that development and the aesthetic are inherently fused. What it means to develop is to achieve ever more complex states of unification, of harmonic interrelationships. Beauty is the unification of diverse elements into the harmonious.

Seeing the quantitative energy of the self as eros not only allows us to make better sense of Kohut's self, but also provides a deep connection between self psychology and the later Freud. Freud's shifting from libido to eros indicates that he was intuiting the presence of the self, intuiting the presence of a psychic sector that was longing for development and loving connections with the world.[3] That is, he was sensing the presence of a psychological agency—the self—that differed from the ego and id and which had its own motivational source that was not an id drive but an entirely different kind of pressure—the urge to expand and grow. If this is true, then we can see Kohut's self psychology as a legitimate development of Freud's late insights into the human psyche. And, of course, identifying the energy of the self as eros ties Kohut to Plato's *Symposium*, considered by many to be one of the most profound works ever written on what it means to be human.[4] In short, in recognizing the energy of the self as eros, we can see Kohut as the legitimate heir of two of the most profound explorers of the human soul—Plato and Freud.

There are other important benefits to positing that the energy of the self is eros. It can explain why persons with fragmented selves tend to compensate by sexualizing and why they fill with narcissistic rage. Further, if we see empathy as a form of eros, we can explain why empathy can be so powerful in generating, sustaining, and repairing self-structure, and it can help clinicians understand why erotic transferences are really forward-edge/selfobject transferences and not self-negating defenses. Finally, and most important, identifying eros as the energy of the self gives us a strong phenomenological marker for discovering and knowing who we really are. It is the key that unlocks the door to the hidden self.

3.3 Eros, Sexualization, and Rage

Kohut writes that when a person's self is injured or traumatized, there frequently ensues a sexualization of the self's defects and needs. For example, Kohut says of a patient who developed a tendency towards disturbing sexual fantasies which he sometimes acted out, that "The sexualization of the patient's defects was due to a moderate weakness in his basic psychic structure, resulting in an impairment of its neutralizing capacity" (1971, 70). He goes on to say that for such patients, "the sexualization of their defects and needs serves a specific psycho-economic function, i.e., it is a means for the discharge of intense narcissistic tensions" (1971, 72). Rather than directly seeking to satisfy the self's needs for selfobject responsiveness, a person with a traumatized self will often identify his lack as a sexual one and transform the self's needs into sexualized desires.

A second breakdown product of injuries to the self is narcissistic rage, which differs from anger in that "there is an utter disregard for reasonable limitations and a boundless wish to redress an injury and to obtain revenge" (1985, 143). When a person's self is injured, there erupts an aggressive urge to destroy the person who injured the self and, when this is not possible (the usual case), to be revengeful against all who happen to get transferentially connected to the original perpetrator.

In short, when a person's self is injured, the basic motivational forces in the psyche shift from an internal pressure to develop and sustain the self to what appear to be sexual and aggressive drives. On this view, what Freud discovered in his later work is not a psyche developing under normal conditions, but one whose self has been traumatized.

Although these themes of sexualization and narcissistic rage as disintegration products caused by injuries to the self are common throughout Kohut's writings, they are deeply problematical, for they seem to re-instate Freud's drive theory. If the need to develop and sustain self-structure can be replaced by sexualization, it implies that there is a sex drive—libido—that now takes over the psyche. And if injuries to the self unleash a rageful aggression, it seems to imply that there is some kind of aggressive drive ready to be released. In short, it appears as though the Freudian drives are still in play. Are we now thinking there might be three fundamental motivational forces at work in the human psyche—a narcissistic pressure to generate a self, a sexual drive, and an aggressive drive, with the latter two being released, like monsters from their cages, when the self is injured? This interpretation makes sense of Kohut's claim in *The Analysis of the Self* that one of the functions of the self is to modulate the drives (see Chapter 2), but raises a difficult question: how can we have a new self psychology with such a Freudian underlay? I think that when we see the primary energy of the self as eros, we can solve this problem, for both sexualization and rage can be seen as transformations of eros.

Kohut is surely right in saying that when a person's self is injured, there is a strong tendency to sexualize the self's deficits and needs. This sexualization is quite apparent—many persons with injured selves have a driven sexuality with fantasies and actings-out that can be interpreted not as having to do with sexuality but with an attempt to express both the self's injuries and its desperate needs. However, as clinically evident as this claim about sexualization is, it is theoretically problematic, for we are not given reasons as to why the psyche should want to express injuries to the self as a sexual neediness and transform its need to nourish self-structure into sexual compulsiveness.

I think that we can most adequately address this problem if we think of the self's energy as eros. Since sexual arousal is a natural expression of eros, sexualization makes sense as an expression of an injured self. The erotic self in its transformed state of sexualization is still trying to get its narcissistic needs met, but now in a compensatory and compulsive way. In the most important analysis of Kohut's understanding of sexualization, Charles Strozier et al. write that:

> The key idea for Kohut is that sexualization is a phenomenon whose functions attempt to soothe the self that is both vulnerable and predisposed to fragmentation, by eliciting archaic sensate experiences, whose quality is one of undifferentiated merger with a caregiver, in an attempt at sustaining psychic cohesion. As this self persists into adulthood, grounded upon a structural enfeeblement, it is unable to engage adequately life's complex challenges to internal cohesion, demands for agency, and needs for authentic self esteem. Sexualization is an attempt at soothing these tensions brought on by the threat of psychic fragmentation. It operates as a compensatory substitute for internal resources, which when not

absent or are unimpinged would more adequately support the self's relatedness and cohesion.

(2016, 172)[5]

The erotic energy of the self is still seeking to perform the self's functions of granting the psyche vitality and soothing its inner chaos but cannot do this by seeking out selfobjects in empathic and reciprocal ways and so seeks them through sexualization. Eros becomes sexualized when it unites with sexual desire, or what Panksepp calls LUST (see Chapter 4). Sexual desire is not an ever-present Freudian libidinal drive, but a desire that is aroused under certain circumstances. That eros and sexual desire are different is made evident by the fact that we can be sexual without being erotic (sex without love) and erotic without being sexual. Eros is the pressure to unite and bond with another; sexual desire makes this pressure take the form of a sexual union. It is eros arising from an injured self that gives sexualization its compulsive nature, for the self is desperate to have its needs met.

In short, sexualization is best understood as the self's transformed erotic energy fusing with sexual desire to get the self's needs met. It is both a defense against the pain being harbored in an injured self and an expression of that self. Rather than erotic/self energy being at the core of the psyche, we now have erotic/sexual energy at its core, attempting to fill the empty space where is a self is supposed to be. Because eros is embodied love, there is no problem with grasping how and why it transforms into sexualization, and this explains why persons with injured selves so often try to repair their selves with a driven sexuality.

The erotic energy that might have gone into the realization of the self now pours into a compulsive sexuality and we become assaulted with fantasies and driven sexual desires to fuse with others in hopes that such fusion might bring cohesion to the self. We often find a strange idealization at work in driven sexuality in which we fantasize about how union with a desired object will be bring us into an archaic state of bliss, a state of re-unification with the self. Seeing sexualization as a fusion of the erotic energy of the self with sexual desire allows us to see why persons often feel most like themselves when they are engaged in acts of driven sexuality, whether this be in masturbation or seduction.

This theory of sexualization can also help us understand the difference between healthy sexuality and sexualization. Charles Strozier, et al. differentiate sexuality and sexualization beautifully:

> Sexuality consists in the full range of genital and bodily enjoyment in the other who is empathically experienced as a separate center of initiative…Sexualization on the other hand, eliminates the other as a separate center of initiative with whom one empathizes in a tender, loving way. Sexualization can turn genital sexuality into a deadly game of manipulation, control, and even violence and often subsumes body parts or symbolic substitutes as in fetishes into sources of stimulation. Fantasies played out in these realms provide a form of self-soothing.
>
> (2022, 168–169)

When sexual desire arises in a person with a healthy self for an appropriate other person and fuses with eros, the experience can be one of tremendous self-affirmation for both persons, an aesthetic experience of wild delight—full of intense sexual pleasures for both. When one has a healthy self and feels sexual desire for an inappropriate object (but not eros), the desire can be set aside without repression, fragmentation, or even a sense of loss. However, if the erotic energy of the self gets transformed into a compulsive sexualization, then the other is objectified and controlled. We are so desperate to restore the psychic coherence, soothing, and vitality that a self provides that we cannot allow our sexual partners to be free. Their independence represents too great a threat to our sanity. We need to control them as we once tried to control our very first selfobjects. Hence, in sexualization we express a distorted eros, an eros longing to devour its objects in a desperate attempt to fill a core inner emptiness. We have a self both expressing its deficits—its depletion—and desperately attempting to fill the absence of a self with sexual excitement. The reason that such activity is so common is that the extra energy that makes sexual desire feel driven is none other than the erotic energy of the injured self.

My guess is that for many persons there is a mixture of genuine sexuality that affirms the full independent worth of their partners and a sexualization that needs to use them to shore up the self. Since many, if not most, contemporary adults have suffered unrepaired injuries to the self but have also developed enough self-structure to be empathic and respectful, a mixture of sexuality and sexualization seems almost the norm in the world today.

We can also interpret narcissistic rage as transformed eros. The world's literature is replete with stories of how wronged lovers transform their eros into such rage that they seek to annihilate those who jilted them. Perhaps the most famous is Euripides' *Medea*. When Jason (the leader of the Argonauts) decides he needs a new wife to enhance his political aspirations and abandons Medea, she kills their two children, gives Jason's fiancée a poisoned wedding dress that consumes her with fire, and flies off laughing in a chariot driven by black horses, leaving Jason a ruined man. Medea's eros has transformed into a rage that seeks to utterly destroy Jason. Spinoza, the great 17th-century philosopher who has one of the most profound understandings of the human emotions, says

> If anyone has begun to hate the object of his love to the extent that his love is completely extinguished, he will, other things being equal, bear greater hatred towards it than if he had never loved it, and his hatred will be proportionate to the strength of his former love.
>
> (Bk. 3, prop. 38)

He adds, "He who hates someone will endeavor to injure him" (Bk. 3, prop. 39).

Narcissistic rage seems to be a fusion of injured eros with the emotion of anger. Anger gives narcissistic rage its attacking character while injured eros gives it its all-consuming compulsive character. What is erotic in narcissistic rage is the urge to unite with the other, while anger makes the act of uniting one in which we seek to destroy the other. Narcissistic rage is especially acute when our selves are injured by a selfobject whom we have loved and trusted. Self-injuries from such persons are experienced as betrayals, and, as Spinoza says, we will hate those who injured us with as much passion as we once loved them. This rage feels enlivening, and insofar as it is all-consuming, it unifies the psyche and hence grants a kind of coherence to the self. The rage can feel erotic, for we love taking revenge. We are loving to destroy that which once destroyed us.

While sexualization and narcissistic rage are two different break-down products of an injured self's eros, they can be, and often are, fused such that a person's behavior exhibits both sexualization and rage in the same act. This is, of course, a way of understanding many of the sado-masochistic pre-occupations in sex.

Narcissistic rage, like sexualization, reduces others to objects—but rather than using them for sexual gratification, seeks to utterly annihilate them. In both cases the other is de-humanized. That is, it is persons with injured selves who are responsible for much suffering in human life, for the loving eros that is the core of their selves has been converted into sexualized and revengeful motivations that objectify others so that we can use or destroy them. This is a further amplification of the claim I made in the last chapter (and two previous books) that the foundation for a community's being populated with ethical persons is those persons' having intact selves.

Finally, I think that injuries to the self are not typically injuries to the idealized pole or to our ambitions—although both can happen—but to our eros. It is not a pole of the self that is injured in traumas, but the self itself. When we are shamed, abused, neglected, or objectified, it is not a sector of the self or even a sector of the psyche that is injured, it is the whole self, the whole erotic self which now finds itself less able to love—to love itself, love its ideals, or love others.

3.4 Leading Edge or Selfobject Transferences as Erotic Transferences

In her memoir about her analysis with Freud, H.D. (Hilda Doolittle) writes that one day Freud exploded at her "'The trouble is—I am an old man—*you do not think it worth your while to love me*'" (1956/2012, 16), indicating that unless an erotic transference emerged, the psychoanalytic therapy could not progress. And in "Observations on Transference-Love" Freud says that the key to any analysis is the appearance of and working through erotic transferences (1915). Freud thought that erotic transferences were important because they re-enacted unconscious sexual desires, allowing them to be brought into the light of consciousness where they could vanish in the bright sunshine of Freud's brilliant interpretations. What Freud didn't understand was that he was in fact meeting and affirming the presence of his patients' selves when he welcomed their eros into the consulting room, and this is what had the curative effect.

That is, the presence of eros in the consulting room is not at base the re-enactment of oedipal love, but the presence of a self longing to unite with the therapist in order to repair its fragmentation. That erotic transferences are often sexualized and experienced by the patient as a longing to sexually merge with the therapist is to be expected, as sexualization is a major form eros takes when the self is injured. Even negative transferences that are intended to hurt and destroy the therapist can be interpreted as transformed eros. They are not at base the attempt to destroy the homogenital parent in order to be an oedipal victor, but expressions of a self's love that has been betrayed—of a love that was scorned, neglected, or abused. Underlying the hate and abusive rage is eros—a betrayed eros that has been injured, but eros, nonetheless.

In both sexualized and enraged engagements with patients, therapists can feel a high degree of vitality, energy, and desire to connect— even if the connection is meant to be destructive—and these are the qualities of the erotic self that is letting itself be present in the consulting room and longing for the kind of connection that can let the self out of its prison to be free to develop once again.

That is, rather than seeing sexualized and rageful transferences as defenses or resistances to the therapy, they can be interpreted as leading-edge transferences carrying tendrils of hope that the development of self might be re-ignited. They are longing to connect to the therapist—in distorted ways for sure—in hopes that the connection will restore the self. Obviously, these transferences also carry trailing-edge trauma in that they express the pain of an injured self. They fuse tendrils of both hope and despair, and that is why they are so difficult to work with. Insofar as this kind of transference longs to connect with a restorative selfobject, it is what Peter Zimmerman calls a *generative transference*.

> The generative transference refers to the dimension of the therapeutic relationship that promotes growth and healing… It entails the establishment of the development-enhancing experiences in the relationship with the analyst that the patient yearns for and needs to reinstate a process that results in the unfolding, consolidation and vitalization of self experience.
>
> (2019, 38)

Generative transferences need to be affirmed, even though they might be carrying very uncomfortable sexual and/or aggressive aims.

Although sexualization and narcissistic rage tend to push therapists out of an empathic modality and put them into a defensive orientation, it is important to recognize that what has entered the room is someone's self in a distorted way, but still a way that carries vital energy and purpose. Richard Geist gives a vivid example of how sexualized behavior can be seen as an expression of the self's needs in his therapy with Judy (2009). While in a session, Judy, a young woman who had a history of sexualization, suddenly and without warning stripped naked and approached Geist, offering him various possibilities for attaining sexual satisfaction with her. Rather than imposing rules, telling her to get her clothes on immediately, or getting up and leaving, Geist took hold of her wrists and out of a depth of empathic responsiveness said, "You want to be special to me." Judy turned around, put on her clothes, went to the section of the room with child's toys to re-engage her childhood, and continued the session. Geist had correctly interpreted Judy's sexual desire as longing for a selfobject to help her feel special, and it was this very understanding that made her feel special.

Patients full of narcissistic rage are, obviously, not easy to work with, for they are seeking to destroy the therapist's self-esteem and sense of competence. David Terman describes them: "The patient is relentless. Attacks on the weaknesses and defectiveness of the analyst are made with utter conviction, and they are accompanied by a feeling of enormous disillusion" (1975, 241). One of the important ways that Terman recommends for transforming the analytic situation is to acknowledge that one has the deficit recognized by the patient and affirm the distress it must have caused, for when this happens "the patient's rage subsides, and he can recall the appropriate genetic situation; the analyst as idealized self-object is once more restored, and the reaction may eventually be seen as belonging more appropriately to the past" (1975, 242). That is, the rage has transformed into love in the form of idealization. Kohut and Terman both write that such patients have typically had their grandiosity injured by an idealized selfobject. If the analyst can keep in mind that underlying the rage coming at them is a person's experience of having their erotic love betrayed or rejected by an early selfobject and that the rage is actually a transformed form of love, it might be easier to affirm the rage not simply as a breakdown product from an injury to the self, but a profound expression of the self, a leading tendril of health.

3.5 Eros and Self Knowledge

The most important benefit that comes from identifying the energy of the self as eros is that it gives us a crucial phenomenological marker for knowing which experiences are truly self-experiences and which are not. Since both the ideals and ambitions of the self are largely unconscious, we typically do not know what they are and, hence, are often at a loss to say who we really are or what we truly want. The self's ideals are often veiled and hidden behind socially introjected ideals. What we really want to succeed at is often obscured by a generalized need to be successful at everything we try. How are we to find our "true selves"? The self is not an object that can be found like a lost ball; nor is it an identity that is consciously created like the avatars that appear on social media. If the self is not an object; not a social construction; not an identity structure whose contours are available to consciousness, how are we to find it?

If we think of the self's energy as eros, then we can discover who we are by seeing what we erotically love. We find our selves in moments of erotic eruption, as what happened to me in my first philosophy class, or when I first visited Colorado, or when I first met Marcia. These moments of falling madly in love typically involve intense idealization, a heightened sense of agency, and the feeling that this is really me. We often don't know what our ideals are until we fall in love with an activity, person, or place. It is in loving that we find our ideals, not the other way around—finding our ideals and then loving them.

Since eros is aroused by beauty, these moments in which we discover our selves tend to be moments of intense aesthetic depth in which the self is both expressing itself and being nourished by the beauty of what we are falling in love with. These moments often occur in the kind of events that John Dewey calls "an experience" in which a set of elements seamlessly flow into a unified aesthetic whole, making the event one that is memorable for a lifetime. One such experience stands out vividly for me. When the annual self-psychology conference was held in Vienna in the fall of 2018, we were all invited to a grand dinner in the Orangerie of the Schönbrunn Palace. The palace is, of course, full of history—the Hapsburgs, the glorious dances that occurred when Vienna was the seat of the Empire, the extraordinary grandness and beauty of the palace itself. The food was exceptional, the small string band was playing elegant music, and we loved ballroom dancing, and then they played our favorite dance—a Viennese waltz. The air was soft even though it was late autumn, the food delicious, the company esteemed, and for a moment they watched as Marcia and I swirled effortlessly around the floor as Strauss's ethereal music flowed through us, each taking in the beauty of the other's face, each glowing with life. Life and our selves at that moment, were complete.

When the erotic self is intact, it seeks and lives such harmonious and fulfilling experiences. However, while each might express something deep about the self's ideals, there are some in which the essence of the self is so profoundly expressed that they can ground and structure an entire lifetime. Eros is often criticized for being fickle; but I have not found this to be the case—at least not when eros is fully robust rather than being infatuated. I fell in love with philosophy at the age of 18 and now over 60 years later, I am still insanely in love with it. I fell in love with Colorado when I first saw it in my mid-20s and am still deeply in love with this place of wild mountains, alpine flowers, light brilliant air, crashing waterfalls, huge snowstorms, and dazzling sunshine. I turned down several offers from other schools that were more strategically located in the academic world and have never regretted my decision. My eros soared when I first kissed Marcia, and that was over 40 years ago. We are still madly in love. I have also had experiences in which I was "kind of" in love or was "trying to be in love" and they never worked out. If eros is the self and the self is our eros, then this kind of erotic stability makes sense. Eros is not like the desires which tend to come and go with some fickleness, but an expression of the depth of our selves, selves that have a coherence and stability.

In the traditional Anglican and Episcopalian wedding ceremonies, the marriage partners say to one another, "I plight thee my troth." "Troth" is a rich, powerful word, for it means both "truth" and "trust." In plighting one's troth, one promises that one can be trusted because one is marrying out of the truth of who one is. "Being true to one's self" means nothing if there is not a self to be true to; but this is the same as being true to one's erotic loves, for these loves are one's self.

In sum, who I am is what I love, for the activity of loving expresses my ideals, my ambitions, and my core narcissistic libido—eros. In the search for my self, I don't find an entity or even an identity, I find when, where, and who I am loving, and it is in these relationships that I locate myself. This account of the self as eros can also explain how selfobjects can be an essential part of the self. Since we typically love our selfobjects, we find our selves in them.

We are assaulted all the time by a myriad of desires, emotions, needs, and social pressures. We need to find some way to distinguish what pressures truly need to be responded to and which can be shoved to the side or abandoned. That is, we need a phenomenological marker to tell us what motivations are coming from our selves and which are coming from other motivational centers. Emerson, Nietzsche, and Heidegger thought that distinguishing motivations which were coming from one's unique self from those that had external sources was the most important ability a person could have. I can think of no more visceral, experiential marker for finding the self than the feeling of being in love—with someone, an activity, a place, an art object, a pet, a way of being in the world. Eros is the way the self presents itself to the ego— to the person; it is how the being of the self reveals itself. In sum, the self is a kernel of swirling erotic energy at the core of psychic life. The eros expresses itself in terms of love of myself, love of emergent ideals, love of being special, love of selfobjects, and when the self is fully realized/recognized, a profound love of life itself and the world.[6]

I cannot leave this chapter without asking the question as to why Kohut himself did not come to the conclusion that the self is fundamentally erotic energy structured around ideals and ambitions. He had to have known that since he was inquiring into the nature of "narcissistic libido" that he was dealing with "embodied love," and it is not a far stretch to realize that this is best conceived as eros. I think he stayed away from this kind of claim because *eros* in ordinary parlance is so closely associated with sexual desire that it would have made self psychology too close to classical Freudian theory. He wanted to explore narcissism and the self, not the vicissitudes of libido. However, in bypassing the question of what *libido* really is, he bypassed the nature of what the essential energy in narcissism is. I hope that this chapter makes full sense to Kohutians as to why and how seeing the self's energy as eros not only does not collapse Kohut's self psychology into

Freudian drive theory but becomes a way to interpret the later Freud as a precursor to Kohut. Psychoanalysis is, in essence, the exploration of the erotic self.

Notes

1 Quoted by J. Lear (2005). P. 196. Note that while Freud adopts Plato's notion of eros as longing to unite with wider forms of connectedness and its seeking of harmony, he does not follow Plato into his mystical realms. That is, he does not think that eros is only fully satisfied when united with the eternal, ethereal form of Beauty.
2 See Jane Ellen Harrison's *Themis* (2012/2010) for an account of who the *daimones* were in ancient Greek ritual practices that existed before the invention of the polis.
3 For a full development of this Freud/Kohut comparison, see Riker (2017), chapter 4.
4 Plotinus in the Hellenistic Age and Ficino in the Florentine Renaissance were two philosophers for whom the *Symposium* was crucial, and both these philosophers deeply influenced their ages and subsequent epochs.
5 Also see chapter 6 of Strozier, et. al.'s *The New World of Self* (2022).
6 Eros has a number of doppelgängers, including infatuation and mania. See chapter 5 of my *Exploring the Life of the Soul* (2017) for an exploration of these erotic look-alikes.

References

Doolittle, H. (1956/2012). *A Tribute to Freud*. NY: New Directions Publishing.
Emerson, R. (1836/1982). *Nature* in *Nature and Selected Essays*. Ed. L. Ziff. New York: Penguin.
Freud, S. (1953–1974). *Standard Edition of the Collected Works*, tr. & ed. James Strachey, et al., 24 vols. London: Hogarth Press. Hereafter: SE.
———. (1910). "Wild Psychoanalysis." SE 11, 219–230.
———. (1915). "Observations on Transference Love." SE 12, 157–171.
———. (1921). "Group Psychology and the Analysis of the Ego." SE 18, 65–145.
———. (1923). *The Ego and the Id*. SE 19: pp. 1–66.
———. (1924). "An Autobiographical Study." SE XX, 7–70.
———. (1925). "The Resistances to Psychoanalysis." SE 19: pp. 213–222.
———. (1930). Civilization and Its Discontents. SE 21: pp. 59–145.
Geist, R. (2009). "Empathy, Connectedness, and the Evolution of Boundaries in Self Psychological Treatment." *International Journal of Psychoanalytic Self Psychology*, *4*(2), 165–180.
Harrison, J. (1912/2010). *Themis*. Cambridge: Cambridge University Press.
Kohut, H. (1966). "Forms and Transformations of Narcissism." In C. Strozier, ed. *Self Psychology and the Humanities*. New York: Norton (1985).

————. (1971). *The Analysis of the Self*. New York: International Universities Press.

————. (1977). *The Restoration of the Self*. New York: International Universities Press.

————. (1985). *Self Psychology and the Humanities*. Ed. C. Strozier. New York: Norton.

————. (1996). *The Chicago Institute Lectures*. Eds. P. Tolpin & M. Tolpin. Hillsdale, NJ; Analytic Press.

Lear, J. (2004). *Therapeutic Action*. New York: The Other Press.

————. (2005). "Give Dora a Break: A Tale of Eros and Emotional Disruption." In S. Bartsch & T. Bartscherer (Eds.), *Erotikon* (pp. 196–212). Chicago: University of Chicago Press.

Nietzsche, F. (1883/1978). *Thus Spoke Zarathustra*. Tr. W. Kaufmann. NY: Viking Press.

Riker, J. (2017). *Exploring the Life of the Soul: Philosophical Reflections on Psychoanalysis and Self Psychology*. Lanham, MD: Lexington Books.

Spinoza, B. (1677/2002). *Ethics*. Tr. S. Shirley. Indianapolis, IN: Hackett.

Strozier, C., Strug, D., Pinteris, K., & Kelley, K. (2016). "Sexualization in the Work of Heinz Kohut." *Psychoanalysis, Self, and Context, 13*(2), 171–185.

Strozier, C., Pinteris, K., Kelley, K., & Cher, D. (2022). *The New World of Self: Heinz Kohut's Transformation of Psychoanalysis and Psychotherapy*. Oxford: Oxford University Press.

Terman, D. (1975). "Aggression and Narcissistic Rage: A Clinical Elaboration." *Annual of Psychoanalysis, 3*, 239–255.

Zimmerman, P. (2019). "The Therapeutic Action of Intersubjective Self: Part One." In *Intersubjective Self Psychology: A Primer*. (pp. 37–56). Eds. G. Hagman, H. Paul, & P. Zimmerman. New York: Routledge.

Chapter 4

Metapsychology
The Self, the Ego, and Personhood

4.1 The Need for a New Metapsychology

When Plato set out to explore what kind of persons could live the best kind of human life, he found that he needed to develop a metapsychology which identified the best arrangement of the different motivating sectors of the psyche. That is, he theorized that those persons with the best psyches could live the most deeply satisfying and distinctively human of lives. In the *Republic* he claims that persons who develop souls in which their rational capacities, with the help of a high spirit, achieve control over their emotions and desires are those who can live the most satisfying lives, for they can "have lives" rather than being tossed this way and that by impulses and shifts in social pressures. That is, Plato held that the best kind of lives are lived by persons with the best organization of the parts of their souls. I think that this is a profound truth—one that provides a major thematic for this book.

In contrast to Plato, I will develop a metapsychology based on Kohut's notion of the self in distinction from the rational ego and hold that persons who have intact selves at the core of their psychic functioning will, *ceteris paribus*, have the best possibilities for living the most fulfilling of lives. As such, this self psychological metapsychology will stand as a radical critique of the Western philosophical tradition that has largely identified the self with the ego. I believe that this identification has led to the dangerous idealization of the autonomous, masterful, power-seeking individual that has become so predominant in the capitalist world of today. It was Kohut's monumental discovery that the self is a particular configuration within the psyche that has its own developmental path, structure, energy, needs, aspirations, and functions that differ drastically from those of the ego. Indeed, I think

DOI: 10.4324/9781003303657-6

this differentiation is, along with his discovery of the self's intrinsic need for selfobjects, his greatest conceptual accomplishment.

Kohut first indicates that the ego and the self are different at the very beginning of *The Analysis of the Self* by asserting that we need a "conceptual separation of the self from the ego" (xiii), and later adds, "The ego's ability to perform a variety of tasks (e.g., professional pursuits) increases hand in hand with the increase in the cohesiveness of the self" (1971, 297), indicating that he thinks that the two are different.

The distinction between the ego and the self is drawn, perhaps, most vividly in his essay "On Courage:"

> I am strongly inclined to think, however, that it is more appropriate (i.e., more in tune with the clinical facts, and more advantageous from the heuristic point of view) to conceptualize the normally integrated nuclear self not as occupying only a delimited portion within the ego, but as forming a whole sector of the psyche in depth.
>
> (1985, 29)

He goes on to differentiate those who "rationally resisted" the Nazis from those who resisted out of the ideals of their core selves by saying of one group that they had made the ego the sole source of resistance (and, hence, shallow), while, in contrast, for others, "the ego is not the autonomous source of the motivations. The ego is here in its decisive activities guided by the deeply anchored pattern of the nuclear self and is drawing its power from it" (1985, 23). It is clear from this passage that the ego and self must be different.

In *The Restoration of the Self* Kohut asks, "Is it necessary now to add a psychology of the self to the psychology of the ego?" (1977, xviii), again indicating that he thinks of the ego and the self as different sectors of the psyche.

While Kohut holds that the self and ego are different, he never develops this distinction or constructs a new metapsychology to replace Freud's ego, id, superego model. The closest he comes to producing a metapsychology is in the beginning of *The Analysis of the Self*:

> The notions of self, on the one hand, of ego, superego, id, on the other, as well as those of personality and identity are abstractions which belong to different levels of concept formation. Ego, id, and

superego are the constituents of a specific, high-level, i.e., experience-distant abstraction in psychoanalysis: the psychic apparatus. Personality, although often serviceable in a general sense, like identity, is not indigenous to psychoanalytic psychology; it belongs to a different framework which is more in harmony with the observation of social behavior and the description of the (pre)conscious experience of oneself in the interaction with others than with the observations of depth psychology. The self, however, emerges in the psychoanalytic situation and is conceptualized, in the mode of a comparatively low-level, i.e., comparatively experience-near, psychoanalytic abstraction, as a content of the mental apparatus. While it is thus not an agency of the mind, it is a structure within the mind since (a) it is cathected with instinctual energy and (b) it has continuity in time, i.e., it is enduring. Being a psychic structure, the self has, furthermore, also a psychic location. To be more specific, various—and frequently inconsistent—self representations are present in the id, the ego, and the superego, but also within a single agency of the mind... The self, then, quite analogous to the representations of objects, is a content of the mental apparatus but is not one of its constituents, i.e., not one of the agencies of the mind.

(1971, xiv–xv)

This dense, abstruse passage is full of important ideas that are never developed into a robust metapsychology. Strangely, none of Kohut's close followers, such as Arnold Goldberg or Ernest Wolf, ever developed a metapsychology.[1] Why? I think it is because within the self psychology movement, there is a strong predisposition to favor concepts that are experience-near rather than the experience-distant, and metapsychology is seen as experience-distant. However, Robert Stolorow and George Atwood not only think that metapsychology is unnecessary because it is experience-distant, but downright condemn it:

psychoanalytic metapsychologies [including Kohut's] ... are actually a form of metaphysics [that] represents an illusory flight from the tragedy of human finitude. Metaphysics transforms the unbearable fragility and transience of all things human into an enduring, permanent, changeless, reality, an illusory world of eternal truths.

(2019, 17)

While I agree with Stolorow and Atwood that humans need to fully immerse themselves in the transience of life to feel fully alive, I find their critique of metapsychology highly problematic. Neither metapsychology nor metaphysics can remove us from the world of change, finitude, loss, and suffering. Discourses like metaphysics and metapsychology might try to conceptualize structures that map stable patterns in the universe or psyche, but they have no power to transform the mutable into the unchangeable. While it is true that belief in metaphysical systems which posit a spiritual eternal realm as existing beside our changing ephemeral world—a belief in some form that many peoples, if not most, throughout human history have held—can ease the pain of loss and the terror of death (is this so horrible?), such beliefs cannot erase the actuality of loss, suffering, and death. Nor can metapsychological maps of the mind erase finitude, trauma, despair, or experiential turmoil from psychological life.

I can understand why Stolorow is against metapsychology if he sees it as dealing with "the material substrate of experience and couched in the natural science framework of impersonal structures, forces, and energies" (2021, 352), but I do not see why he thinks of metapsychology in this way. I prefer to see metapsychology as arising out of an attempt to map the motivational sectors of our psyches in order to explain why we have the complex lived experience that we do. These theorized motivational sectors are not impersonal forces or mechanisms but an attempt to chart the intrinsic psychological make-up of who we are. Just as it is very difficult to find one's way through an unmapped territory, it is hard to grasp the dynamics of psychological experience without some kind of metapsychological map to tell us what is going on.

All attempts to map the complexity of psychological phenomena are, of course, speculations that can never be proven. And yet they are of utmost importance for several reasons. First, metapsychological maps can allow us to see phenomena that might otherwise not be observable. Freud's id/ego/superego metapsychology allows us to see and grasp the dynamics of guilt and repression better than we could before he proposed this model of the mind. I think that Kohut's positing the existence of a metapsychological "self" and his speculating about how it arises from narcissistic libido, how it can be injured, and how it can be repaired have transformed how therapy is being conducted and allowed us to see and understand psychic phenomena with more clarity and power than ever before. If Kohut had not hypothesized about the existence of "the self," his ideas would not have had the impact that they have.

Not only does theory allow us to see and grasp patterns of psychic functioning, it is, according to Kohut, necessary to grasp the nature of any psychological activity. "[A]n observer needs theories in order to observe ... these theories must be the helpmates of the observer, not his masters" (1985, 67). There is no such thing as "theory-free" observation, as much as the phenomenologists would like there to be. To paraphrase Kant: experience without theory is blind; theory without experience is empty.

There are further problems for refusing to do either metaphysics or metapsychology, namely, that it dooms us to accept the metaphysics and metapsychology that are already regnant in the culture. Whether we like it or not, we have semi-conscious theories of what is real and how our minds work. I think that following Stolorow's advice to perform a *"radical theorectomy"* (2021, 352) prevents us from questioning the highly problematical—indeed, highly destructive—metapsychology that underlies modern Western society's construction of persons into spectacularly rational, incredibly self-controlled, emotionally shallow, disconnected human beings.

It is humans with this kind of modern rational soul that have transformed the world with science, technology, and liberal politics. They have created the modern world with its medical miracles, extraordinary opportunities, immense freedoms, and an unfathomable amount of goods and services. However, the metapsychology that underlies how modern persons are constructed must also be implicated in much of the massive human suffering of contemporary persons. While homelessness, chronic loneliness, depression, deaths of despair, suicides, addictions, racism, and global climate change have numerous roots from which they emerge, one of these roots is a profound misunderstanding of the human psyche.

At the heart of this misunderstanding is the failure to recognize the vulnerable self and its need for selfobject connectedness. When the self is displaced from the center of our lives, we feel a profound emptiness or void—a hopelessness and despair that leads to loneliness, desperate attempts to fill the emptiness with a massive consumption of goods and power, an attempt to soothe the inner pain with drugs, food, gambling, etc., a narcissistic clinging onto racial superiority, and so on. That is, I believe that modernity's deficient metapsychology which confuses the self with the ego is implicated in many of our social and personal ills and that these problems cannot be fully alleviated unless we replace the ego-centric metapsychology with a Kohutian self-centric metapsychology. With this shift of metapsychologies we will be better able to understand why our souls so often feel empty in a world teeming with plenty, why life can descend into nihilistic hopelessness, and why we cannot seem to know who we are despite all the kinds of personality inventories that we can take. The key to this shift in metapsychologies—this shift in the ideal of how our souls should be arranged—is the recognition of how the self differs from the ego.

4.2 The Ego and the Self

We have the ineffable sense that there is a subject, an "I," who is having our subjective experiences. However, this subject never itself appears in experience. As soon as we think we might have located the subject as an object of consciousness, we realize that there is still a transcendent subject looking at us looking at that object. And, in truth, the subject in its subjectivity can never appear as an object to itself, for it is sheer activity and not a thing. The inability to perceive the subject of experience as an object led David Hume to doubt that there really is a subject of experience at all. He hypothesized that there is just experiencing without an experiencer. Immanuel Kant countered that the sense of having a singular subject unifying experiences into "my" experience is so universal that we must posit a "transcendental unity of apperception" as a necessary pre-condition for the possibility of any experience (1781/1998). While for Kant we must postulate that there is some kind of being that is unifying experiences into the experience of a singular subject, he refused to speculate about what this being might metaphysically be.

I will follow Kant in not proposing some kind of metaphysical soul or mental substance as the unifier of experience. Instead of doing metaphysics, I will attempt to answer the question of who the subject of experience is by probing into the two metapsychological agencies that have the strongest claims to be who we most are: the ego and the self.

While both the ego and the self have formidable claims to be the subject of experience, it is the ego that has the far better claim, for it is the arena of consciousness and self-consciousness. It is the realm of our experiencing subjectivity. The self, on the other hand, is a structure that can infuse the ego and make us feel most like ourselves. While the ego, by necessity, is always present as the subject of experience, the self can be either present or absent. We can have experiences in which "I am just not myself today" or "I lost myself in that job." That is, we can have experiences in which we do not feel as though they are really ours. In these experiences of the self's absence, there is still a subject having experiences—an "I" that is present. Given experiences in which the ego is actively experiencing but the self is missing, it must be the case that the ego and the self differ. The ego is the subject of experience; the self is a configuration of subjectivity which, if structuring the experience of the ego, makes us feel most like ourselves; and when it is not structuring experience, we can feel that we are not really present or actively engaged in life. Also, as Kohut indicated, the self is in part a structure of our unconscious subjectivity and thus cannot be equated with self-conscious experiencing.

Along with its being the realm of conscious/self-conscious experience, the ego can be defined by its set of functions. Freud (1923) elaborated these functions well: to negotiate the organism's relations to its social and natural environments and to establish a coherent equilibrium within the psyche without which the ego cannot perform its primary task of environmental mediation. The ego can also function unconsciously in establishing psychic order when it uses such defensive mechanisms as repression and dissociation to rid itself of traumatic emotions and experiences.

The conscious ego has been extensively explored by philosophers from Plato through Jean-Paul Sartre and Freud, almost all of whom have held that for the ego to function well, persons need both to develop character traits that moderate the passions and cultivate their rational capabilities, mainly through education. No one analyzes these concepts better than Aristotle, who carefully shows why the moral virtues are needed for us not to be over-or under-whelmed by our emotions/desires and why we need to cultivate the deliberative powers of reason to optimally interact with our environments. If our desires/emotions are compulsive or if we are ignorant of crucial knowledge about what we are doing, then we cannot engage in the most important of human acts: choice. When we have "right reason" and "right desire," we can then be agents choosing our own lives.

Philosophers have discovered other key truths about ego consciousness. First, the ego is not just a servant to satisfy the needs of the id, as Freud posited, but an agency that has its own needs: freedom and power. From the time that Athens became a fully democratic society and the Greek philosophers began to explore the possibilities of living a self-determined life, through the democratic movements of the modern world, to the existentialists proclaiming openness to be the essence of the human soul, freedom has been hailed in the Western tradition as the highest of human values. The rallying cry for most marginalized peoples is the demand to be free—free from oppression by dominating populations and their prejudices. The quest for freedom—at least a *freedom from*—comes out of the very essence of the ego.

The ego's esteeming freedom makes sense if our ego's fundamental task is to optimally resolve problematic situations in our internal and external environments. To think clearly about how to transform problematical situations into resolved ones, the rational ego needs freedom from emotions/desires that can hinder clear thinking. Since the ego seeks to be as self-determining as possible, it separates the organism's needs from those of others and seeks to satisfy them as efficiently as possible. If the ego is excessively pressured, either by compulsive inner drives or external demands, then it does not have free reign to negotiate with its environments. The freedom the ego seeks is best identified as *independence*, or *freedom from*. The ego wants to be free from unnecessary constrictions and impediments.

What Nietzsche discovered, however, was that freedom and knowledge are only subsidiary goals for the ego, for what the ego most cherishes is power. For many post-modernists (e.g., Foucault), the quest for power is the essential force lying behind all human activity. While power and freedom are not conceptually equivalent, they certainly imply one another. The more power one has, the freer they seem to be. In short, the ego's values of achieving knowledge, rational abilities, freedom, and power all imply one another and define the ego's essential activity. When we find ourselves seeking to control situations, deliberating about how best to free ourselves from situations of bondage or control by others, disciplining our emotions and desires, and increasing our abilities to cognitively understand the world and our selves, it is the ego which is the foremost motivating sector of our psyches.

For Nietzsche, what is most important is attaining power over ourselves, for if we cannot follow our own values and dictates, we will be dictated to by others. He was deeply concerned about the power of our social environments to infiltrate and colonize our souls. To be powerful we need to rid ourselves of society's values, and we can do this, for Nietzsche, only if we can see through every attempt to establish an objective authority for values and the "right way to be human" (1978). That is, the critical rational power of the ego needs to see through all the fallacious arguments for God, categorical imperatives, Platonic forms, or any other ground that purports to be the right way to be human and live a human life. Insofar as the need for power undermines the legitimacy of all structures of meaning, it leads to the brink of the abyss: nihilism.

And this is the last crucial truth that existentialist philosophers have discovered about the ego: its fundamental openness means that it cannot produce meanings that can ground life. Sartre (1956) claims that no matter what identity we choose, we know that its ground is our act of choosing, and, therefore, we can question it, put it into play, choose to be otherwise. Conscious subjectivity can never reduce itself to an object, to a set identity structure. This is why Sartre and Hegel call consciousness "nothingness," for it is not a thing but a ceaseless activity. It is this openness that is the basis for seeking freedom (to be unbounded) and the ability to critique any form of life or any set of values that claim objective validity. Even psychoanalysis participates in this quest to be free in its attempt to release us from bondage to unconscious structures that constrict experience and make it endlessly repetitive.

There is an essential subjective activity that underlies and gives birth to the freedom, power, and knowledge that the ego seeks: the act of *questioning*. All living things—and probably all things, organic and inorganic—perceive and process information, but questioning seems to be a strange, unique activity which rather than receiving and processing information refuses to go along with it or separates from it in order to negate its authority or its very being. It is the act of questioning that lies behind Hegel's claim that the Geist (subjectivity) always involves negativity and Sartre's claim that subjectivity is essentially a nothingness. It is questioning that allows us to disaffirm the world of actuality and open the realm of possibility. Since questioning is the ur-activity of the ego, it means that there can be no final ground of meaning within the ego.

We can see the ego being born in the two-year-old who questions the authority of the caretaker and loudly proclaims, "No!"; who all at once runs away when called; who starts asking endless "why" questions; who now openly dissents from having to go to bed at the set time. The ego is birthed in acts of negativity. While questioning opens the world for creative exploration and change, it is also the origin of separation. When we question someone or something, it destroys our unquestioned immersion in them. Questioning allows us to separate and individuate, but also causes us to lose a home of immersive bliss.

When we turn the act of questioning on ourselves, we separate from ourselves and in so doing become self-conscious. It is not our consciousness which is definitive for who we are as humans, but self-consciousness, for it is in the self-conscious awareness of ourselves that we become able to critique ourselves, change ourselves, be open to new possibilities, and become mortal. In self-consciousness the "I" separates from itself, establishing a "nothingness" between itself as subject and itself as object, so that it might appear to itself. The question that most opens this species-defining internal space is "Who am I?" "What does it mean to be a human being?" It is our self-consciousness that more than anything else defines the species, and it is in this wrenching open of our subjectivity so that it might not only be aware but be aware of itself being aware that defines our species. It is because we are self-conscious that openness, questioning, nothingness, and freedom are definitive of our egos.

The act of questioning lies behind the ego's pursuits of knowledge, freedom, and power. It opens the doors of freedom by negating structures of power over us such that we can pursue our own power. Questioning also allows us to creatively interact with our environments, making reasoning and knowledge necessary rather than instinct and a mere following of set patterns. One of the negative sides of questioning is, of course, the possibility of criminality; both criminals and geniuses refuse to be boxed-in by the codes.

The appearance of ego consciousness and self-consciousness in the universe is one of the final mysteries, if not the ultimate mystery. The coming into being of the self-conscious ego seems to be an evolutionary miracle, not explainable by reference to neuroscience or evolutionary theory. While I will hold that the self is the key to psychological health, it is not what is most definitive about being human. Having self-conscious subjectivity is.

Having a well-functioning ego—one that can creatively entertain new possibilities, think clearly and critically, gain power over inner and outer turmoil, and assert a separate individuality—is crucial for one to engage fully in life. The ego is so definitive of human life that it has completely overshadowed another psychic structure—the self. Indeed, it has been almost universally equated with the self in the West. However, the ego's values and needs are in many ways deeply opposed to those of the self.

If the ego seeks independence, the self seeks connectedness. The ego might desire to detach from its caretakers, but the self wants to remain as close to them as possible. While the ego seeks power over its inner and outer worlds, the self seeks loving relations, vitalized emotions, and empathic affirmation. While the ego seeks to be successful in its relation to the world (a world in which success equals socioeconomic triumph), the self seeks to realize its organic ideals and sustain its selfobject relationships even when they do not optimally position one to be successful in the world. The ego questions everything; the self offers answers—answers as to who we really are and what we want most in life. The ego has a primal emptiness; the self has a primal structure of meanings. The ego needs to formulate an identity through which it can be recognized by society and which usually includes adopting a set of social roles (Erikson, 1960/1980); the self, on the other hand, often finds that accommodation to social structures destroys its singularity and vitality. The ego's energy is often cool, dispassionate, and pragmatic; the self's energy is erotic and aesthetic.[2]

However, a significant problem arises in this contrast of the ego and the self insofar as the self also seeks freedom and power. Since the self emerges out of an early state of narcissism in which it feels itself to be omnipotent, it retains a sense of power in the grandiose pole and seeks the freedom to express its ideals rather than conform to what others what it to be. Hence, both the ego and self seek freedom and power, but the freedom and power they seek are very different.

The freedom that the ego seeks is *freedom from*—freedom from any pressures that could limit its choices or distort them. The freedom the self seeks is *freedom to actualize itself*, the freedom to be myself. The ego seeks freedom from constrictions—including the constriction of having to realize the self's ideals; the self seeks to freely realize its destiny. These conflicting senses of freedom are one of the profound complexities in human motivation. We want both to be fully open to possibilities but also want to be grounded in a purposeful journey of actualization. The ego's mantra is "You can be anything you want to be;" the self's mantra is "Be true to yourself."

The key difference surrounding the ego's value of freedom and that of the self's is that the self is not merely a psychic structure within a person but a fusion of this structure with a person's selfobjects. It is a self-selfobject system, not just a self-system. Given the profound connectedness of the self with its selfobjects, it cannot seek freedom from them. Hence, it values the freedom of self-actualization and this will include the actualization of deeper forms of connectedness. The ego, on the other hand, seems to value freedom as autonomy. The ideal of autonomy is expressed in the contemporary capitalist world's emphasis on achieving a self-sufficient independence. "I am the master of my fate; the captain of my soul." Dependence is seen as immature; independence mature. The ego's sense of freedom as autonomy has gained predominance in the Western world over the self's longing to actualize its ideals and achieve a full interconnectedness with others.

This difference is mirrored in the ego's and the self's two different senses of power. The ego *"seeks power over"* internal and external environments, while the self *"seeks power to"* realize its ideals. That is, the power the ego seeks is one to *control* circumstances to get the organism's needs securely met, while the self seeks to develop *agency* to realize its ideals and establish selfobject connectedness.

The two kinds of power are obviously interconnected and often fused, but we can see their different senses in several kinds of situations. In a love relation, the self needs to feel mirrored and affirmed by another who freely offers affection, affirmation, and closeness. The ego, worried about whether the other will always be available, seeks to control the other—to limit their ability to leave or change the relationship.

Hence, many intimate relations struggle between issues of control and love. In a second example, we can look to persons who have developed an immense amount of ego power and become CEO's or other kinds of leaders, but whose selves seem absent. There are countless case examples of therapists' treating persons who have become extremely powerful and wealthy, but whose lives feel empty and whose love relations are shallow because the self is absent from their lives. They have power to be dominant in their worlds, but don't have a sense of agency—of having the courageous strength to assert the values of their nuclear selves.

The tensions between the two senses of power and freedom are often experienced as a conflict between different sets of values in the ego: we want independence but also want to belong; we want success but also want just to be our selves; we want to be thoroughly pragmatic but also romantic. That is, these conflicts are experienced as a conflict of values within ego consciousness. What I am doing in finding their roots in a tension between two psychic configurations is to validate each set of values as expressing the deep needs of these different psychic sectors. That is, the conflict of values represents a conflict of two essential psychic processes and is, hence, not to be resolved by allegiance to only one side of the values. Both the ego and the self need to be recognized and nourished. These conflicts occur because of our human nature, not because we are confused.

Given the opposing values of the self and ego, we can see why there is a great deal of tension between them, and why so many persons in our egocentric world lose track of their selves. While the ego and self are psychological sectors that often conflict with one another, they can, and often do, work in harmony, becoming so fused that we cannot separate them and simply feel like ourselves most of the time. In optimal cases, the self is providing ideals and erotic energy that make life feel meaningful and vitalized, and the ego is locating social situations in which the self's values and selfobject needs can best be satisfied. The self acts as an inner gyroscope calming and organizing the desires and emotions, and the ego finds out how best to satisfy them. In sub-optimal cases when the self is traumatically injured, the ego must provide inner harmony through rigidifying mechanisms and often sequesters the self and its chaotic pain behind defensive walls, making it unavailable to experience. In such cases the ego takes full domination of life, seeking freedom, power, and control, and producing the kind of egocentric, driven, isolated autonomous individuals that are so common in today's world. Part II of this book will explore these deformations in detail.

4.3 Ego Identity vs. Self-Structure

One important outcome of our differentiating the ego and the self is that it allows us to distinguish what Erik Erikson calls an "ego-identity" from what Kohut calls "the self." An ego identity is a semi-conscious construction for how an individual desires to be recognized by society and involves a choice of key social indicators such as profession, marriage status, recreational priorities, etc. It is typically formulated in late adolescence/early adulthood (Erikson, 1960/1980). As already noted, there is strong social pressure to adopt those markers that give one the most status within market society. However, the identity that one attains is not simply a matter of individual choice, for societies also force identity-markers on individuals according to gender, sexual preference, level of education, race, and income level. The identity markers that society imposes on its members typically carry a set of prejudices and stereotypes that turn persons into tokens of social categories and grant them undeserved privileges or derogations. Insofar as these social markers are typically ranked, one can find oneself in the lower brackets in terms of gender (women), race (non-whites), education, or sexual orientation (non-heteronormal), and thereby be subject to institutionalized violence and shame, which in turn lowers the ability to live a vitalized life.

The self, as different from an ego identity, is a largely unconscious psychological structure that comes into being in childhood though selfobject interactions and expresses something singular and unique about the individual—something that might not fit easily into what our social worlds esteem or recognize. Selves are peculiar and need not be straightforwardly recognizable by society, while identities must be socially recognizable.

Selves are who we are—they are in Christopher Bollas' terms, destinies (2011). Identities, on the other hand, are negotiated ways for us to appear and be recognized by society. Identities can be abandoned, shifted, augmented, and changed depending on contexts and social pressures without psychological harm. The same is not true for selves.

At present there are extraordinarily important conflicts concerning the "politics of identity," as many persons who have been negatively treated because of certain identity features—such as being non-binary, transgendered, belonging to a racial minority, etc. are exposing the prejudices of their culture and demanding changes in social justice. Some conservatives are fighting back and wanting to impose regulations that limit or prevent a number of the "woke" exposures to be recognized. This important discourse about the nature of social justice concerns "identity-formation," not "self-formation," and has had, as an unintended consequence, the tendency to equate identity with the self.

Differentiating the ego from the self also means that we can respond to Phillip Cushman's critique that Kohut's theory of the self unwittingly supports and justifies the "masterful, bounded, empty selves" that consumerist society is creating (1995). They are "masterful" because they are supremely self-disciplined; "bounded" because they think of their individual realities as being separate from all other persons; and "empty" because of "a significant absence of community, tradition, and shared meaning" (2019, 10). Economic society needs such masterful, bounded, empty persons, for they keep insatiably consuming the disposable, non-essential goods of capitalist production in an attempt to fill the emptiness they experience at their cores. And, to keep insatiably consuming, they have to keep ceaselessly working. That is, capitalist society is creating just the kind of human beings it needs to sustain its feverish productivity and lifestyles. Cushman sees Kohut's "nuclear self" as fostering the deficient individuals of capitalism because it advocates the primacy of singular selves abstracted from traditions and communities, thereby fostering the emptiness and isolation of modern persons, deficiencies that can be filled only through the usual capitalist method of solving problems: endless consumption of goods, including selfobject supplies.

This critique of Kohut is based on a confusion of "self" with "ego identity." Cushman is criticizing how modern humans go about constructing their ego identities, not their selves. In short, there is a great deal of pressure in today's highly competitive world to gain advantage by constructing an identity that is, indeed, masterful, abstract, and supremely talented in rational problem-solving. Kohut's understanding of the self not only does not support the production of such individuals but constitutes the main critique of this way of forming human beings. Rather than being bounded, Kohut says the self extends into selfobject others. Rather than being masterful, the self is erotic and closely tied to emotions; rather than being empty, it provides the ideals that can make life meaningful. The self must not be identified with an ego identity. In optimal cases, a person will adopt an ego identity (a *persona*) that expresses and incorporates the self's ideals and ambitions.

4.4 The Social Unconscious

As crucial as the ego and self are as sectors of the psyche, they are not its only motivational structures. To complete our metapsychology we need to consider revised versions of Freud's superego and id, or what I term the *social unconscious* and the *basic drives*.

The social unconscious is our introjection of the codes, practices, and mores that infiltrate us and make us automatically members of a culture, sub-culture, and/or a society. The social unconscious is larger than Freud's superego, as it includes all we unconsciously ingest from the social world that informs how we go about living our everyday lives. Freud describes the superego as containing both an ego ideal, as represented mainly as an identification with the father, and as a set of prohibitions—"You may not be like this (like your father)—that is, you may not do all that he does; some things are his prerogative" (1923, 34). That is, the superego is an agency that imposes moral commands on the ego and will aggress against it if it fails to abide by these decrees, often causing guilt and depressiveness. In the metapsychology I am elaborating here, Freud's superego and its dynamics are retained but seen as part of a much wider range of social mores and practices that we unconsciously ingress and which instruct us how to become recognizable members of our society. The social unconscious tells us what objects to seek, what kind of life is best, how to be a boy or girl, a man or woman, young or mature, rich or poor, a professional or worker, how to rebel against the culture, etc. It includes a knowledge of our native language (and other languages, should they be taught), which gives us our ability to make sense of the world and ourselves. We are all embedded in our

cultures and encoded by them; without this immersion, we could not
be human. As Herbert Fingarette says in writing about Confucius'
philosophy:

> The forms of life, even when viewed in their aspect as intelligent
> convention, cannot be invented and accepted en bloc; they rest pri-
> marily on the inheritance by each age of a vast body of conven-
> tional language and practices from the preceding age. Only as we
> grow up genuinely shaped, through and through by traditional
> ways can we be human.
>
> (1972, 69)

It is the ingression of social codes, traditionally formed and elucidated
in practices, that enable us to be human. While we might be able to
alter this piece or that of our social construction, we can never, and
ought never, to throw it all off, as Nietzsche and other existentialists
seem to advocate.

What needs to be acknowledged is that there is often a tension, even
an opposition, between the ideals of the self and those of society.
Emerson's, Nietzsche's, and Heidegger's claim that the major obstacle
to actualizing our selves is conformity to socially imposed ideals of
who we should be is reverberated in Kohut's claim that we can lose our
selves if we are too opportunistic (1985). Following social ideals typically does not cause trauma or the need for psychological defenses—
the problem is that they come too easily to us, with too little tension.
In short, we can lose ourselves both to traumatic ruptures in our selfobject relationships and to failures to distinguish our organic ideals
and ambitions from those received from society.

Hence, while it is neither possible nor desirable to flee society, it is
crucially important is to discriminate between the self's ideals and
those that have been socially ingested. One of the keyways to distinguish between the two is that we love the activities which are motivated
by the self's ideals but feel we "ought to" abide by the social ideals.
Freud was right that we feel as though our superego values are aggress-
ing against us—they pressure us to do their bidding with the threat of
social censure and guilt if we don't. When children say, "Oh, mom, do
I have to clean up my room?" they are expressing what it feels like to
have an ideal thrust upon them by the world. We feel put upon,

obligated, and lose some vitality. But when we are engaged in activities in which we are realizing the ideals of the self, we love what we are doing, lose track of time, and become increasingly vitalized, although we are expending lots of energy.

However, as much as the existentialists want to make a strong differentiation between self and society, in reality they are often so fused as to be inseparable. It is not uncommon for someone to try on a social persona and find that it fits them perfectly. It is by trying on the persona that they find their self's ideals. For the existentialists we could only be our authentic selves if we find ourselves alienated from society; in a Kohutian self psychological world we can authentically be ourselves while being immersed in the roles of society. We can be authentic without being thoroughly alienated. For sure, there are persons who are so non-alienated, so socialized without any expression of a genuine self, that they feel fake or shallow. My supposition is that we must achieve some distance through questioning, rejecting some norms, etc. in order to be genuine selves; but we do not have to flee to the mountain tops as Zarathustra did.

4.5 The Id and the Basic Drives

In *How Does Analysis Cure?* Kohut says that self psychology more or less replaces a psychology of the drives; yet he never abandons the notion that we have biologically wired needs and pressures. He just doesn't see them as the fundament of psychological life, as Freud did. Rather, it is the narcissistic pressures to develop and sustain a self that constitutes the foundation of psychological life. We obviously need to take account of our biological needs, but when they pass through the self, they become part of our personhood rather than being the impersonal biological forces—the "it"—that Freud postulates as being the essence of our mammalian existence.

While it is not part of the project of this book to delve deeply into recent work that is attempting to re-define what the basic id drives are, I think it is worthwhile to briefly note the important contributions of Jaak Panksepp (1998) and Mark Solms (2021), who are updating drive theory on the basis of recent neuroscientific and evolutionary evidence. By studying the behavior and brain activity of mammals and birds, Panksepp posits that there are seven basic affective systems located in the subcortical regions of all mammalian brains: SEEKING, LUST, FEAR, RAGE, CARE, PANIC/GRIEF, PLAY, and SELF (Panksepp fully italicizes these terms). Solms accepts Panksepp's affective systems but integrates them into psychoanalysis by seeing them as "drives." He says that "The fundamental mechanism of drive is *homeostasis*" (2021, 1048). Solms further states that our psycho/somatic systems are set to a homeostatic equilibrium and when any of its components registers an error (a failure to stay within the homeostatic regulative measures), it then signals a *demand for work*—and this is experienced as a drive. Drives are attempts to reach *satiation* (not pleasure), which comes about with the restoration of homeostasis. Drives seek to take us out of *uncertainty* and restore us to a world of high *predictability*. *Affects* are the consciously experienced subjective aspects of drives.

Since all drives are associated with affects, Solms can connect his theory of drives with Panksepp's theory of affective systems. For Solms, "the sources of our emotional drives are 'the inmost interior' of the brain itself" (2021, 1064). That is, "it turns out that *seven* of them [Panksepp's affective systems] can be reliably elicited by electrical or (specific) chemical stimulation at exactly the same brain sites, in all mammals, from mice to men" (2021, 1064).

SEEKING is the drive to explore environments to satisfy the organism's needs but can come into play even when there are no needs that are pressing to be satisfied. We get pleasure from simply exploring our environments. LUST is akin to Freud's sexual drive, except that it is not constant but evoked by opportunities and can be pushed aside if other basic affective systems are more pressing. FEAR is the affect we feel when we sense danger; RAGE is what we feel when we find ourselves blocked by obstacles. PLAY is the drive to find out who we are, what we like, how we rank with others, etc. It is a way of learning about the world without the serious consequences of dealing directly with reality. The final three affective systems are very close to the basic findings of Kohut. Our caretakers (primary selfobjects) are so important to us that we have a basic affective system that throws us into PANIC when they are absent and then into grief, despair, and hopelessness when they do not return. We are hardwired to relate to our caretakers and suffer these emotions when our basic selfobject bonds are severed. However, we not only need care, we also need to give it.

CARE is the affective system that comes into play especially in regards to our young but also with all of those whom we love. We are biologically wired to care.

Finally, Panksepp posits that we have an affective SELF system that feels the affects, organizes them, and gives a sense of singularity to the organism. It is the least developed of Panskepp's affective systems. What is important for us is that it locates the biological urge to develop a self in the subcortical regions of the brain—the region that is closest to and interrelated with the other affective systems. Locating the self here is further evidence that it is different from an ego structure that is mainly operative in the cortical regions of the brain. Locating the self neurologically in the realm of the affects is further reason to think that the energy of the self is erotic. Finally, insofar as Pankseep and Solms see the self as a system that organizes the other affective systems, it must have some ascendency over the rest in importance. This fits perfectly with the concept of self and psychological dynamics that I have been developing in this book: that a well-formed self is the fulcrum of a well-organized psyche.

4.6 Persons and an Optimally Functioning Psyche

Experience does not come nicely compartmentalized as to what is motivating us; rather it is a jumble of attitudes, temperaments, moods, ideas, plans, emotions, wants, pressures, memories, etc. And it is not egos, selves, the social unconscious, or biological drives that think, experience, and act; it is persons. What is most evident in persons is not the various structures of the psyche, but their "personalities." "Personality," like "identity," is not indigenous to psychoanalytic psychology, as "it belongs to a different framework which is more in harmony with the observation of social behavior" (Kohut, 1971, xv). Hence, I will not attempt to review the massive literature on personality construction, but just say that our personalities are the ways we put together not only the self, ego, social unconscious, and id, but favored defenses, unconscious organizing principles, habits for dealing with various situations, etc. For instance, many people have as a major personality attribute "being a nice person" in which niceness is a character trait for defusing aggression and conflict, encouraging positive approbation, fending off criticism, a strategy for being liked and getting to belong, etc. All of these tendencies probably began in childhood as a way of dealing with parents, drives, integrating the social unconscious and getting the self's needs met. It is a way that tends to be strongly reinforced by society and family. However, it is also a trait that could be an essential part of what Winnicott calls "the false self" in that we have to be nice regardless of what we are actually feeling.

Like each of the sectors of the psyche, personalities do not act, think, suffer, or die; persons do. However, who a person is, how that person experiences life, whether that person can robustly engage with the world, and whether they find a sense of deep meaningfulness will depend a great deal on how their psychic agencies and structures function and intersect one another. It is how we put together in our strangely unique ways the ego, social unconscious, self, and id, plus various other voices that motivate our subjectivity, such as unconscious organizing principles, that make up our personhood.

Let us assume that humans, in general, would prefer to live lives that feel fully vitalized and meaningful; lives in which we feel deeply actualized and real; lives in which we engage the world with hope rather than excessive shame or guilt. The kind of metapsychological arrangement that most fosters this kind of life is one in which the self acts as the nucleus of the psyche around which all the other motivational sectors revolve. Another way of saying this is that in an optimally functioning psyche, the self infuses all the other sectors with its values and erotic energy. In such a psyche, the ego uses its intelligence, sense of power and freedom to find optimal ways for the ideals, ambitions, and selfobject needs of the self to be realized. It is the self that has organic ideals, which, when we are actualizing them, make us feel zestfully alive and meaningful, but it is the ego that can think and locate the right social practices that will foster the realization of the ideals. For instance, I have ideals that revolve around bringing philosophic thinking to the world, but I cannot do this by standing on a corner and corralling people to listen to me. In today's world, I need a position in an educational institution for this self-ideal to be recognized. I am thankful that my thoughtful ego could locate and affirm this ideal and then figure out how to get into and through graduate school, and finally locate an educational institution that most agreed with how I wanted to do philosophy. The self without the ego is lost; the ego without the self is empty. When the ego is locating social opportunities for the actualization of the self's ideals, ambitions, and selfobject needs, society is a field of opportunity; when the self is not being realized, then society can appear, as it did to Emerson, Thoreau, and Nietzsche, to be oppressive and limiting.

When the drives of the id pass through the gateway of the self into the ego, they, too, become transformed. We don't simply want lustful sex, we desire to have sex with a special person with whom we share a profundity of selfobject relations. We become erotic not just about a body on whom we want to release our tensions, but for a person who constitutes a deep source of meaning, stability, and reciprocal love. Those we are closest to also tend to be those with whom we are most likely to be enraged. But when rage passes through the self and into the ego, it is modified because it now is intertwined with the drives of care and our narcissistic need for stable and abiding selfobject connectedness. We find ways to express our anger that do not cause an irreparable rupture or hurt our partner/friend in ways that undermine their self.

Without a self as the fulcrum of psychic life, the ego will tend to align with the social unconscious and attempt to be highly successful in ways that might have very little meaning. Without a strong self anchoring the psyche, the drives have more of a chance of bursting forth and demanding satisfaction. Hence, one engages in sexual escapades/affairs that ruin stable selfobject relations and families; or rage breaks out with such magnitude as to shatter any possibility of repair; or grief overwhelms us with such a sense of despair and hopelessness that we retreat from life.

What this metapsychology teaches us is how important it is to construct social practices that foster the chances of selves developing at the core of psychic functioning. Yet, because modern culture has profoundly misidentified the self as the ego and asserted that the best way to be human is to be independent, autonomous, driven to attain socially valued goods, and ultra-rational, it has developed social practices that not only do not foster self-development but lead to its being undernourished and/or injured. We will explore in detail how the practices and values of modern society tend to undermine self-development and sustenance in the next part of this book.

Notes

1 It appears that, as a philosopher, I am the only one to attempt such a new self-psychological metapsychology (see my *Why It Is Good to Be Good* (2010, chapter 4) and *Exploring the Life of the Soul* (2017, chapter 3), but no one seems to have noticed or cared much.
2 While the self might seem to be a kind of subject that has its own desires, needs, aspirations, and ways of experiencing, I prefer to think of subjectivity as a unified whole that is always structured. It can be structured by the ego's energy and values, the self's values and erotic energy, or the energy and values from other motivational sectors of the psyche.

References

Bollas, C. (2011). *The Christopher Bollas Reader*. New York: Routledge.

Cushman, P. (1995). *Constructing the Self, Constructing America: A Cultural History of Psychotherapy*. New York: Da Capo.

———. (2019). *Travels with the Self: Interpreting Psychology as Cultural History*. New York: Routledge.

Fingarette, H. (1972). *Confucius—The Secular as Sacred*. New York: Harper & Row.

Erikson, E. (1960/1980). *Identity and the Life Cycle*. New York: W. W. Norton.

Freud, S. (1923). *The Ego and the Id*. In *Standard Edition of the Collected Works*, tr. & ed. James Strachey, et al., 24 vols. (1953–1974). Vol. 19, 1–66. London: Hogarth Press.

Kant, I. (1781/1998). *Critique of Pure Reason*. Eds. P. Guyer & A. Wood. Cambridge: Cambridge University Press.

Kohut, H. (1971). *The Analysis of the Self*. New York: International Universities Press.

———. (1977). *The Restoration of the Self*. New York: International Universities Press.

———. (1985). *Self Psychology and the Humanities*. Ed. C. Strozier. New York: Norton.

Nietzsche, F. (1978). *Thus Spoke Zarathustra*. Tr. W. Kaufmann. New York: Viking.

Panksepp, J. (1998). *Affective Neuroscience: The Foundations of Human and Animal Emotions*. New York: Oxford University Press.

Riker, J. (2010). *Why It Is Good to Be Good: Ethics, Kohut's Self Psychology, and Modern Society*. Lanham, MD: Jason Aronson.

———. (2017). *Exploring the Life of the Soul: Philosophical Reflections on Psychoanalysis and Self Psychology*. Lanham, MD: Lexington Books.

Sartre, J-P. (1956). *Being and Nothingness*. Tr. Hazel Barnes. New York: Simon & Schuster.

Solms, M. (2021). "Revision of Drive Theory." *JAPA, 69*(6), 1033–1091.

Stolorow, R. & Atwood, G. (2019). *The Power of Phenomenology: Psychoanalytic and Philosophical Perspectives*. New York: Routledge.

Stolorow, R. (2021). "Does Psychoanalysis Need a Metapsychology? A Reply to John Riker." *Psychoanalysis, Self, and Context, 16*(4), 352–354.

Chapter 5

A Self Psychological Understanding of Psychopathology

5.1 From Conflict to Deficit

Kohut offers both a novel understanding of psychopathology as caused by injuries to the self and a new vision of the therapeutic space needed for the restoration of selves.[1] To see how radical Kohut's shift is for understanding psychopathology and its cure, we need to compare it with Freud's classical model.

For Freud, psychopathology results not from some external event (the seduction hypothesis) but from the psyche's struggles to deal with intense inner conflicts.[2] In his early work, the conflicts involve a person's having a libidinally transgressive wish (e.g., an oedipal desire) that is opposed by moral and social standards, the upholding of which is required for a person to "survive" in society. Lying behind the clash between libidinal desire and social propriety is a deeper clash between two basic drives—sexual libido and survival. If the conflict between the two drives is so intense as to produce massive anxiety and threaten psychic cohesion, endangering the very ability of the psyche to function at all, then the wish, conflict, and anxiety are cast out of conscious awareness into the prison house of the unconscious, where they will be placed behind a repressing wall (the censor).

The psyche has now fragmented into conscious and repressed unconscious sectors, with the unconscious sector working according to primary process logistics independently of the ego's secondary process. In secondary process—conscious—thinking, the law of contradiction rules, time is sequential and real, and things that are alike are understood as similar but different. In primary process thinking, there is no law of contradiction, time is obliterated, important meanings can be displaced into insignificant items, and things that are alike are condensed

DOI: 10.4324/9781003303657-7

into an identity. In consciousness Amy is like my mother; in the unconscious, she is my mother—let the oedipal transferences loose!! As unconscious primary process is timeless, we can be subject to such transferential identifications and their experiential distortions for a lifetime.

The pathologized psyche will now suffer from depression, as psychic energy that would ordinarily be available for work in the world must now be used to keep the conflict repressed. And we develop a sense of not being quite real—of living an "as if" kind of life, because we are pretending that the repressed trauma never occurred; but it did! Further, the repression causes a regression to the last stage of psychosexual development that was reached before the repression. As such, development in these areas of psychic life is stultified. And, of course, debilitating symptoms develop—often psychosomatic—which express both the wish and the counterforce to the wish. These symptoms are repetition-compulsions that distort reality and compromise creative and nuanced ways of engaging with the world. The symptomized person becomes frozen in time, unable to grow and develop in crucial ways. Since symptoms express the anxiety-provoking conflict, it is dangerous to have them challenged, as the traumatizing tensions might be re-evoked and send the psyche back into chaos. To prevent such a re-traumatization, the psyche sets up defenses and then adds an extra layer of protection by developing resistances to having the defenses challenged. These resistances and defenses rigidify experience, often making it brittle, tense, and prevent a person from creatively adjusting to the changing conditions of life.

In his later work Freud complexifies his model of psychopathology as he introduces further internal conflicts. In *On Narcissism: An Introduction* (1914) he says that there is a profound conflict between how much libido to retain for oneself and how much to send out to the world. If too much libido is retained in the ego, we can become psychotic; if too much is sent out to the world, we can be deficient in taking care of ourselves. In the *Ego and the Id* (1923) he still has a conflict between two drives—now Eros and Thanatos—but adds a structural conflict between the ego, id, and superego. It is with the structural conflicts that Freud is best able to describe the tensions that lead to a guilt-ridden psyche, one in which the superego mercilessly condemns the ego (using the death drive of the id) for not living up to the superego's ideals (typically social standards). He summarizes: "When an instinctual trend undergoes repression, its libidinal elements are turned into symptoms, and its aggressive components into a sense of guilt" (1930, 139). He finds that the "sense of guilt [is] the most important problem for the development of civilization ...the price we pay for our advance in civilization is a loss of happiness through the heightening of the sense of guilt" (1930, 134).

To relieve the psyche of its pathology, the analyst needs to work backwards—through the resistances to the defenses, then to the symptoms, then to the original conflict in which the transgressive wish that caused the whole mess is finally uncovered and owned by the patient. This wish is best brought to light in an analysis of the transference, for the wish/conflict tends to be replicated in the therapeutic relation, and the interpretation of the wish/conflict as it appears in the transference is the best way for the client to experience the unconscious dynamics that are causing such pain. Freud famously compared the analyst to a surgeon, who would take their psychoanalytic surgical tools, cut through the defenses, and, at a time when the patient could tolerate it, expose the psychic infection and excise it with brilliant interpretations, as the repressed material cannot survive the brilliant light of consciousness.

What is most important to take from this insufficient thumbnail account of Freud's theory is that all pathology arises from internal conflicts—between two drives, two objects at which to direct libido, or among the id, ego, and superego, and all the complex variations that occur when these three kinds of conflicts interact. This inner turmoil is the fate of human beings who are creatures with typical mammalian drives for sex, survival, and aggression, but whose primary environment is a civilized social one that disallows open expression and satisfaction of the drives. We are a rather sorry animal whose fate is always to have to deal with inner conflict and turmoil. As Freud famously said, what psychoanalysis can do for us is to replace neurotic suffering with everyday ordinary suffering.

Kohut does not, in his earlier works, deny the usefulness of Freud's model for what he calls ordinary neurotic problems; he simply denies its usefulness for disturbances in the narcissistic sector of the psyche. However, by the time Kohut writes *How Does Analysis Cure?* he thinks that his self psychological model for understanding psychopathology and its cure can completely replace Freud's model.

> Self psychology is now attempting to demonstrate ... that all forms of psychopathology are based either on defects in the structure of the self, on distortions of the self, or on weakness of the self. It is trying to show, furthermore, that all these flaws in the self are due to disturbances of self-selfobject relationships in childhood.
>
> (1984, 53)

That is, psychopathology is not the result of an inner conflict between a wish and its prohibition but is caused by failures of external others (the child's chief selfobjects—almost always parents) to adequately tend to the child's narcissistic needs.

While the failures of parental selfobjects to adequately nourish the nascent selves of their children can be due to many factors, such as untimely illnesses and death, Kohut attributes most failures to self-defects in the parents themselves. In Kohut's case studies, we typically find as the cause of traumas to the self a cold distant mother, a depressed out-of-work father, a psychotically disturbed mother, a mother "whose face does not light up at the sight of her child" (1984, 21)—the kinds of caretakers who are unable to joyously mirror the child or affirm its idealizations. "What leads to the human self's destruction ... is its exposure to the coldness, the indifference of the non-human, the non-empathically responding world" (1984, 18). Indeed, Kohut goes so far as to say that children's selves can be fully nourished only by caretakers who themselves have coherent selves. Parents cannot overcome their deficiencies by acting on the latest childrearing advice or by having good intentions: "The capacity of a parent to respond empathically to the unusually great or highly specific selfobject needs of a child is, in the last analysis, a function of the firmness or the cohesion of the parent's self" (1984, 33). "It is less important to determine what the parents *do* than what they *are*" (1984, 15). Given the number of parents/caretakers who have injured selves, one need look no further than the ordinary conditions of family life to find factors that lead to narcissistic vulnerability and pathology.

Kohut says that parents should not be judged "from a moral point of view" for their selfobject failures. "Such an attitude would be foolish since the parental disability is an outgrowth of the deepest early experiences that influenced the development of the parent's responsibility and is thus beyond direct control" (1984, 33). "[T]he self psychologically informed psychoanalyst blames no one, neither the patient nor his parents" (1984, 25). That is, Kohut takes moral judgment out of the realm of psychopathology and keeps therapy within the realm of understanding and empathy.

Kohut explicitly states that the difference between his understanding of psychopathology and Freud's is that the Victorian household of Freud's era was one of "emotional overcloseness between parents and children and intense emotional relationships between the parents" (1977, 269); while the household of the late 20th century is so absent of close relationships that it "is now experienced more and more as threateningly distant; where children were formerly *over*stimulated by the emotional (including the erotic) life of their parents, they are now often *under*stimulated" (1977, 271). In short, what is most likely to traumatize contemporary children is an unbearable *lack* of selfobject responsiveness. This traumatic deficit in selfobject responsiveness is a major cause of ill-formed or injured selves in modern persons.

> And, again in contrast to the personality structure of the fin de siècle patients whose investigation led Freud to his formulation of the dichotomized psyche and later of structural conflict, the prevalent personality organization of our time is not typified by the simple horizontal split brought about by repression. The psyche of modern man—the psyche described by Kafka and Proust and Joyce—is enfeebled, multifragmented (vertically split), and disharmonious.
>
> (1984, 60)

5.2 The Traumatized Self

Although Kohut discusses cases of hyperarousal in which overly stimulated emotions cannot be metabolized, he deals mainly with pathology caused by a deprivation of selfobject nourishment. Kohut died before trauma theory emerged in the 1980's connecting the symptoms of men who went to Vietnam with those of women who had been sexually assaulted. Trauma theory focused not on situations of lack but on events that are so emotionally overwhelming that one is not able to process their meanings and/or the emotions they evoke. Philip Bromberg offers the following definition of trauma:

> Psychological trauma occurs in situations, explicitly or implicitly interpersonal, in which self-invalidation (sometimes self-*annihilation*) cannot be escaped from or prevented and from which there is no hope of protection, relief, or soothing. If the experience is either prolonged, assaultively violent, or if self-development is weak or immature, then the level of affective arousal is too great for the event to be experienced self-reflectively and given meaning... At its extreme, the subjective experience is that of a chaotic and terrifying flooding of affect that threatens to overwhelm sanity and psychological survival.
>
> (1998, 12)

While this conceptualization of trauma (one that reverberates with most trauma theory) works best for events that overwhelm our capacities to process them, we can use it for the traumas of deprivation by positing that there is an excessive point at which the absences or impoverishments so shatter expectations that they cannot be processed. We seem to have an inbuilt expectation as infants that we will be born into an empathically responsive world; when the world fails to be responsive in ways that are unendurable, trauma ensues. For instance, a child left alone for much longer than it can tolerate will be overwhelmed with panic (Panksepp & Biven, 2012) and not be able to process why their world is the way it is. Such absences can traumatically invalidate the selves of children, giving them the sense that they are not valuable or good enough to be of concern to the caretakers.

While Kohut does not discuss cases of sexual abuse/rape/aggression or the experience of traumatic violence as in war or school shootings, we can certainly see these as traumas to the self, for such events tend to shatter self-structure insofar as they destroy the homeostatic baseline in terms of which life feels safe and makes sense. Affective flooding of the psyche tends to sweep the self into a psychic whirlpool of chaos in which the self's need for its ideals and ambitions to make sense is annihilated. For instance, in the case of the sexual abuse of a child, the child's sense of self is shattered insofar as the child feels thoroughly objectified— turned into an object for the use of another. Its subjectivity is negated;

its specialness as a singular subjective being annihilated—it has been turned into a thing for the use of others. If the perpetrator is a family member—especially if it is a parent—idealization crashes traumatically and a sense of worthlessness pervades the psyche. Both poles of the self are crushed and a subterranean pathology can set in.

Kohut says that when a person is traumatized, the self "*fragments*," by which he means, first, that when the self is injured, we experience a deep sense of incoherence. We feel disoriented, at sixes and sevens, unable to find a center for our experience. Especially in moments when we are re-traumatized, we feel as though our minds are going haywire, as though they had no ballast, no gyroscope to keep them on an even keel. We find ourselves assaulted by emotional turmoil and nothing seems to provide a solid ground for producing meaning or an orientation to the world. We literally feel "*fragmented*." The experience of feeling fragmented is often translated into a hypochondriacal experiencing of one's body falling apart (1971).

Second, *fragmentation* is a structural concept. The traumatized self, which is now the source of unbearable pain, becomes separated from ego subjectivity and no longer infuses it with its vitalizing presence. The self that has been fragmented off from the ego has been cast into a largely inaccessible unconscious prison where defenses surround it, keeping it safe from further traumas. There are cases in which the traumas are so severe that the self simply disintegrates, leaving the person in a state of psychotic chaos; but in less severe cases, the self and its traumatic injuries are sequestered behind defenses that protect the injured self but also prevent it from interacting with the world. The self becomes dissociated from conscious experience. This lack of interaction means that the self cannot develop in a normal way. It is not unusual for the ego to compensate for the self's frozen development by accelerating its own development. Traumatized children often become "little adults" very quickly. Their ego development is often praised as the sign of precocious abilities rather than as a symptom of injuries to the self (see Alice Miller's *The Drama of the Gifted Child* (1979) for a brilliant depiction of this phenomenon). Not only does the self not develop when it has been traumatized, it often regresses to earlier levels of development. Self-esteem can plummet into a shameful archaic grandiosity and the sense of perfection can collapse into a primitive narcissistic identification. Hence, not only is the self a site of traumatic pain, but is also a place of shame, as it contains primitive ambitions to show off and be center stage—to be admired as the greatest thing ever.

There is a further reason why the injured self is a danger to ego consciousness and needs to be held apart from it, namely, that it is filled with narcissistic rage. This murderous rage constitutes a danger in its need to destroy the perpetrator of its injury, for this typically is a parent or sibling or close relation. Hence, one's self is now a place of danger, for it harbors unbearable pain, murderous rage, and a pressure to shamefully show off. Rather than having our selves as the ground of experience, we need to flee from them.

Although injured, the authentic self still has a vitalized erotic energy that wants to continue to develop. Like a caterpillar, it has been cocooned and is awaiting the time when it might once again be safe to re-enter the world, to take wing and shine forth. The growth will probably involve compensations and distortions, but it will grow out of the core self's original ideals, loves, and ambitions. As a young tree that is blocked by an obstacle will adjust to grow around it, so a person with an injured self can learn how to adjust and grow in ways that are possible.

I have had the strange—even unfathomable—experience of having my self erotically announce its ideals, needs, and values, even though it had been severely injured in childhood and was for the most part sequestered behind massively distorting defenses and symptoms. When I was 19, my self erotically signaled that I should major in philosophy and, indeed, devote my life to it. After I received my Ph.D., it made me fall in love with Colorado College and accept a position there rather than at more prestigious institutions. And when I first saw Marcia, my eros told me that this was the woman I had been waiting for my entire life. These were erotic eruptions expressing the deep needs and values of my genuine self, even though it had suffered debilitating traumas of abuse and neglect. The only way I have of understanding these events is to say that an injured self is still a self—it still contains an erotic fusion of ideals and ambitions. But it is so infiltrated with pain, regressive pulls, rage, and turmoil, that it must, for the most part, but not always, attempt to get its narcissistic needs met in symptomatic ways such as by engaging in addictive activity, sexualization, or by fully adopting social values and achieving great ego successes in the world.

There is one further kind of fragmentation that Kohut explores in an original and important way: the vertical split. A person suffers a vertical split when they engage in an activity or attitude towards the world that is so antithetical to their self-image that it must be disowned or disavowed. Unlike a horizontal split in which emotions/thoughts/experiences are cast into an unconscious realm, persons with vertical splits are conscious of what they are doing but deny that what they are doing belongs to them. For instance, if an upright member of the community also has a perversion to flash his genitals to children, he knows that he is doing it—there is no repression to the unconscious—but, nonetheless, does not know, for he refuses to see himself as a pervert, refuses to own what he is doing. Kohut defines a vertical split in the following way:

> The ideational and emotional manifestations of a vertical split in the psyche—in contrast to such *horizontal splits* as those brought about on a deeper level by repression and on a higher level by negation (Freud, 1925)—are correlated to the side-by-side, conscious existence of otherwise incompatible psychological attitudes *in depth*.
>
> (1971, 176–177)

Vertical splits are not an uncommon way of expressing a traumatized self, for the disowned behavior is attempt to get the self's narcissistic needs met but in ways that are incongruent with the person's idealized self-perception.[3]

Kohut says that when the self has been fragmented off from experience, we feel a sense of *"depletion."* Like fragmentation, *depletion* is a term that is phenomenologically appropriate ("experience near") and structurally descriptive. Depletion refers to feeling a lack of "vitality"—feeling that we are not fully alive in our lives. When the self is present, it vitalizes experience—makes us feel zestfully alive. When the self is absent, we lack a spring from which flow the waters of life. Kohut often uses the word *enfeeblement* to describe the state of depletion, indicating that in this state one lacks not only vitality but also agency. He says that persons with injured selves often attempt to compensate for the lack of vitality/agency by generating manic energy or hypervitality. Manic energy is not true vitality because it is not grounded in the organic ideals/ambitions of a self. When we manically accomplish tasks, we usually do not feel the profound satisfaction that comes when we use the self's erotic energy to achieve its ideals.

Kohut says that this sense of depletion is often experienced as having a profound *deadness* at the core of subjectivity. The emptiness or deadness that one experiences due to the absence of self-structure is very different from the "nothingness" of consciousness that was discussed in the last chapter. The nothingness of consciousness is openness and freedom—the ability to allow the world to flow into experience and the ability to choose new possibilities. Although Sartre declares that the experience of our essential nothingness makes us nauseated (1956), and Fromm believes that we wish to desperately flee from freedom (1941), it can also evoke senses of exhilaration, agency, and creativity. We are not doomed to be just who we are; we are also what we are not yet—we are essentially open to possibility. The nothingness of ego consciousness/self-consciousness is the essence of being human and, as such, is both problematical and joyful. It is otherwise with experiencing the *"emptiness"* caused by the absence of a self, for this is felt as an inner "deadness." Such experiences are utterly horrifying, for they are like going to the center of one's existence and finding a black hole sucking up all the light. Rather than locating a substantial core, there is a void. A death at the center of life. It feels like the icy pit Dante describes as the very bottom of hell where Lucifer dwells, freezing all the life and love out of existence. This lifeless emptiness is so painful, so unbearable, that, once experienced, we must defend against being able to encounter it ever again.

In response to injuries to the self, the psyche can unconsciously produce either *compensatory structures* and/or *defensive structures*. Although both are meant to protect the self from further injury, the difference between them is of vast importance. A structure is compensatory "when, rather than merely covering a defect in the self, compensates for this defect." A defensive structure, on the other hand, is one whose "sole or predominant function is the covering over of the primary defect in the self" (1977, 3). Kohut will go on to hold that "every self, not only in the narcissistic personality disorders but also in the structural neuroses and in health, consists to a greater or lesser extent of compensatory structures" (1984, 44). That is, most everyone receives traumatic setbacks, injuries, failures, roadblocks, etc., in childhood

and develops subsidiary compensatory structures to get their narcissistic needs met. Strangely, suffering significant traumas and developing
structures to compensate for them can result in more profound lives
than otherwise might have been:

> On the basis of impressions gleaned from observing people who, I
> believe, are (or were) able to live especially meaningful and creative
> lives, I have come to assume that a self characterized by the pre-
> dominance of compensatory structures constitutes the most fre-
> quent matrix of the capacity for high achievement. Stated in
> different terms, it is my impression that the most productive and
> creative lives are lived by those who, despite high degrees of trau-
> matization in childhood, are able to acquire new structures by find-
> ing new routes toward inner completeness.
>
> (1984, 44)

Kohut gives an extended example of how compensatory structures
work in the case of Mr. M, who had a primary defect in the grandiose
sector of the self, due to his mother's faulty empathy, and a secondary
defect in the idealizing sector due to the unavailability of his father
(1977). However, he deeply idealized his father's love of language—
the father had collected dictionaries and talked endlessly about words.
Mr. M developed this love of language in himself as a compensation
for not being able to fully bond with his father but was unable to fully
actualize it in life. When he started therapy with Kohut's supervisee,
he had a professional job that used his ability with language but in a
critical capacity rather than a creative one. The therapist focused the
therapy on strengthening the compensatory ideal of Mr. M's self, and
eventually he gained enough self-confidence and inner security to
start his own writing school, and, in so doing, regained the vitality of
his self.

Defensive structures, in distinction from compensatory ones,
cover over the injured self with its pain/fragmentation/deadness/
rage and attempt to deal with the narcissistic needs in ways that are
not growth-promoting. They can attempt to mask the devastating
sense of inner deadness by, for instance, compelling a person into
an unrelenting pursuit of pseudo-excitement, such as compulsive
masturbation, driven sexuality, excessive drug and alcohol use,

gambling, hypersociality, etc. The void can also be counteracted by the adoption of such narcissistic defenses as thinking of oneself as overly great (rather than, in fact, worthless), entitled to more than others, taking center stage whenever possible, etc. These defenses, of course, are dangerous in that they can put one into situations of being shamed and often need to be defended against themselves by such defenses as pseudo-humility and retreating to positions of insignificance—never taking center stage, but harboring fantasies of how great one would be if they did. Kohut remarks that it is not unusual for his narcissistically injured patients to alternate between being haughtily arrogant and being overly humble or retiring. "And every analyst is familiar with the two phenomenological faces of the narcissistically vulnerable person's behavior: his tendency toward timidity, loss of heart and shrinking retreat, on the one hand, and toward boastfulness, arrogance and provocative aggressiveness, on the other" (1985, 47).

For Kohut and self psychology, the defenses and resistances need to be understood as the psyche's attempt to protect the self from further trauma. They are positive, life-affirming strategies for both shielding the self and getting narcissistic needs met, although in less-than-optimal ways. Patients are reluctant to surrender their defenses because they fear re-traumatization and further fragmentation. Hence, one attractive therapeutic strategy is to simultaneously build up self-structure while diminishing defensive behaviors. It is akin to a sculptor's realizing a form from a block of marble. As the form appears, simultaneously the enclosing marble is chipped away.

5.3 Typology of Injured Selves

Kohut and Wolf generate a typology of injured selves in their seminal article, "The Disorders of the Self and their Treatment" (1978). Their inventory of the disorders is overly simplified and not meant to be exhaustive of the types of narcissistic disorders that can occur. Many, if not most, persons with narcissistic disturbances will have a mixture of the experiential and behavioral symptoms of the types listed below. What is important is to see how, with Kohut's understanding of the self, narcissistic injuries of various kinds result in different types of symptomatic formations and how these narcissistic symptoms are different from the neurotic ones with which Freud dealt.

The understimulated self. Persons with understimulated selves lack vitality and "experience themselves as boring and apathetic and they are experienced by others in the same way." They "will use any available stimuli to create a pseudo-excitement in order to ward off the painful feeling of deadness that tends to overtake them," including such activities as compulsive masturbation, daredevil actions, and addictive sex, gambling, shopping, drinking, drugs, etc.

(184–185)

The fragmenting self. Persons with fragmenting selves tend to fall apart and feel incoherent with even small blows to their self-esteem. While all humans tend to feel out of whack when our self-esteem has been taxed during the day and there is no source of replenishment available, persons with fragmenting selves will experience "a deep loss of the sense of the continuity of the self in time and of its cohesiveness in space. They will tend to symbolize these feelings hypochondriacally and become obsessed with body parts which "are beginning not to be held together anymore by a strong, healthy awareness of the totality of the body-self."

(185–186)

The overstimulated self. Persons with overstimulated selves have had their grandiosity in various activities overly praised or affirmed, but not the whole selves performing the activities. Such people "are subject to being flooded by unrealistic, archaic greatness fantasies which produce painful tension and anxiety" and "will try to avoid situations in which they could become the center of attention" (186). Selfobjects have responded to the performances of the self and not the total self and, hence, the performances get separated from the self. "Such people will tend to shy away from giving themselves over to creative activities because their self is in danger of destruction by being siphoned into its own performance or the product of its shaping."

(186–187)

The overburdened self. Persons with overburdened selves have "not been provided with the opportunity to merge with the calmness of an omnipotent selfobject. The overburdened self, in other words, is a self that had suffered the trauma of unshared emotionality" and will lack the ability to self-soothe. Such persons often experience the world as hostile and can be oversensitive to small noises, odors, or things slightly out of place in the therapist's office. They tend to be overly suspicious and irritable. A mistimed interpretation, even if on target, can be experienced as an attack or an intrusion.

(187–188)

Mirror-hungry personalities "thirst for selfobjects whose confirming and admiring responses will nourish their famished self." They seek to be noticed by others in order to try to ward off the feelings of worthlessness. They are compelled to display themselves in hopes of gaining confirmation of their greatness.

(190)

Ideal-hungry personalities "are forever in search of others whom they can admire for their prestige, power, beauty, intelligence, or moral stature. They can experience themselves as worthwhile only so long as they can relate to selfobjects to whom they can look up." Since idealized objects always have flaws, this can lead to lives of crushing de-idealizations and forever searching for new idols to worship.

(190–191)

Alter-ego personalities "need a relationship with a selfobject that by conforming to the self's appearance, opinions, and values confirms the existence, the reality of the self. Like the mirror-hungry and ideal-hungry personalities, the alter-ego hungry personality will soon find failures in the other to be the same as they are, break-off the relation, and seek for new alter-egos in an endless quest.

(191)

Merger-hungry personalities "need to control their selfobjects in an enactment of the need for structure." These personality types have selves that are much more enfeebled/injured than the previous personality types and "seek selfobjects in lieu of self-structure." They have difficulty discriminating "their own thoughts, wishes, and intentions from those of the selfobject. Because they experience the other as their own self, they feel intolerant of his independence" and can "demand—indeed, they expect without question—the selfobject's continuous presence."

(192)

Contact-shunning personalities "avoid social contact and become isolated, not because they are disinterested in others, but, on the contrary, just because of their need for them is so intense. They fear both rejection by others but also being "swallowed up and destroyed by the yearned-for all-encompassing union."

(192)

These thumbnail descriptions of various pathologies of the self that result from selfobject failures and responses to them reveal how differently psychopathologies are understood from the perspective of self psychology rather than a classical model.

5.4 Stoicism

There is another personality constellation that is a common way for persons to deal with a fragile self in relation to a difficult world: Stoicism. Stoicism arose in the chaotic era of the Hellenistic and Roman Empires in which one's fortune and status could change dramatically at almost any time, depending on which faction gained the upper hand in politics. Stoicism was adopted as a form of life by both those enslaved (Epictetus) and those who ruled (Marcus Aurelius). The stoic way of being human seeks to reduce the pathos in life by withdrawing from the chaotic circumstances of embodied existence and retreating into an inner world over which we seem to have control. The hero for Stoicism was Socrates, who in his trial and death showed no emotional turmoil, regret, or even concern over what was being unfairly done to him by the state. He kept a cheerful visage and proclaimed that "Nothing can harm a good man either in life or after death" (*Apology*, 41d). Socrates refused to allow the world to determine his inner state; he was thoroughly self-determining.

When ancient Stoics withdrew from the world, they tried to find some universal principle, such as the laws of Nature, by which to respond to the world to help them negate the vicissitudes of transient particularity. The universality gave them freedom from the world; freedom to live without pathos. Pathos—suffering—simply means that what one experiences is determined by forces acting on one; freedom is acting out of the universal ground in one's inner self, unaffected by what the world is doing. Rather than being passive in relation to the world, the Stoics were active.

I first read about the Stoics when I was just ten years old and was captivated by their ability to escape from the pain and turmoil of the world simply through an act of dismissing the importance of what the world was doing to them. I found that I when I adopted the stoic attitude, I did not need to let my mother's craziness or my father's sadistic sexuality throw me into pain and chaos. I could invalidate them with a mere act of choosing how to respond to them. I went into an attitude of "I just don't care what happens." "Don't let anything get to you." Becoming a stoic at a very young age helped salvage my life. I am, of course, hardly alone in turning to stoicism.

Given that many, if not most, persons today have either very fragile or injured selves and given that the contemporary world is one of vast uncertainties, a stoic approach to life is attractive for many. Climate change is making the important emotional surround of weather unpredictable and raising scenarios of impending doom. The upheavals around systems of social injustice makes affirming American life very difficult. There is the socio/economic/political upheaval caused by rogue nations such as Russia and North Korea. We are still recovering from the ravages of COVID and do not know how it will twist and turn to once again disrupt our patterns of life. There is the radical right threatening the very existence of democratic government. There are endless mass shootings. And aside from all of that, we live in a technological capitalist age in which ceaseless change destroys all that is familiar. How can one live in a world in which disaster seems to be lurking around every corner? The answer for many is turning to a stoic way of being in the world.

Contemporary persons trying to be stoical in relation to the vicissitudes of existence tend not to search their souls to find some universal principle, but instead transform stoicism into a kind of not-caring, in which the fundamental response to the world is "whatever." This kind of practiced indifference has the effect of not getting emotionally involved with the world and thereby protecting oneself against the anxiety that one's life might be thoroughly derailed. It is a retreat into a narcissistically protected world in which one's concerns basically come down to my arranging my little world so as to attain my pleasures and keep out the disruptive negativities of everything else.

The price one must pay for adopting this wonderfully insular way of being is simple: give up emotions. The Stoics thought of emotions as deficient perceptions that were likely to lead one into untruth. Cease having emotional responses to the world; live a life of reason. Stoicism typically involves developing enhanced ideational abilities to deal with the world rather than emotional ones. Kohut does not think that such intellectualization need be disastrous, as ideational structures "can be a protection against these disorders of self-cohesion, which the rigorous, cohesive intellectual systems help to overcome (1996, 329).

> The coexistence of the capacity for abstract thought and deep disturbances in the cohesion of the self is not at all an accident. If you investigate the greatest minds in theoretical physics or astronomy disciplines of that type, I have no doubt that in these areas of outstanding intellectual functioning you will find a much higher percentage of people with very, very vulnerable, if not protracted, disturbances of self-cohesion.
>
> (1996, 329)

However, stoicism is more than intellectualization, for it constitutes a whole way of being in the world, an entire personality constellation. While intellectualization is an ego defense that originates unconsciously, stoicism is often a conscious choice for a way to be in the world. When it is consciously adopted as a way of being in the world, it can both characterize all experience or act as a kind philosophical escape hatch, as it was for me. That is, when life got tough, I could escape into a world of stoic indifference—a place of untouchability and narcissistic invincibility. By not caring about what the world was doing, I was safe from the dreaded vicissitudes of existence. In contemporary parlance, stoicism as an escape hatch is a "self-state," a way of being oneself that the ego can run to when it needs to. The penalty for always having the possibility of becoming indifferent is that one cannot commit to being fully alive, commit to living in the depth, complexity, and vivacity of existence. When one is always ready to flee emotions when they seem difficult means that one cannot have a robust emotional connectedness to life.

It is easy to see why a stoical way of being in the world is a preferred defense for the ego that values power and freedom. It frees the ego from highly disruptive emotions and painful neediness and allows the ego to pursue aims of power and success because it has a built-in safety net of not-caring if things go wrong. Not-caring is a muscular, almost impenetrable defense against inner and outer chaos and the pain of loss or failure. It is also a fabulous way to get narcissistic needs met insofar as it puts one above the fray in a place of imperturbable invincibility.

Stoicism is not only a common way for contemporary persons to consciously choose for how to live in the precarious world but can be an elaborate unconscious defense to protect a traumatized self, a defense in which a person has dampened emotions, loses concern about the actualization of the self's nuclear program, and avoids failures in selfobject relations by establishing an insular independence. Stoicism is a supremely fine defense for narcissistic injuries because it not only limits the vulnerability of a person to further injury but asserts a primitive sense of omnipotence, perfection, and grandiosity, thereby satisfying our basic narcissistic needs. Stoics are omnipotent in the sense that they are above the world and distain it; they are perfect in the sense of attaining an ideal of imperturbability (*apatheia*); they are great in that they believe that nothing in the world has power over them.

Stoic patients will be a hard nut for therapists to crack. They desperately fear dependency on the analyst and keep wondering why they are there at all. Only a deep failure in some aspect of life and a concomitant sense of desperate emptiness is likely to send a stoic to therapy in the first place and constant reminders of this pain will be needed to keep them there. It might take a good while for the narcissistic transferences to develop, but once they do, empathic forward-edge/trailing-edge selfobject responses—a kind of therapy that has been well-explored in the self psychological literature—might lead to the repair of the self. However, not only does the self need repair, so also does the ego, for it needs to adopt a new outlook on life, one which is willing to engage more deeply and suffer more profoundly. To live tragically rather than stoically is an entire shift in how to be in the world and is very difficult to achieve. I suspect that in the end, it will take an identification with the therapist's commitment to living fully that is needed.

5.5 Eros, Empathy, and Repair

That a therapist's empathic responsiveness can repair damaged selves and fragmented psyches has been empirically documented and is well-known (Bohart & Greenberg, 1997). What is less well understood is why empathy seems to be the medicine an injured self needs to heal. Why is it that empathy, delivered in the right way at the right time by the right person, can help restore an injured self? Kohut, himself, offered that empathic responsiveness might cure because it was a "corrective emotional experience," thereby going against the psychoanalytic hegemonic dictum never to satisfy a patient's desires (1984). However, when we change from a conflict model to a traumatized-self model of pathology, it makes sense to say that the provisioning of empathic responsiveness will help fill the deficit. But the question remains as to why empathy is the food the self needs to grow in the first place. Why is empathy the psychological protein out of which selves can develop?

Empathy is a form of mimesis—a form of mimicking in which one person replicates what another is feeling. Mimesis is a kind of human activity that seems to unify one with whatever is being mimicked. In the ritual dances of tribal peoples, it is not unusual for them to do dances that mimic what they are trying to become: an eagle, a bear, a rainstorm. Jane Ellen Harrison quotes an ancient Greek hymn in which we must imagine tribal persons mimicking what is being sung about in a leaping dance: "Leap for full jars, and leap for fleecy flocks, and leap for fields of fruit, and for hives to bring increase" (1912/1963, 8). She imagines that the tribal dance is mimicking the leaping into life that occurs in spring to magically help this miraculous event occur. And Aristotle says that one of the key ways we become virtuous is by mimicking those who are virtuous. We become just by acting the way just people act (*Nicomachean Ethics*, 1105b). Indeed, the young of many species develop social skills and character by mimicking their elders; it is a crucial way that they become a member of its species. However, the reverse, at least for humans, is also true. We develop self-structure by being empathically mimicked.

It is the grandiose pole of the self—the pole which needs to be anchored in a firm and substantial sense of self-esteem—that most needs empathic mirroring. We develop self-esteem by being affirmed, and empathic mirroring can affirm one's worth in the most profound ways, for it says, "You are so wonderful that I make myself just like you." "If you are sad, I am sad with you." "If you are happy, I am happy with you." "You are so important I duplicate you in myself." These meanings, of course, are not spoken, but emotionally understood; empathy does not reverberate with the ego, but with the self. In Edward Tronick's still face experiment we see the mother perfectly mirroring the facial expressions of her child and can see how the child feels fully affirmed and full of herself. When the mother's face goes still and is unchanging in response to the baby's changing face, the baby gets upset and panicked at first and then goes into a kind of despairing hopelessness. When the mother then restores her empathic mirroring, the baby once again becomes vitalized (YouTube).

To connect with the injured self and repair it, empathy is needed. However, the kind of empathy that is transformative is not simply empathy for the person and what the person is feeling, but for the self-states that have been dissociated. That is, the injured self that is dissociated from consciousness is a particular instantiation of the self at a particular time with its own particular way of being itself and relating to the world. A self-state is a "narcissistic configuration" and to an extent can be treated as a fully formed little self—a subjectivity with hopes, sufferings, dreads, a primitive relation to narcissistic needs, and a relation to selfobjects. Bromberg sees each self-state as "organized around a particular self-other configuration that is held together by a uniquely powerful affective state" (181) and as having its own sub-narrative. That is, each self-state is a "way of being in the world"—a way of being the self that one once was and which needs to once again be integrated, rather than dissociated, into the psyche for development to fully re-emerge.

Dissociated self-states are aspects of the self that the person has disavowed as truths about who they are. Since these states have such pain and shame connected to them, we are not likely either to empathize with them or admit their reality. For the psyche to achieve integration and achieve a sense that one is real rather than fake, a person needs to reclaim the parts of the self that have been lost. To help them do this, therapists need to empathize with the dissociated self-state fragments. The patient can then start to mimic the therapist's empathy and become empathic with these split-off parts of himself. This self-empathy for the disowned segments of the self is what allows them to rejoin the self and make it robust, although now with a deepened sense of the suffering one has experienced.

We can add depth to this understanding of why and how empathy can build and repair self-structure if we understand the energy of the self as eros. As we have seen, eros is simply love—the kind of love that seeks to connect with the other, to be one with the other. It is the kind of love that gleams through the eyes. I believe that empathy is a profound form of erotic love because it is the one form of knowing who another is that does not objectify the other but affirms the other's subjectivity in the deepest way—by duplicating it in one's own subjectivity.

Since empathy is a form of eros and eros is the energy of the self, when someone empathizes with us, we feel loved by another self. The love pouring into us is actually the erotic self of another person; hence, we are building self by ingesting self. Empathy validates the worth of the self as nothing else can because it is the flowing of self into self. If the energy of the self is love and we feel most like our selves when we are loving, then there is little else in life that makes one feel more like loving than finding one's self being loved. And in loving the other who loves us, we are empathically mirroring them, establishing a kind of loving reciprocity. This loving reciprocity is the fertile soil in which self-structure can be repaired. That is, empathy is the self's sharing its substance (its eros) with another, and this is why empathy can nourish the other. It is literally a person's self's sending itself into the self of another and giving it the one nourishment it needs: love—a love that understands the other because it is empathic.

When therapists empathically respond to their patients, they are sending their loving selves into the injured selves of their patients. However, the selves of the therapists are more organized than those of their fragmented patients, and so a kind repair to the developmentally arrested self can occur. As Freud said, psychoanalysis is a cure through love. What kind of love? A love that is inherently connective, aesthetic, and developmental: empathic eros. This is the basis for why intersubjective self psychology has the right set of presuppositions for how to do psychoanalytic therapy. Insofar as the forward-edge of both patient and therapist are engaging one another, the patient's self can re-awaken because it is loving and being loved. To feel as alive and awake as the dawn, one needs to feel oneself loving and being loved.

The metapsychological distinction that I have drawn between the self and the ego allows us to see why psychoanalytic empathic approaches to therapy have the best chances of repairing fragmented, injured selves, and why CBT is not as effective for long-term transformation of injured selves. CBT seems to presuppose a metapsychology that identifies the self with the ego. As such, it focuses on the conscious ego and its interactions with the world, using methods that involve cognitive speech and problem-solving techniques in attempts to improve patterns of behavior and thinking that are ineffective or self-negating. While this kind of therapy can be effective in improving choices for interacting with the world, it cannot reach the depths of the unconscious psyche where the injured self resides. Behavior might improve; thinking might improve; but the feelings of emptiness, worthlessness, and meaninglessness will likely still haunt the person who will need to find other symptomatic ways to try to fill the emptiness. Some will be improvements. I know someone who used drugs to soothe their inner pain and transformed their addictive activity to working out in the gym—multiple hours every day. This is a genuine behavioral shift that reaps great benefits, but the person still deals with chronic senses of emptiness and shame.

Even so, CBT and most other forms of therapy can have some positive effect on the injured self, for therapists in general seek to understand their clients and help them. At an unconscious level this concern can be experienced as love, even if it involves structures of objectification. At least someone is taking an interest in me! However, since the self lies largely in the unconscious and is deeply embroiled in unconscious dynamics, it needs someone with psychoanalytic understanding and empathic resonance to transform it.

5.6 Psychological Health

This chapter has delineated what constitutes psychopathology; we need to conclude by giving a notion of what constitutes psychological health. Freud, of course, offered his famous definition of psychological health as the ability to love and work. This is a behavioral definition;

Kohut and other self psychologists disagree and point out that some persons who have healthy psyches are not necessarily involved in intimate relationships or satisfying labor. In contrast, Kohut wanted to posit a more psychological definition of health, one that goes to the internal experience of a person. In Chapter 4, we gave a metapsychological definition of health: a psyche in which the self is at the core of psychological activity, a rational and informed ego locates opportunities for the actualization of the self's ideals and knows how to get selfobject support, the emotions and drives of the id are modulated by the self, and the social unconscious offers possibilities for self-actualization rather than insisting on a false persona. However, while this definition is psychological, it is not phenomenological. How does a person feel who has a healthy soul?

Kohut offers five experiential criteria for identifying a psychologically healthy psyche: coherence, firmness, vitality, vigor, and harmony (1984, 65). People with healthy psyches feel coherent in that they are not pulled in myriads of directions but feel that they have a core which holds them together, which gives a pole star to psychological life around which the other elements can revolve. The core is felt as firm—as not easily shakable by the vicissitudes of everyday life. That is, persons with intact core selves do not feel excessive fragility but have a deep sense that they can withstand the ups and downs of life. Persons with firm, coherent selves also feel vitalized—full of the zest of life. They are full of vigor in that they have a strong sense of agency and efficacy. They have a confidence that their actions will be productive. And their psyches feel harmonious in that they are using the self's ambitious energy to actualize the self's ideals. That is, life harmoniously revolves around the pursuit of the self's most meaningful ideals rather than fantasies or empty statuses. We can add that persons with healthy psyches that are anchored in an intact self will be able to establish and pursue meaningful goals guided by their heartfelt ideals and be able to regulate their emotions, self-esteem, and desires. They will also be able to engage in meaningful relationships with others, relationships that exhibit mutual empathy and care.

But, finally, we must say that we agree in part with Freud: one's soul is healthy to the extent that it can love—love the self's ideals, love selfobject friends, love beauty in whatever forms are most compelling. For some, this will involve the love of nature and the love of life.

For some, it is love of God or a like spiritual presence that fills them with vitality and meaningfulness. And, of course, the most essential love is the narcissistic one—love of our selves and our lives. Nietzsche said that to live as a free spirit, we need *amor fati*—love of our fate. This is a love that accepts and affirms all that has happened to us, all that we are. It ceases judging and longing that life might have been otherwise. It is the full love of oneself and the universe into which we have been strangely thrown.

Persons who are psychologically healthy live according to ideals rather than fantasies, are efficacious rather than passive, are singular rather than socially generalized, are empathic rather than judgmental, affirm creativity over repetitiveness, accept fate rather than fighting it, and love themselves, others, and life to the fullest.

Notes

1 Several fine books have been written on the clinical implications of Kohut's self psychology, the most recent being Charles Strozier, et al.'s *The New World of Self: Heinz Kohut's Transformation of Psychoanalysis and Psychotherapy* (2022) and George Hagman, et al.'s *Intersubjective Self Psychology: A Primer* (2019). What I hope to add to this literature is a careful analysis of the concepts involved in understanding what happens when selves are injured and how they can be repaired.
2 There is, of course, a massive literature on Freud's concept of psychic dynamics and therapy. What follows in this section is the briefest of thumbnail sketches.
3 See Arnold Goldberg's *Being of Two Minds* (1999) for an in-depth analysis of the vertical split.

References

Bohart, A., & Greenberg, L. (1997). *Empathy Reconsidered: New Directions in Psychotherapy*. Washington, DC: American Psychological Association.

Bromberg, P. (1998). *Standing in the Spaces: Essays on Clinical Process, Trauma, & Dissociation*. Hillsdale, NJ: The Analytic Press.

Freud, S. (1914). "On Narcissism: An Introduction." In *Standard Edition*, 14, pp. 73–102. London: Hogarth Press, 1961.

———. (1923). "The Ego and the Id." In *Standard Edition*, 19, pp. 1–66. London: Hogarth Press, 1961.

———. (1925). "Negation." In *Standard Edition*, 21, pp. 149–157. London: Hogarth Press, 1961.

———. (1930). "Civilization and Its Discontents." In *Standard Edition*, 21, pp. 64–145. London: Hogarth Press, 1961.

Fromm, E. (1941). *Escape from Freedom*. New York: Farrar & Rinehart.

Goldberg, A. (1999). *Being of Two Minds: The Vertical Split in Psychoanalysis and Psychotherapy*. Hillsdale, NJ: The Analytic Press.

Hagman, G., Paul, H., & Zimmerman, P. (2019). *Intersubjective Self Psychology: A Primer*. New York: Routledge.

Harrison, J. E. (1912/1963). *Themis: A Study of the Social Origins of Greek Religion*. London: Merlin Press.

Kohut, H. (1971). *The Analysis of the Self*. New York: International Universities Press.

———. (1977). *The Restoration of the Self*. New York: International Universities Press.

———. (1984). *How Does Analysis Cure?* Chicago: University of Chicago Press.

———. (1985). *Self Psychology and the Humanities*. Ed. C. Strozier. New York: W. W. Norton.

———. (1996). *The Chicago Institute Lectures*. Eds. P. Tolpin & M. Tolpin. Hillsdale, NJ: Analytic Press.

Kohut, H., & Wolf, E. (1978). "The Disorders of the Self and their Treatment: An Outline." In *Essential Papers on Narcissism*. Ed. A. Morrison. New York: New York University Press.

Miller, A. (1979). *The Drama of the Gifted Child*. New York: Basic Books.

Panksepp, J., & Biven, L. (2012). *The Archaeology of Mind: Neuroevolutionary Origins of Human Emotions*. New York: Norton.

Sartre, J-P. (1956). *Being and Nothingness*. Tr. Hazel Barnes. New York: Simon & Schuster.

Strozier, C., Pinteris, K., Kelley, K., & Cher, D. (2022). *The New World of Self: Heinz Kohut's Transformation of Psychoanalysis and Psychotherapy*. Oxford: Oxford University Press.

Part II

The Concept of Self in the Modern World

Chapter 6

The Construction of Individuals in Modern Society

6.1 Constructing Persons in the Economic Age

Persons had to change how to be human because a new environment came into existence, one that would eventually dominate every aspect of human life: *the market*. While humans have always exchanged goods and services, this activity was typically in the support of life, not the essence of life. In the modern economic era engaging in market activity—working, making a living, and consuming goods and services—has become the central focus of life around which all else revolves. Since the market is the crucial environment that must be both negotiated and generated, modern society needs to produce the kind of human being who can best sustain and propel the economy. To do this, it must first create a new ideal for how best to be human and how to live the best of human lives—a revolutionary ideal that has helped birth a very different kind of human being than what has existed previously in the West (or to my knowledge anywhere else): the modern person.[1]

The market is structured around several central principles that make it different from previous ways in which humans exchanged goods and services. First, everything—all goods, services, positions, salaries, etc., are competitive. Competition is the key to prices stabilizing at the lowest level, new products and services being innovated, and productivity increasing exponentially. Competition is the crucial factor making market society extraordinarily dynamic—probably the most dynamic in all of human existence. However, competition is not the only factor making modern society so volatile. Capitalism's principle of re-investing profit into production rather than spending it, as former aristocrats had done on luxuries, has been crucial in making the market stunningly dynamic. If profit is re-invested in production, then production must

DOI: 10.4324/9781003303657-9

expand, and if production expands, then markets must expand to consume the goods. It took almost no time from the beginning of the economic world in Western Europe for the European countries to colonize most of the rest of the world in search of both raw materials to transform into finished products and to find markets for those products. It was toward the end of the 19th century that the West discovered that the ultimate, infinite market for goods and services is *desire*. Insofar as customers desire ever more and newer goods, the capitalist economy could keep dynamically and volatilely expanding. Hence, the center of the capitalist world became Madison Avenue rather than Wall Street, for the art and science of stimulating desire through advertising became the foundation for the new economic world. Insofar as the market depends on its members to be continually purchasing goods and services, it needs persons to desire—incessantly. And insofar as one needs money to purchase the goods one desires, one needs to work. And work we do! For most modern persons, work is the center of life. What we do to make a living more or less defines who we are and where we rank in society.

In previous ages, stability reigned over change; now change reigns over stability. In the famous words of Karl Marx and Friedrich Engels,

> Constant revolutionizing of production, uninterrupted disturbance of all social conditions, everlasting uncertainty and agitation distinguish the bourgeois epoch from all earlier ones. All fixed, fast-frozen relations, with their train of ancient and venerable prejudices and opinions, are swept away, all new-formed ones become antiquated before they can ossify. All that is solid melts into air, all that is holy is profaned.
>
> (1848/1994, 161–162)

Modern persons living in this world must be able to adapt to rapid, never-ceasing change, and this adaptability requires them to abandon traditions and stable practices. They need to become modern nomads who cherish geographical and social mobility to take advantage of market opportunities as they arise.

Given that modern society revolves around competition, profit, and change, it needs to construct persons who can both generate this kind of world and flourish in it. The key characteristic for such persons is that they think of themselves as self-contained *individuals*, each out to optimize their own welfare. It is individuals, not collectives, who are in competition with one another both in Darwinian evolutionary theory and capitalist economics. It is mobile individuals who are best able to deal with the changing vicissitudes of the market, and we are raised to be this kind of independent person able to negotiate life on our own.

A society based around competition must by necessity become stratified into winners and losers—must become a society of classes based on how well one does in the market rather than on whether one was born into the aristocracy or peasantry as in previous eras. The crucial new class that comes into existence is the middle class or the bourgeoise. Unlike peasants or aristocrats who were more or less born into their status, middle class persons must earn their status by engaging in market competition, and since competition is always in play, no status is guaranteed to be permanent. Winners can suddenly become losers. Hence, life in the middle class tends to be filled with anxiety and the question arises with great poignancy about what kind of human being is most likely to succeed and remain successful in such a world. And, of course, before defining such an ideal, we need to know what constitutes winning and losing. In the old religious world these might be defined as salvation for the morally good and damnation for the evil; but in a market world, winners are those who attain the most wealth, power, and status; losers are those who become poor.

6.2 The Ideal Market Person

Let me summarize and expand on the traits of the kind of person best able to be successful in advanced technological market interactions. The successful market person will have an amalgam of key characteristics:

- *Desire*: It seems strange to say that becoming a "desiring human being" is part of an ideal, but without desire, there can be no market economy. The kind of pious person populating the religious era—one who was not interested in material well-being—is not the kind of person who can propel an economic world. The modern world desperately needs desiring persons and so has convinced us that desire is life. To not be desiring is to be dead, empty. Since the fulfillment of desire is pleasure, modern utilitarian ethics redefines the purpose of human life as the attainment of pleasure. The more pleasures, the better the life. Although many pleasures can come from non-market sources (the beauty of nature, the joys of intimate love, etc.), modernity creates needs that can only be satisfied by engaging in market exchanges. Since what allows one to optimally engage in the market is wealth, having money becomes the ultimate desire. Money not only allows us to satisfy desires but also allows us to expand them, and (supposedly) the more expansive one's desires, the more one can fill one's life with pleasures. In sum, the economic society conceives of humans as pleasure-optimizing organisms and idealizes those who not only have expansive desires but who also have enough money to satisfy them.

- **Being productive and technologically savvy**: Since the goal of the economy is to generate goods and services, it needs persons who highly value being productive. It has convinced us that we are good when we are productive; worthless when we are non-productive. Leisure time has steadily decreased, as work pours electronically into weekends and evenings, asking us to be evermore industrious. Work has become so important that what we do for a living is the foremost component of our social identity. Where before we might have had as the central feature of our social identity what congregation or clan we belonged to, now it is what we do for a living—where and how we work. Indeed, we no longer have mere social identities, we now have socioeconomic identities.

  Crucial to our being able to be productive is our ability to use technology. In his brilliant essay, "The Question Concerning Technology," Heidegger says that technology is not to be thought of as tools we use but as a whole way of "being-in-the-world," for it touches how we perceive the world, treat its inhabitants, and treat ourselves (1954/1977). In the technological way of being human, we tend to see everything in terms of its usefulness—its use-functionality. We are concerned not so much with what something is doing for us now, but what it could do for us when we need it. That is, we turn everything into what Heidegger calls "*standing reserve*." In this way of experiencing the world, everything loses its actuality—its Being—and becomes potentiality. Rather than being able to experience the oak tree that stands before me in its singular being, I reduce it to its various potentialities—it is where I could hang a swing, place a bench under it for shade, cut it down for lumber, trim it to fit my aesthetic tastes, etc. That is, everything gets reduced to its ability to do work for us. We even reduce ourselves to standing reserve insofar as we think of ourselves as essentially productive individuals. We develop skills, knowledge, credentials, and know-how to make ourselves able to be productive members of society—to be attractive commodities in the market. This technological way of being in the world makes full sense in an economic world in which every part of life is quantified, measured, and assessed to see how productive we have been and might be. To be is to be productive; and to be optimally productive, one needs not only to be adept with the newest technology but to adopt technology as a way of being in the world.

A technological way of being-in-the-world has as a necessary consequence the tendency to treat subjects as objects, to treat everyone as *standing reserve*. The question "what can you do for me?" almost automatically arises upon meeting others. Can you entertain me with jokes? Are you available for some hook-up sex? Can you help me get promoted? Even for those close to us, the question arises, "What have you done for me lately?" Others exist for what they can do for us; for their ability to produce desired results. That is, the extreme emphasis on productivity in modern individuals tends to make us into objectifying persons who negate the subjectivity of others and ourselves.

• *Rationality*: Since the complexity of economic society and the technology needed to run it keep expanding exponentially, modern society needs incredibly intelligent, rational, problem-solving members at its highest levels. It has invented a vast system of schooling to produce such persons, with many starting their schooling by three or four years of age and continuing through graduate school several decades later. What is understood by rationality has changed dramatically from earlier epochs in which reason was given the task of gaining knowledge, especially knowledge about eternal verities. In response to the dynamic changeableness and instability of modern life, the American pragmatic philosophers re-defined the nature of rationality from having a storehouse of knowledge to being able to practically solve problems. Charles Sanders Pierce, William James, and John Dewey not only changed how we think of truth, knowledge, and rationality but changed the nature of American education to foster this new kind of rationality—the kind of rationality needed by the new economic society. For James, every idea has a "cash value;" namely, how it works in lived experience. He hates abstract metaphysical ideas that do not make a difference in how we interact with our natural and social environments. Ideas need to work (1907/2000). While there is a spiritual dimension to James' thought, it always has a pragmatic tonality: spiritual ideas need to transform experience and/or open new realms of experience. For Dewey, rationality is defined as the ability to engage in inquiry, which is defined as "the controlled or directed transformation of an indeterminate situation into one so determinate in its constituent distinctions and relations as to convert the elements of the original situation into a unified whole" (1938/1981, 226). That is, thinking is for the sake of negotiating problematic situations in real life. He conceives of humans as "organisms in environments" (a Darwinian articulation of what Heidegger calls "Dasein"—being-in-the-world). For Dewey, life is always lived in environments which de-stabilize in relation to our needs, continuously presenting us with problems that must be solved. "Thinking" is problem-solving.

The pragmatists were impressed not so much by the discoveries of modern science, but by the methodology that kept producing new discoveries and new knowledges about the world. They wanted to bring the scientific methodology of empirical experimentation to everyday life—to have us not ground life in a set of traditions or accepted regularities, but to experiment with how we might make our lives better, more fulfilling, more in-tune with who we empirically are rather than fantasies about who we metaphysically might be. They asked us to abandon speculative rational metaphysics and live with our empirical bodies in this empirical world, experimenting on how best to interact with our environments so as to attain embodied satisfactions in this life—not some imaginary eternal afterlife.

Of course, there is a price to pay for this shift from rationality as a body of knowledge to rationality as the ability to solve problems, namely, that one's mind needs to be empty of old learning in order to process new learning. For instance, when I teach Plato, I get terrific papers that have solved the problem of how to write a terrific paper on Plato. But when I meet my students a month later, they have very little idea what Plato said. They have cleared their minds to work on the next set of problems that must be solved—perhaps learning about Zoology. The postmodern critique of the Western canon exacerbates this problem for it reveals that there is no essential knowledge for people to have. Hence, the rational minds of modern persons tend not have a treasure trove of ideas that are always there to be thought about, mulled over, challenged, put in tension with other ideas, etc.—ideas that might make minds feel full rather than empty. But modern minds do have brilliant techniques for solving problems, whether they occur in life or in the classroom.

As Frank Summers says, this kind of rationality leads us a predisposition to objectify everything—including others, quantify everything so that it is measurable and comparable, and commodify everything so that we know its market value (2012). To be rational is to be scientific: to objectify, quantify, commodify.

- *Plasticity*: Modern persons need to be able to deal with a world that is rapidly changing all the time. They need openness to change, adaptability to new circumstances, a willingness to embrace the new, a willingness to adjust who they are to best deal with the changes they are encountering. Whereas previous cultures valued stability and doing things the ways they always have been done, economic culture needs its members to embrace change because it needs its markets to be ever expansive with new products, new tastes, new experiences. Indeed, the word "new" had negative connotations at the beginning of the 19th century and positive ones at its end. Something used to be problematical and the source of some scorn if it was new; now it is a selling point. Modern persons dread being bored; they need change, adventures, explorations to keep them feeling alive.

- *Competitiveness*: Modern society is constructing persons not only to be competitive but to love competition and to look at the world and everything in it with competitive eyes. It seems that everything needs to be competitively ranked: sports, schools (where does a school stand in the U.S and World Report?), restaurants, possible mates, etc. Everyone wants to know who is number one. We have contests for everything, from who can play football best to who is deemed the most attractive woman (Miss America, Miss Universe) to who can eat the most hot dogs at a county fair.

Today cities and nations do not build new churches; they build sports arenas and stadiums. The national Sunday litany—at least in the fall—is not going to church but watching NFL football teams battle one another. From grammar school through high school, sports are central to both personal identities and the school identity. If your school wins some kind of championship, narcissistic glory rains down on all. The classroom is also an arena of competition as students strive to attain the highest grades and stand out from all others. For those not physically talented, there is now the burgeoning field of electronic sports. Indeed, the electronic game industry was estimated to make $200bn in 2022.

Since market society is, in essence, competitive, learning how to compete, how not to shy back from aggression, and how to aggress against others within rules are crucial traits for the modern economic person. This aggressiveness, like that of technology, comes with a tendency to objectify one's opponents and to divide the world into us vs. them. It promotes a predisposition to divisiveness and violence against those who are on the other side (as unfortunately can be witnessed in current American politics).

Of course, many other societies have cherished competitiveness—witness the ancient Greeks and lacrosse-playing tribes of North America. However, the competitiveness present in contemporary society is so pervasive as to infiltrate every aspect of life and has become an essential part of how modern persons are built. To be is to compete!

• *Independence and self-sufficiency*: Capitalist economics is based on each person independently seeking their own good. As Adam Smith famously said, "Individual Ambition Serves the Common Good." We are to think of ourselves as independent agents and seek to become as self-sufficient as possible. The more we can provide for ourselves, the better we can think of ourselves. Neediness and dependence are frowned upon. I have spoken with several college students who were wondering whether to break-off a satisfying love relationship because they feared they were becoming too dependent on their partner. While I counseled strongly against giving up one of the great joys of life—an intimate relationship—they were too concerned about dependency and broke off the relation. One of the reasons why "hook-up sex" is so prevalent on college campuses and elsewhere is that it is a way of satisfying sexual desire without giving up one's independence. Young persons often see committed relationships as "baggage" that limit their opportunities to explore the world and enjoy a variety of partners. To be fully independent is to attain "self-sufficiency" in which one, like Thoreau, can produce or buy everything they need for themselves. To be self-sufficient is good; to be needy is bad. It is OK to be married or part of a committed relationship so long as each person is given a wide breadth to be themselves and seek their own well-being—even if that means living in different cities because optimal employment demands it.

To be independent and self-sufficient is, for modern persons, to be free, and, above all, modern persons seek to be free—free to live the kind of lives they most want, the lives which can most satisfy their desires. One of the reasons that money is so highly valued is that it is equated with freedom. Restriction in a market society is understood as not being able to afford something. Freedom means that I can buy anything I desire to. Hence, the wealthiest people are seen as the freest. Note that there are other ways to define freedom than as the ability to do what one pleases, such as the Socratic and Emersonian notion that one is free when one is not influenced by outside pressures but acts from an integrity of one's own soul, or Kant's claim that we are free only when we act on universal moral principles, for when we act on desires, we are acting on what has been socially and/or biologically determined.

- *Abstraction*: It is preferable for modern persons to be "abstract" in the sense that they do not bind themselves to any tradition, place, or position. They need to be ready to abstract themselves from wherever they are and whatever they are doing to take advantage of market opportunities that arise. It is strange to think of having weak ties and connections to friends, extended family, and place as part of an ideal, but to be able to be fully successful in the modern economic world, one must be opportunistic, and this means being mobile, and to be mobile means to make oneself abstract. One of the great rituals of modern culture, at least for the middle and upper classes, is sending their adolescent children off to college, and if the best college they get into is far away from home, they must go there. Indeed, it is almost a ritual test of adulthood to be able to leave home, friends, pets, and family to go away to college. Not establishing strong ties to friends, family, or place is crucial if one is going to be an optimal modern person.

Abstractness also involves abstracting economic values from all other values. It used to be that one would buy goods from friends or family—staying true to and supportive of the clan. But to be a rational market agent means to engage the market solely on economic terms without taking into account how the economic transaction is related to other values, such as those of politics, religion, family, or friendship. If Uncle Fred is selling apples at a price higher than Walmart, buy from Walmart, even if it ruins Uncle Fred.

The desiring, rational, technologically-savvy, ultra-competitive person who is mobile, quick to change when opportunities arise, and highly self-sufficient is the ideal kind of person to thrive in modern economic society. However, this ideal is intrinsically tied to success in the market and the values of wealth, property, power, and status. It is because this ideal became so overwhelmingly strong as to dominate how middle-class persons were constructing themselves and their lives that two extraordinary philosophical movements arose in the 19th century to confront the social ideal: transcendentalism and existentialism. Strangely, while these movements were meant to counter the middle-class conformity that had become so pervasive, they actually played into the hands of society with their essential value of radical individualism. Our picture of the ideal modern person cannot be complete without including these philosophical ideals, for they have become highly influential in how many think they should be living their lives.

6.3 Emerson, Thoreau, and Nietzsche

I believe that the transcendentalists and existentialists discovered and advocated what Kohut was later to term "the self" and distinguished it from the rational, pragmatic ego and its capture by social values. Yet, while they anticipated Kohut's theory of the self, there are crucial differences—differences that make all the difference.

Unlike Kohut who held that we get nourishment for our selves mainly from other human beings, Ralph Waldo Emerson declared that we must go alone into nature to discover our selves and free them from social pressures that seek to make us mere conformal beings. In nature we can be our natural selves without social pretenses and can discover who we really are, namely, singular selves who can organically birth truth out of our particularity. Each self is unique and its voice is non-rational, non-pragmatic, non-socialized:

> *Whoso would be a man, must be a non-conformist... Nothing is more sacred but the integrity of your own mind... No law can be sacred to me but that of my own nature... I shun father and mother and wife and brother when my genius calls me. I would write on the lintels of the door-post Whim. I hope it is somewhat better than whim at last, but we cannot spend the day in explanation.*
>
> (1841/2003, 178–179)

He will further reverberate with Kohut's notion that the self is non-derivative by saying that it is "aboriginal ... the essence of genius, of virtue, of life, which we call Spontaneity or Instinct" (1841/2003, 187).

As close as Emerson's notion of self is to Kohut's, there is one major difference: Emerson insists on "self-reliance" and advocates a strong independence of character. There is no notion of a "selfobject." This concept of the independent individual is taken even further by Thoreau, who not only advocated independence of the self but lived it at Walden. He keenly detected the profound problems with the new economic form of life and famously said that "most men live lives of quiet desperation" (1854/2000, 8). He thought new economic persons were slaves to their property, to their desire, and even to how they had to discipline themselves to operate in the market.

> The laboring man has not leisure for a true integrity day by day; he cannot afford to sustain the manliest relations to men; his labor would be depreciated in the market. He has no time to be anything but a machine... It is hard to have a Southern overseer; it is

worse to have a Northern one; but worst of all when you are the slave-driver yourself.

(1854/2000, 6–7)

Rather than adopting the "desire and work" way of being human, he revealed that one could live a perfectly fine, deeply alive form of life if one had few material desires. He claimed he needed to work only six weeks out of a year to get all the goods and services he required for that year. Of course, Thoreau was a vegetarian, never drank, never married or had children, and so was quite content to live with very few desires other than sauntering for four hours each day into nature and poking his nose into whatever was calling to him.

Like Emerson, Thoreau captured the essence of Kohut's notion of the self as an organic singularity. He articulated this singular core by proclaiming the importance of wildness: *"Life consists with wildness. The most alive is the wildest...in Wildness is the preservation of the World"* (1861/2000, 644–645). By "wildness" Thoreau does not mean being chaotic or having crazy emotions, but simply being who you singularly are. The wild bear is simply being a bear, not artificially trying to be some kind of ideal bear. What Thoreau adds to Emerson's value of self-reliance is the ideal of total self-sufficiency, an ideal that will become romanticized and heroized in the American frontiersman. There is no concept of the selfobject as essential to life; indeed, it almost seems inimical to it.

Nietzsche, who avidly read Emerson, also champions fleeing the middle-class herd and discovering a vitalizing source of creativity at the core of one's self. However, unlike Kohut and Emerson, there is no ground to this creativity in terms of organic ideals. Rather, the act of creation itself—a willingness to bring a world and oneself into existence and then abandon that world if it ceases to be a creative vitalizing one—is what defines a free spirit. Kohut's creativity is grounded in the ideals of the self; Emerson's creativity is deeply connected to a universal creative spirit—the Over-soul. Nietzsche's free spirits or overmen rid themselves of all grounds, all constrictions, all limitations and creatively will new values simply for the joy of willing. Nietzsche does find (as Schopenhauer did) that there was a final ultimate value lying behind willing: power. Having power means that one is fully self-determining rather than determined by powers outside of oneself. This radical self-determination goes even further than Thoreau's self-sufficiency in proclaiming the complete independence of the self from everything else, even earlier instantiations of one's self. Thoreau at least wanted to be close to nature and be natural himself; Nietzsche wants total openness. As such, he valorizes not so much the self as the openness and emptiness of self-consciousness. He discovers the essential nature of ego consciousness—its freedom, its emptiness, its questioning, its quest for power, and its tottering on the brink of the nihilistic abyss. As with Emerson and Thoreau, Nietzsche's ideal person is in full flight from selfobjects. Zarathustra sits alone on his mountain top, content to converse with a serpent and an eagle.

Although these transcendental and existentialist philosophers railed against the dominant middle-class values of economic society, they soon became co-opted into the ideal of the kind of person most favored by that society. Self-reliance, self-sufficiency, and even becoming a god in one's own little world became important features of the new ideal of the person best able to negotiate the market environment. In short, the ideal of individualism developed in transcendentalism and existentialism became part of the social ideal of modern society. We moderns seek to be individuals—keenly differentiated from others, independent, self-sufficient, and each responsible for constructing their own lives.

This co-opting of individualism into a social ideal makes the ideal, at best, an ambivalent one, for to become an individual is to not be an individual, as one is simply obeying the social code. This ambivalence in the heart of American individualism is both confusing and enervating—the more one attempts to be an individual, the more one feels they are being just like everyone else. When ideals have this kind of internal self-contradiction, they de-vitalize experience, for they make meaningful life seem somewhat impossible. The only way to rebel against the ideal seems to follow it. There is no escape from the social codes.

The above critique of modern individualism is part of the reason why Kohut's concept of the self is so refreshing and invigorating. It is not part of the social ideal; developing and being one's self is not the same as being an independent, self-sufficient individual. It does not require the assertion of difference or the attainment of economic and emotional self-sufficiency. Indeed, in its emphasis on selfobject connectedness and acting to attain organic ideals rather than social ones, it is a truly rebellious ideal for how best to be human.

6.4 The Ideal Market Person, Democracy, and the Wondrous New World

In sum, the ideal modern person is one who is full of desires, technologically savvy, an efficient and productive worker, self-disciplined, pragmatically rational, competitive, independent, self-reliant, adventurously creative, abstract, and bent on living a life of freedom—a life in which we choose how to construct our lives. Modern persons are little gods creating their own worlds within a massive economic system in which each of these little worlds intersects all others, supposedly producing an optimal general welfare. I can certainly recognize a lot of myself in this description of the modern person and I suspect that it will fit many of the readers of this text (especially if they are men—see section 6.6).

While I will raise criticisms of this new kind of human being, I first must say that this modern kind of person and society have transformed the globe in many positive and extraordinary ways. Economist Deirdre McCloskey says that the per capita expenditure for humans had not increased from the start of recorded history until the modern era. However, it has increased for all humans a stunning 10 times in the past 200 years, led, of course, by improvements in the West but helping to bring others along, too (2010). The new economic human being has produced hitherto unimaginable wealth and material well-being for millions—even billions—of human beings, including miraculous advances in medicine and hygiene. Life expectancy in the West was 35–40 years before the economic age fully blossomed in the 19th century; it is now over 80. In 1800 almost half of all human beings born in America died before reaching adulthood; now the percentage in negligible. There is no doubt that this scientific, rational, competitive, desiring human being has made the world a remarkably different and, in many ways, a supremely better world than in earlier ages.

These new human beings have not only generated an unprecedented world of material well-being, they have also been responsible for the rise of modern democracies. As middle-class persons gained wealth and became increasing self-sufficient, they demanded more say in the systems of political governance. No longer would they let arbitrary hereditary powers control taxes, courts of justice, and other affairs of state; they demanded a system of self-governance and the wealth they gleaned from their market interactions gave them the power to get it.

The English, French, and American revolutions led the way to democracies and WW I dealt the final blows to autocratic government, as the German Kaiser, Austrian Emperor, and Ottoman Sultan, were defeated by the democratic states to the West, while the Russian czar capitulated in the Russian Revolution. The modern person not only is responsible for the rise of democratic states, but these states foster this kind of person coming into being. Insofar as democracies claim that all persons have a right to construct their own lives with minimal interference from church or state, they proclaim that the best way to be human is to establish one's independence and self-sufficiency, thereby joining the pressures we have seen from economics and philosophy.

In short, these new human beings have both been created by democratic economic society and keep creating it with their extraordinary abilities to self-discipline, work, solve problems, and enjoy the pleasures they reap as rewards. They have created a dazzling new world with skyscrapers soaring into a realm once occupied only by gods and houses of parliament attempting to do what is good for the populace rather than just the elite. And, perhaps most important for us, these new humans have created a world with such an astounding proliferation of opportunities for employment, recreation, and social interactions that we can find activities that readily fit our selves' idiosyncratic talents and predispositions.

But we now must ask, what is the cost of this new world and this new kind of person? Always the piper must be paid, and we need to see the price we are paying for these stunning advancements and whether it is worthwhile to keep paying it.

6.5 Metapsychology and the New Ideal Human

To understand what is problematical about this new kind of human being and new economic society, we need to recall the metapsychology we developed in Chapter 4. Modern persons will have highly developed rational egos and endorse the ego's needs for power and freedom. There will be a strong alliance between the ego and social unconscious because the most important factor in attaining power and freedom is securing one of the esteemed socioeconomic positions. That is, modern persons buy into the new ideal of human excellence that has been developed in economic culture.

In this kind of psyche the self is either not well-developed or shunted aside, for modern persons need to have a rational, assertive ego to operate the machinery of a post-industrial technological economy. Skills and talents are praised and developed; successes applauded, but not the self of the person who has the skills and talents, not the part of the psyche that might have eros for activities and ventures that have little to do with being able to successfully compete in the socioeconomic world.

We know that the self needs love, affirmation, connection, and especially empathic resonance—the kind of consistent and constant mirroring that children so desperately need to develop their erotic, self-affirming selves. Unfortunately, these crucial psychological goods are in short supply. As will be detailed in the next chapter, America has constructed social practices in the home, schools, and workplace that diminish the ability to give and receive selfobject supplies, thereby starving the self of the necessary nourishment it needs to grow and remain vital.

And so it appears that modern economic agents have a psyche that is under the full dominance of the ego. The ego will not only keep the voice of the self in abeyance but will carefully control id desires and emotions as they can hinder its ability to gain control over the vicissitudes of its environments. Modern economic persons attempt to satisfy their primary narcissistic needs by becoming little gods creating their own worlds. However, we can ask whether this form of life is sufficient to satisfy our primal narcissistic needs to relate to perfection and grandiosity. The first indication that this kind of psyche is in trouble is the amount of anxiety modern humans experience. Even in the mid-19th century Thoreau noted that this new kind of human being suffered from heightened anxiety: "The incessant anxiety and strain of some is a well-neigh incurable form of disease" (1854/2000, 10). Anxiety has, of course, increased significantly since then. A recent survey found that 86% of college students said that they suffered from high anxiety. Almost 20% of Americans suffer from a clinical anxiety disorder. The high presence of anxiety might be explained by the fact that everything in life is a matter of competition and that one can lose out at any time—whether it be in the world of work, play, or intimacy.

But anxiety is not caused simply by the intense and massive amount of competition in modern society, for people with strong selves can handle a great deal of change and even defeat. Anxiety seems to be the differential between the internal and external pressures on an individual and the individual's sense of inner strength to deal with these pressures. What the high levels of anxiety indicate is that the world is too much for the fragile selves that people have. Kohut identified the root anxiety as disintegration anxiety—an anxiety caused by a self that is so fragile that it might fall apart at any time. Anxiety is the experience of self-fragility—of a hole at the center of psychic functioning rather than a self.

Anxiety and other narcissistic symptoms indicate that the self is suffering in the modern world. While there are millions who achieve ego successes in the contemporary marketplace, these need not be experiences in which the self is actualized and nourished. While it is a caricature, there is truth in the common example of the highly successful businessman being deeply depressed and even suicidal, as so many case studies indicate.

In short, the grandiosity of the ego and its relation to social ideals of perfection can never make up for the absence of a self with its organic ideals and its sense of self-esteem built on empathic responsiveness. As egos get bigger and bigger, the self seems to get smaller. Egoism reigns, but the self goes wanting.

However, I want to make stronger, more devastating, claims about the problems caused by modern society's having de-centered the self. I want to show how such a loss of self is implicated as an essential component of many of our most serious social and cultural problems. This will be the subject of the next chapter. However, we cannot leave this chapter on the construction of the modern self without saying how it has related to gender and race, for it affects women and people of color quite differently than it affects privileged white males.

6.6 Racism, Sexism, and the Ethical Underside of the Modern Ideal

It appears that the modern ideal is available to everyone who lives in a society, and this is not the case. There is an ethical underside to the modern ideal that significantly diminishes the possibility for several sub-populations from attaining it and participating in its vision of the ideal life. The competition in economic society is never fully fair, for it never starts from ground zero with everyone having an equal chance at success or failure. Privileged persons will have initial advantages in terms of resources (money, education, social status) that will make them the likely winners and others because of initial disadvantages will likely be the losers. Two of the most important advantages in American society have been race (being white) and gender (being male). Not only will persons with these privileged attributes have unearned advantages to succeed in the market, but they will also tend to carry prejudices against those who are different, often seeing them as deficient and not deserving of success. Insofar as the modern ideal for humans has been produced by a competitive market society, the ideal has, implied within it, racist and sexist prejudices.

Feminist authors have revealed not only how women have been discriminated against within modern culture, but how the whole ideal of self-sufficient individualism that governs the society is inherently patriarchal. In its proclamation that separation, freedom, power, mobility, rationality, and control over circumstances are good, it posits what many feminist authors have found to be a characteristically male way of being in the world. According to such feminist authors as Carol Gilligan (1982, 2018), Nel Noddings (1986), and Virginia Held (2006), women tend to favor connectedness, relationships, and emotional responsiveness rather than an abstract rational approach to the world. They tend to seek co-operation rather than competition and prefer loving care for others rather than adopting an aggressive competitive modality.

Carol Gilligan revealed these different ethical orientations in her revolutionary *In A Different Voice* (1982) in which she interviewed young women as to how they would approach the ethical problems posed by Lawrence Kohlberg, who mainly interviewed young men (1981, 1984). Kohlberg was attempting to determine if there is a maturational pattern to the way persons approach ethical life. He assumed that those who reach a Kantian level of applying abstract universal moral laws are at the zenith of moral development. The problem with this study and its Kantian presupposition is that most women do not think this way or try to solve conflicts between humans by applying abstract universal principles. They want to talk, to negotiate, to interact with others rather than simply applying a rational rule. That is, men are quite used to living in a world in which there was intense aggressive competition bound within a structure of rules. Women live more in caring relationships. Gilligan concludes that Kohlberg discovered only one kind of ethical trajectory—that of men. For women, ethical life concerns itself not with universal rules dealing with abstract others but with caring for those with whom we have special relationships (Held, 2006). That is women favor living from the needs of the self rather than the values of the ego.

In *Why Does Patriarchy Persist?* Gilligan and Naomi Snider find that patriarchal society imposes a gender binary in which human capacities are divided between the "masculine" and "feminine," and which privileges the masculine over the feminine. This binary "Forces a split between the self and relationships so that in effect men have selves, [by which Gilligan means the ability to be independent and assertive] whereas women ideally are selfless, and women have relationships, which surreptitiously serve men's needs" (2018, 6). Men can be assertive—even aggressive and can speak what they believe—even if it is contentious—without fear of being shamed. Women who are aggressive and speak their minds are often put down as "too demanding," or "too assertive" or "too loud." This gender binary results in men having shallow emotional lives with tepid connections to others, while women lack the permission to develop strong selves. But men really can't have selves without relationships and women can't really have relationships without selves. Hence, the gender binary of patriarchal culture denies both men and women the ability to be fully human.

In her *Metamorphoses of Psyche in Psychoanalysis and Ancient Greek Thought* (2023), Marcia Dobson deepens this feminist critique of patriarchal culture by depicting how patriarchy displaced a matricentric culture in the ancient Greek world and with it a whole way of being human. A fluid way of experiencing in which liminal presences could flow into and out of experience was lost. Emotional vitality, interconnectedness with nature and sacred presences, and the ability to sense subjective realities in the objective world were all cast aside for a rational organizing ego to assume control of psychic life. An interior psyche became separated from an external world and men started on the path to the domination of nature, women, and emotional connectedness. Her book reveals how an openness to more liminal ways of experiencing can deepen and vivify experience and also expand the possibilities for having a nuclear self at the core of experience.

The self psychological ideal that I am promoting in this book (and other writings) is much closer to a feminist ethic of empathic caring rather than a male ethic of rule-following. Insofar as self psychology holds that all humans need to be immersed in caring empathic selfobject relationships, it joins with feminist theorists in proclaiming the centrality of human connectedness over that self-sufficient individuality. However, it also affirms the necessity for all humans to develop singularized selves that have their own strong voices willing to speak the truth of who they are and what they need in life. It affirms the need for strong selves who are in relationship.

The critique from an anti-racist perspective is different from the feminist critique but one that is also very powerful. For many theorists of color, accepting modernity's ideal of excellence is highly problematical because it means desiring to assimilate into a racist culture. It is to accept being the Other who has agreed to be recognizable because they are becoming just like the majoritarian culture. In the words of Homi Bhabha,

> colonial mimicry is the desire for a reformed, recognizable Other, as a *subject of difference that is almost the same, but not quite.* Which is to say, that the discourse of mimicry is constructed around an *ambivalence*; in order to be effective, mimicry must continually reproduce its slippage, its excess, its difference ... *Almost the same but not white.*
> (1984, 126, 130; quoted in Eng & Han, 2000, 676)

Even for the "model minority" of Asian-Americans, attempting to attain the Western ideal of excellence often involves a deep melancholia (Eng & Han, 2000). Many Asian-Americans have been successful at entering the upper echelons of American professional life, but no matter how successful they are, they cannot fully attain the ideal because they are not white. Insofar as the ideal has imperceptively interwoven a presupposition of white supremacy, no one who is not a white male can fully ever attain the ideal. Hence, even though many Asian-Americans have attained high-ranking professional positions and the wealth and prestige that comes with them, they often suffer from a kind of acute melancholia because they cannot really be the ideal they espouse, for they are not white. That is, insofar as they have adopted the Western ideal, they need to look down on themselves as somehow inferior (Eng & Han, 2000).

However, if marginalized minorities living in America do not adopt the Western ideal, then they are likely to find themselves even further marginalized (Akhtar, 2018). They are likely to become, in Ralph Ellison's words, "invisible." To be someone, one must engage with the system that demands a striving for evermore status, power, and wealth; to not engage with this system is to be unrecognizable, and, hence, nobody. In short, the Western capitalist ideal of excellence imposes a terrible dilemma on racial minorities: to adopt it is to acquiesce in a racialized prejudice about white superiority; to separate from it is to cast oneself into a marginalized invisible existence.

Does the ideal of self psychology also involve this inbuilt problem for people of color? Several factors indicate that Kohut's psychoanalytic theory does not have the bigoted underside of the capitalist model. First, it does not proclaim that the best lives are those that do best in the market. Hence, it does not advocate a system which necessitates economic losers and winners and which has an embedded privileging of white men. Second, Freud, Kohut, and many of the great theorists in the psychoanalytic tradition were Jews and hence members of a marginalized group that had suffered devastating violence from the dominant white Christian population. They speak not as the privileged but as those who have been victims of discrimination. Third, psychoanalysis has itself become a marginalized discourse. Insofar as it posits the existence of the unconscious and the irrational as ineradicable parts of the human psyche, it speaks a truth that the rational, power-seeking, controlling white population does not want to hear (Lear, 2000).

Indeed, from a self-psychological point of view, persons in the privileged classes who thoroughly buy into the economic ideal might very well be undermining the conditions needed to produce coherent selves more than those who value family and group connectedness. There will be other conditions, such as poverty, that tend to de-stabilize the family and the ability to address the selfobject needs of children in marginalized populations, but they often do not labor under the ideal of producing hyper-rational, competitive, emotionally impoverished human beings.

With the economic ideal of excellence, persons are by necessity divided into winners and losers. The competition for wealth produces very big winners, some persons who do all right, and a massive number who, although they live in acceptable conditions, nonetheless consider themselves and are considered losers. With a self-psychological ideal, everyone can have a self and the more persons who have selves the more they can help others attain selves. Rather than being a competitive model, a self-psychological ethic offers a profoundly co-operative model of human beings helping one another develop vitalized core selves (Riker, 2010). Can the economic world transform into a psychologically astute one? I believe it can, for the signs of meaninglessness, despair, and unhappiness continue to grow. In the midst of plenty, the wasteland grows.

Note

1 Much, of course, has been written on "the modern person." Many of the analyses find the modern person to be highly deficient—shallow, isolated, narcissistic, materialistic, etc. My account will differ from these insofar as it analyzes the modern person from the viewpoint of self psychology and finds that modern culture is failing to construct social practices that nourish and sustain self-structure. It is not a moral critique of modern persons, but an attempt to understand the depth of their suffering.

References

Akhtar, S. (2018). *Mind, Culture, and Global Unrest: Psychoanalytic Reflections*. New York: Routledge.

Block, J. (2002). *A Nation of Agents: The American Path to a Modern Self and Society*. Cambridge, MA: Belknap Press.

Dewey, J. (1938/1981). "The Pattern of Inquiry." In J. McDermott (Ed.), *The Philosophy of John Dewey*. (pp. 223–239). Chicago: Chicago University Press.

Dobson, M. (2023). *Metamorphoses of Psyche in Psychoanalysis and Ancient Greek Thought: From Mourning to Creativity*. New York: Routledge.

Emerson, R. (1841/2003). "Self-Reliance." In L. Ziff (Ed.). *Ralph Waldo Emerson: Nature and Selected Essays*. (pp. 175–204). New York: Penguin.

Eng, D., & Han, S. (2000). "A Dialogue on Racial Melancholia." *Psychoanalytic Dialogues*, *10*(4), 667–700.

Gilligan, C. (1982). *In A Different Voice*. Cambridge, MA: Harvard University Press.

Gilligan, C., & Snider, N. (2018). *Why Does Patriarchy Persist?* Boston: Polity Press.

Heidegger, M. (1954/1977). "The Question Concerning Technology." In D. Krell (Ed.), *Martin Heidegger: Basic Writings* (pp. 307–342). New York: Harper & Row.

Held, V. (2006). *The Ethics of Care*. Oxford: Oxford University Press.

James, W. (1907/2000). "What Pragmatism Means." In G. Gunn (Ed.), *Pragmatism and Other Writings*. (pp. 24–40). New York: Penguin Books.

Kohlberg, L. (1981). *The Philosophy of Moral Development*. New York: Harper & Row.

———. (1984). *The Psychology of Moral Development*. New York: Harper & Row.

Lear, J. (2000). *Open-Minded: Working Out the Logic of the Soul*. Cambridge, MA: Harvard University Press.

Marx, K., & Engels, F. (1848/1994). *The Communist Manifesto* in *Selected Writings*. (pp. 157–186). (Ed.). L. Simon. New York: Hackett.

McCloskey, D. (2010). *Bourgeois Dignity*. Chicago: University of Chicago Press.

Nietzche, F. (1884). *Thus Spoke Zarathustra*. Tr. W. Kaufmann. New York: Penguin, 1978.

Noddings, N. (1986). *Caring: A Feminine Approach to Ethics and Moral Education*. Berkeley, CA: University of California Press.

Riker, J. (2010). *Why It Is Good to Be Good: Ethics, Kohut's Self Psychology, and Modern Society*. Lanham, MD: Jason Aronson.

Summers, F. (2013). *The Psychoanalytic Vision: The Experiencing Subject, Transcendence, and the Therapeutic Process*. New York: Routledge.

Thoreau, H. D. (1854/2000). *Walden*. In B. Atkinson (Ed.). *Walden and Other Writings*. (pp. 1–312). New York: Modern Library.

———. (1861/2000). *Walking*. In B. Atkinson (Ed.). *Walden and Other Writings*. (pp. 625–694). New York: Modern Library.

Chapter 7

Contemporary Social Practices that Undermine the Self and the Psycho/social Ills that Result from this Destabilization

7.1 Social Practices that Undermine Self-Structure

For modern society to produce its most valuable commodity—persons who can generate and sustain the economic culture—it has developed certain social practices within its institutions to foster such persons. I want to show how these practices in the home, school, workplace, and technosphere, while enhancing our ego's capabilities for negotiating economic culture, either do not nourish the self or injure it. I further want to show how these injuries to self-structure are implicated in many of our most severe contemporary social problems. While homelessness, debilitating loneliness, deaths of despair, addictions, global warming, income inequity, racist and sexist prejudice, gun violence, sexual violence, and the obesity epidemic seem to be entirely different problems, each having multiple causes, there is one common link tying them together: the lack of a vibrant self at the core of modern persons' experience. As we discovered in the last chapter, this lack of self-structure is in part due to modernity's misguided concept of self as a self-sufficient rational individual whose fundamental goal is to achieve success within market society. In other words, modern society is suffering from a profound conceptual confusion, one that we could not fully understand until Kohut produced his brilliant self psychology.

What follows is an analysis of how the practices that economic culture has created in the crucial institutions of society undermine self-structure.

The Home: The home has had its patterns of empathic and emotional responsiveness thoroughly disrupted by market forces. Both parents work in over 60% of households, leaving the home empty a great deal

DOI: 10.4324/9781003303657-10

of the time. They need to work both to sustain the household's level of material comfort and to be recognized as "someone" in the economic world (Foucault, 1979). It used to be before the 1970's that being a mother had an elevated status, but now being "just a mother" or a "just a housewife" is not good enough for women in the middle to upper echelons of society, as these are not "socioeconomic" positions.

Almost half of all children under five have at least some daycare either at a facility or in-home. While children in high-quality daycare actually have slightly higher ratings for cognitive skills than children who are raised entirely at home, they also tend to be more aggressive and more angry.[1] Much fine socialization and learning can take place outside the home, but it is doubtful that the empathic responsiveness given by paid workers is equal to the nurturance that loving parents can give. Babies are deeply attuned to the voice, smell, and face of their mothers, and nothing can quite equal the loving resonance that a mother (if she is healthy) or a father can provide. Parents' narcissistic pride in their children helps them deal with the extraordinarily difficult challenges that young children pose for adults; this tends not be true for non-parents.

Even when parents are home, they are often engaged in household tasks or being captured by electronic media—the TV, computer work, streaming, etc. While the current mantra holds that quality time can replace quantity, I doubt that this is true. A constant and consistent empathic presence seems necessary for the development of strong self-structure. In short, the demands of economic society are disrupting the patterns of extensive and consistent empathic resonance that children need to form healthy selves.

Part of the problem for parents is that they often conceive of their children as a bundle of desires and needs. Insofar as they cannot distinguish the needs of the nascent self from other desires, they often find themselves in the difficult position of thinking that if they frustrate a child's desires, they are injuring the self-esteem of the child. The child's narcissistic needs for empathic responsiveness, merger with idealized others, twinship, and opportunities to explore what natural gifts they might have are important, as are the biological needs for food, sleep, exercise, play, warmth, etc. But most of the other desires can be frustrated without genuine loss to the child. However, due to the conception of humans as pleasure-optimizing organisms that is present today, many parents are held hostage to their child's endless, "I want; gimme, gimme" pressures. They often cave-in; partly because they do not have time in their busy lives to give the child what they really want—prolonged interactions. This is another social practice stemming from the concept of human nature developed in modernity that hinders the development of self-structure.

There is a further problem in the home in that many marriages are failing today. Although statistics vary depending upon the source, the estimate is that almost half of marriages end in divorce. Married partners seem less able to be selfobjects for one another. (A recent study found the empathy between married people declined significantly between 1979 and 2009.) That is, not only are both parents working rather than being at home; but many relationships are so disturbed that partners cannot give one another the empathic resonance they need to sustain their selves. And parents with fragile or traumatized selves cannot offer their children the safety and full empathic resonance they need.

Often, children are given electronic toys or videos to keep them occupied and out of their parents' hair, but these are rarely activities that involve significant selfobject interactions. The child gets stimulation and perhaps occasions to develop skills, but it seems there is not enough interaction in which a gleaming face adoringly watches and helps a child with play.

Current childrearing practices often concentrate on cognitive development and learning self-discipline rather than fostering the emergence of a unique self. The earlier a child can learn their ABC's and 1,2,3,4,5's, the more they are praised, and the parents' anxiety is relieved, for they are showing early signs that they will do well in school and later in the economic world. Self-discipline in terms of early toilet-training, curtailing anger, and controlling sporadic spontaneous behavior are also central features of bringing up baby to be successful. If the self is closely tied to spontaneous erotic eruptions, then it often is not responded to. Rather, variations of what Brandshaft (2007) calls "pathological accommodation" occur, as children are raised to meet the economic ideal of a disciplined, problem-solving, cognitively advanced being. This is, of course, not bad—most of us would love to have self-discipline, advanced cognitive skills, and inventive abilities to solve problems. It is only deleterious when this kind of growth is fostered to the detriment of the emotional surround needed for selves to develop. While it is right and necessary to develop the powers of the ego, it is also necessary to concomitantly foster the development of the self.

In sum, the contemporary home is often empty, emotionally unresponsive, and fragile—an environment that is likely to traumatize the self or, at best, not provide enough nutrients for the nascent self to grow strong.

School: The other major institution with which children engage is, of course, school. For many children, school is a second chance to get the nourishment they need to build sufficient self-structure to go forward with life. A warm, affirming teacher who takes a special interest in a child can make a great deal of difference. (I was fortunate enough to have such a teacher in the fourth grade.) However, the school situation is getting more difficult as a place to receive nourishing selfobject supplies, for it is under pressure to develop rational agents able to run the technological and corporate machinery of modern life. Cognitive skills must be developed early, and self-discipline is crucial. Spontaneous erotic eruptions from the self are discouraged as order must preside in the classroom. Given that homes seem to be less supportive of self-structure than in the past, many children enter school with psychological and behavioral problems causing them to act out, after which they are often shamed, scolded and/or punished, thereby decreasing self-esteem and increasing the problematic behavior.

The possibility of teachers' giving enough care and attention to the emotional needs of their students is also diminished by having to deal with large classes. The national average class size is about 25, about twice as large as an optimal class size. Taxpayers want to keep their money; they do not want to pay for the premier kind of schooling that will genuinely support their children and help them grow. Again, this kind of mindset is easily traced back to the set of values fostered in an economic culture.

Rather than being a co-operative place in which students get to support and sustain one another, the classroom is often a competitive space to see who can get the highest grades, stand out in sports, and be the most popular. Since competition is the heart and soul of capitalist economics, such competition is strongly encouraged. Unfortunately, in competitions there are a few winners and many losers. Only one student can be chosen first for a team; everyone else gets to feel a little less good until you are the last chosen and know what others truly think of you. The emphasis on competition can certainly aid the self-esteem of the winners; but for many, school is a depressing place in which the self steadily loses its erotic vitality.

To add to these difficulties, schools over the past half century have become increasingly focused on standardized tests and the standardized education needed to prepare students for them. While this might be beneficial for cognitive development, it can be crushing for original explorations—for following one's nose wherever it might lead, for finding places of interest in the nooks and crannies between subject matters. And teachers who have to conform to the strict curriculum and are judged by how well their students perform on the standardized tests can lose their eros for teaching and either leave the school system or become deadwood. When teachers lose their enthusiasm for teaching, it is very difficult for students to find their eros for learning. As teachers become dead, students become bored, and the classroom ceases to be a place in which students' selves can come alive. Standardized environments produce standardized humans—robots—and, while such a mechanical existence seems horrible, it fits well with the ideal economic person, who must be ultra-efficient and productive with the impersonal tasks assigned to them.

There is another problem with the grammar school environment in terms of its being an institution in which selves can be nourished and built: the legal dangers of warm physical contact and bullying. Given the heightened sensitivity to physical and sexual abuse that has occurred in devastating ways in schools, teachers need to be super-aware of any kind of physical contact, and, hence, often refrain from hugging or putting a gentle hand on a shoulder. Yet, a hug can mean a great deal more to children than some abstract words attempting to give comfort.

Finally, there is the omnipresent problem of bullying. Because so many children have injured selves by the time they get to school, there is a tendency in some to satisfy their needs for narcissistic grandiosity and the release of pent-up narcissistic rage by bullying others. The more injured selves there are on the playground, the more possibility there is for a victimizing/victimized interaction to take place. This is not meant at all to justify bullying, but to understand why it has become such a common phenomenon. While there has probably always been school bullying, it seems far more prevalent today, especially with the kind of vicious bullying that occurs on social media.

In high school and college, what has changed significantly is the demise of committed love relationships. While experimentation and changing partners is normal for the young, the development of a hook-up culture in both high school and college is highly problematic when looked at from the viewpoint of self psychology. Adolescence and young adulthood are very difficult emotional times, as the source of selfobject supplies shifts from family life to intense new friendships that can often be volatile. This is also the time when pubescent sexuality erupts and needs to be integrated into our personality structures, especially the self. Since this transition to being a sexual being can be frightening and fragmenting, it seems best done in a relationship in which one feels moderately safe and empathically responded to. That is, I think self-structure can best be integrated with sexuality in committed intimate relationships. Alas, it is this kind of relationship that seems to be becoming increasingly rare, as hook-up relations have come to dominate the social scene.

Committed intimate relationships appear too dangerous to many young people for several reasons: they experience their feelings and the world as too volatile for commitments; they want to explore; they don't want to be limited or constrained. Hence, a hook-up culture of casual relationships (not always involving sex) has arisen that is defined by the expectation that the relation need go nowhere and means nothing beyond a casual friendship and the production of pleasure. There is certainly no expectation of exclusivity. Students have told me that hook-up encounters are now so normalized in high school and college that even if two persons want a more committed relationship, they are afraid to ask one another for fear of being rejected. It is doubtful that the young will let their selves—their fragile, probably injured selves—appear and be nourished in such ephemeral relationships. But without the kind of selfobject nourishment that committed love relationships can give, it is hard for self-structure to adequately mature during these years. As a result, I often see our college seniors graduate with brilliant cognitive capacities but immature social abilities—abilities needed to engage in the complex mutual relationships that constitute adult love.

Workplace: Surprisingly, many survive home and school well enough to become young adults with somewhat intact selves—but selves that still need selfobject responsiveness in order to grow and flourish in the adult world of work and love. And here further problems arise that constrict the exchange of selfobject supplies. It is probably a caricature to think of corporations or companies a half century or so ago as being friendly places—at least in their white-collar sectors—in which co-workers became friends, had some loyalty to the company, and believed that the company had some loyalty to them, but there also appears to be some truth to it. This ethos seems to have changed, as companies assess and evaluate the performances of their members with objective criteria and a willingness to release anyone not performing to expectations. Employees can also be let go if new technology makes them expendable or if market volatility means the company must downsize to stay profitable. Since advancement is highly competitive, one's co-worker is not a friend but an opponent with whom one is competing for the next promotion. Neither company nor employee have a commitment to loyalty. In short, many workers experience job insecurity and this undermines security in establishing a home. We need the world to be predictable to feel safe; the contemporary economic world seems inherently unpredictable and, hence, contemporary persons must deal with both an inner and an outer chaos. It comes as no surprise to learn that a great percentage of young adults experience debilitating levels of anxiety.

One of the great shifts that has happened over the past half century is the entrance of women into the workplace and with it the rise of uncomfortable/illegal/immoral sexualization of the workplace. However, when the law and general business culture finally addressed this horrendous issue that deeply problematized the workplace for women, it had the side-effect of dampening personal warmth and non-sexual caring feelings. Insofar as expressions of such feelings can be interpreted as "come-ons," they are considered inappropriate and even dangerous. A cool business demeanor that assesses according to standards has become the norm. Even in small colleges such as my own, hugging a favorite student is frowned upon, and advice is given not to become friends with students or talk with them about anything other than the material of the class. We are to be professionals first, humans second—and this means that one is never quite able to interact with those in the classroom as anything other than as students. Selfobject nourishment is becoming rarer in the workplace; common everyday human warmth and emotional connectedness are being eliminated as dangers both to individuals and to companies.

Technosphere: Humans today live in a sphere that transcends home, school, and the workplace; they often enter it at a very young age (early childhood) and remain in it until death: the *technosphere*. The average American spends over seven hours each day using the Internet with nearly four of those hours being spent using a smartphone. Add to Internet time the time people engage with other electronic media, such as television (average three hours a day), and we can see that most of our waking hours are spent in the technosphere. This arena of life is so important to contemporary people—especially the young—that disruptions in it can cause trauma. Some 73% of people experience something like minor panic inducement when they do not have a smartphone at hand (Haynes, 2018). Even when the young know that they are becoming depressed spending so much time in the technosphere, they cannot stop their engagement with it. They are addicted.

The question arises as to what effect this massive engagement with the virtual world has on the self. In *Alone Together* (2011), Sherry Turkle finds that many of today's youth have trouble conversing face-to-face because they are so hooked on online communication. Indeed, a number of high-school sophomores said that they preferred online communication to direct communication because it was safer. Studies have shown that persons who were on the Internet for more than four hours a day tended to become depressed—that is, de-vitalized—a crucial sign that the self is not engaged. Although much of the time spent on Facebook, Instagram, etc., is communicating with others, this communication is disembodied, and, hence, at best able to give only partial selfobject nourishment. There are no gleaming eyes, no inviting body postures, no alluring or comforting smells, no hands touching yours. That is, there is communication; there is recognition; there might even be some empathic responsiveness; but it usually feels as though we leave the interaction starved—starved for genuine connectedness.

A century or so ago, almost all communication was face-to-face or by hand-written letters in script that was highly expressive and idiosyncratic. Then came the phone in which we could hear a voice with its nuances, cadences, warmth, or coldness—but not a body, no hugs, no gleams. And now talking on the phone is disappearing as texting replaces it in which there are only typed words and emojis desperately trying to indicate some emotional content. Of course, there is also zooming and facetime, but electronically delivered faces and bodies are simply not the same as in-person, embodied others.

Frank Summers summarizes the devastation to self-structure that the technosphere can cause:

> It is precisely in the interaction with another seen as an experiencing subject that the self grows and flourishes. The use of cyberspace as a means for forming relationships withdraws the nutrients young people need for the growth of the self and thereby depletes self development… Dialogue is what makes us human and without the ability to converse, young people are in danger of losing their very humanity. Cut off from the world of meaningful human conversation, the individual is left in a solipsistic enclosure that remains static and empty. The adolescent will often attempt to fill this void by the stimulation of Internet games and activities, a strategy that ultimately only removes him even further from the world of human relationships.
>
> (2013, 154)

There are reasons other than the dearth of selfobject nourishment for why spending so much time on electronic media is deleterious to the self. The self's most vitalizing activity is a person's erotically pursuing the self's organic ideals. Such pursuit demands commitment to the ideals and the tenacity to work through problems that are painful, and it is difficult to stay true to one's commitments when the siren of the Internet is luring one to wonderous distractions, each giving a bit of pleasure. Rather than undergoing the difficult task of actualizing the self's ideals—that activity which gives life its deepest sense of meaningfulness—we lose ourselves in the pleasant diversions of the Internet. Neuroscience points to the fact that the Internet has similar impacts as drug usage at the neurochemical level, as it provides temporary hits of dopamine, numbing the pain of our existence and taking the edge off life (Haynes, 2018).

Here is a quote from one my students who knew about self psychology:

If I feel the oncoming heat of shame or guilt due to injury of the grandiose pole, I escape to grandiose fantasy by streaming braggadocious pop songs. If I feel the deadening presence of boredom due to a lack of realization of the ideals, I turn to email and text communication to feel productive. I feel the blueness of loneliness arise and start shooting tweets into the technosphere rather than considering how I can more meaningfully tend to my relationships.[2]

Attempts to solve problems of the self electronically tend to cover over these problems rather than work through them. The pit gets deeper and deeper. When we spend a lot of time with electronic media, we also tend to have a shallow emotional life, as disembodied communication does not have a full ability to transmit affects. We can message luscious words such as "I love you" and put in a heart emoji, but without the presence of real bodies, it is difficult to communicate the fullness of emotion that one is feeling (if one is, indeed, feeling it). The Internet is unprecedented in its ability to provide information, but the "I love you" that is messaged is likely to be both sent and received as information by the ego, not as an expression of emotion. The self and the emotions which lie in the limbic brain often never get touched. The authors of *A General Theory of Love* claim that the essential language in which emotions are expressed is prosody—language that fuses neocortex input with limbic inflections. They write, "At night all cats are gray, and in email everyone is aprosodic, because the medium consists of curt sentences lacking emotional inflections" (2000, 59).

There is also the problem that young persons usually construct fantasy avatars to represent themselves, or, as one student said to me, "On social media we are all imposters." Some use the technique of blurring photos so that one's image actually becomes surrounded by an alluring indistinctness, making one open to myriads of projections, and the construction of the avatars—and life itself—is made to look effortless. The image makes one look perfect, as though life has no struggles or imperfections. In order for self-structure to develop, persons need to be engaged in reality—engaged with real problems, real failures, real emotions, and real others; insofar as persons remain in a fantasy world of avatars, their emotional existence remains undeveloped.

The extensive use of electronic media also tends to turn us into technocrats who have a tendency to reduce all subjects to objects.

An object, as we have noted in a previous chapter when discussing the work of Jessica Benjamin, is that which can be "done-to." We do not have to be empathic with objects—they are just things. Insofar as persons tend to objectify themselves and others in the technosphere, extraordinary amounts of cruelty and bullying occur. It is hard to want to destroy a living person who is face-to-face with you; it is much easier to be destructive to a distant objectified other on a screen.

In the digital era not only do people treat themselves and others as objects, they exist as data in the most literal sense. While there is a genuine experiencing "I" that exists, there is also a me that exists as a node of data in the digital realm. The data version of me has been formulated through machines using algorithms that are the beating heart of the technosystem. The data version is what is valued in an economy that is increasingly propelled by big data. The algorithms track every click, every follow, every purchase, the location of my body, and the stretch of time I spend viewing any piece of content. In the technosphere, it is easy to find ourselves swallowed up into a sea of objectifications, struggling to find and affirm our subjectivity, struggling to find and affirm our authentic selves.

As another student said to me, "We all get instant gratification from social media. We are addicted to it. Our egos love it. We are so lost."

7.2 Basic Claims

Given these current trends in institutions and social practices, I want to make five major claims:

(1) *The modern ideal of excellence underlies social practices that are constructed so as to produce human beings capable of advancing the capitalist market economy.*
(2) *These practices systematically enhance the powers of the ego and help make it the dominant agency in psychic life.*
(3) *In their concentration on enhancing the rational ego, these social practices tend to under-nourish the self, shunt it to the side of psychic motivation, or traumatize it by neglecting to provide necessary selfobject supplies.*
(4) *Persons with injured or displaced selves have strong tendencies to feel an inner emptiness, ungroundedness, and desperation.*

(5) *The inner sense of emptiness that many persons feel due to the lack of a vitalized self is implicated in many of the major personal, social, political, and environmental problems that are haunting our society today.*

7.3 Injured Selves and Contemporary Social, Political, and Economic Problems

If I am right in claiming that modern society is systematically under-mining self-structure in its most important institutions, then we should be able to see this negation of the self as implicated in many of the basic problems in contemporary America. What follows is an attempt to show how many of America's most egregious problems have as one of their major factors persons' attempting to deal with displaced, undernourished, or injured selves.

Homelessness: About 0.2% of America's population is homeless. While this is an insignificant percentage in terms of total population, the homeless tend to be highly disturbing to those living in metropoli-tan centers who see them every day. They haunt our urban landscapes; they upset our serenity. We want them made invisible, because they let us know that something is terribly wrong with our society.

Who are the homeless? About one-third suffer from severe mental illness; about 40% suffer from alcohol abuse, and a quarter suffer from drug abuse. These symptoms all point to significant traumas of the self in childhood. In short, the homeless are symbolically expressing that America's homes are failing to sufficiently nourish the selves of their children. While there are a number of reasons as to why the homeless become homeless, including poverty due to insufficient income, lack of affordable housing, lack of affordable healthcare (especially mental health care), violence, parental drug and alcohol abuse in the home, and sexual abuse (90% of homeless women have been physically or sexually abused), it is my contention that one of the underlying causes is conceptual—a failure to understand what a self is and what its needs are, especially the immense selfobject needs of children. That is, today's homes have often been destabilized by the economic environment that causes both parents to work outside the home or causes them to suffer un- or under-employment and fails to provide sufficient selfobject nourishment to the parents who are drained, angry, and often in need of drugs or alcohol to soothe their pain, and who then cannot offer their children the kind of nourishing presence they need to develop selves. If the ideal of independence weren't so prevalent, perhaps parents would not abandon their children to empty homes or babysit them with electronic devices. And these parents themselves probably came from homes that had insufficient selfobject supplies.

In short, one of the major reasons for homelessness is the devastation that is occurring within American homes, a devastation caused in part by a failure to recognize and respond to the selfobject needs of children. These needs go under-recognized because the regnant ideal of abstract individualism fails to affirm the selfobject needs we all have. The homeless represent a deep, uncomfortable truth about our society, and that is why they are so disturbing.

Chronic loneliness: America is experiencing an epidemic of loneliness. The Harvard School of Education reports,

> Alarming numbers of Americans are lonely. According to our recent national survey of approximately 950 Americans, 36% of respondents reported feeling lonely "frequently" or "almost all the time" in the prior four weeks. A startling 61% of young people aged 18–25 and 51% of mothers with young children reported these miserable degrees of loneliness. Survey respondents also reported substantial increases in loneliness since the outbreak of the pandemic. The cost of loneliness is high. Loneliness is linked to early mortality and a wide array of serious physical and emotional problems, including depression, anxiety, heart disease, substance abuse, and domestic abuse.
>
> (Weissbourd, et al., 2021)

Jacob Sweet adds that "the heightened risk of mortality from loneliness equals that of smoking fifteen cigarettes a day or being an alcoholic" (2021, 32). In 2021, 28% of American households were single-person households—more than double what it was a half century ago.

There are numerous reasons for this serious epidemic of loneliness, especially the isolating policies of the COVID pandemic and the loneliness inherent in using electronic media. However, I must implicate as a major cause of loneliness the ideal of the independent, self-sufficient person. When a culture refuses to recognize healthy interdependence as ideal but proclaims instead that the more one can exist on one's own the better one is, then debilitating loneliness would seem to be a natural outcome.

Of course, one can be alone without feeling lonely. Indeed, it is one of the grounding experiences of life to be alone with one's self engaged in inner dialogue, for in these moments. we can come to know our selves in deeper ways. Indeed, the experience of having an inner dialogue with oneself while alone is a great counter to loneliness, for so long as this dialogue is available, one seems always to have a friend to talk to. However, if one's self is injured and harbors shame, deadness, and rage, then this dialogue will be difficult, for we will be afraid to enter the inner sanctum of the self. Without this inner dialogue, we will probably be lonely no matter how many people are around.

Deaths of despair: Princeton economists Anne Case and Angus Deaton coined the term "deaths of despair" to refer to mortalities among Americans from drug overdoses, suicide, and alcoholic liver disease (2020). Deaths from these causes have increased significantly over the past two decades, averaging 70,000 per year. The majority of these deaths are white men without college educations who have lost their jobs or who are highly underpaid for what they do. Hence, the authors find the major cause of this deadly despair to be economic, citing that it is not only income but loss of identity that drives them to a despair so deep that it causes them to become alcoholic, drug-addicted, or suicidal. While I fully agree that the economic world and its inequities stand behind these deaths, I think that the selves of these people had already been decimated, and when the economic identity blows came, they had little inner sustenance to deal with them. That is, many people use ego identities to compensate for the lack of a self. When these ego identities are shattered, life becomes meaningless and hopeless.

It is also true that this kind of person is likely to have bought into the ideal of being self-sufficient and independent. Hence, when they are not able to provide adequate sustenance for themselves and/or their families, they feel intense shame and a concomitant loss of self-esteem. This loss of self-esteem is so painful that it can drive people into opioid and other drug addictions, excessive use of alcohol, and, most painfully, suicide. Once again, we find the ideal of the independent, self-sufficient individual to be implicated in this horrible epidemic of deaths of despair.

Addictions: Kohut says that one of the prevalent responses to an injured, fragmented self is to engage in addictive behaviors. These behaviors are meant to assuage or cover-over an intolerable inner deadness and emptiness by soothing the pain and/or generating pseudo-excitement. While there are many variables that go into addictions such as genetic predispositions, living with others who are addicted, social pressures, etc., I think that most of them have as an essential cause the presence of traumatized selves. It is statistics on the addictions and other compulsive activities that allow us to see how widespread devastations to the self are. Two million American adults are addicted to gambling (0.6%); one out of three adults drinks excessively with 14.5 million adults (4.4%) suffering from Alcohol Use Disorder; 23 million people (7%) have drug addictions; 3–5% have experienced sexual addictive behavior; and 6–7% have a shopping addiction. If one adds up these addictions (and assumes only one major addiction per person), then about 20% of the population suffers from addictive behavior. If one then adds to the addictions that much activity associated with shopping, sex, alcohol, drugs, and gambling is compulsive, but not fully addictive, and further adds compulsive video game playing, working out, and other driven activities, we can see that an incredible amount of behavior tends not to be under one's conscious ego control, but is unconsciously compelled to deal with a fragmented self and the feelings of profound emptiness that accompany it.

How many lives and families have been devastated by addictions? How many bodies ruined by alcohol and drugs? How many families have lost their wealth to gambling and addictive shopping? How many love relations have been shattered by people having compulsive sexual desires that drove them to affairs? The ego attempts to construct a rational life but is undermined by unconscious forces stemming from a depleted, fragmented self-structure. The great hope of the Enlightenment thinkers that rationality could conquer all human problems shatters on the rocky reef of injured selves. And it is the ego's very attempt to gain total dominance in the psyche that causes the reef to rise up and doom its dictatorial attempt at total psychic control.

Cheating: David Callahan has documented how extensive cheating is in the United States—cheating on everything from income taxes, doctor's prescriptions, lawyers' reported hours, car mechanics' finding non-existent problems, people falsifying resumes, etc. (2004). In recent statistics, 60% of college students report that they have cheated at least once in the past year (31% more than once); the IRS estimates that over 15% of Americans cheat on their taxes, costing the government over one trillion dollars a year. Almost half of Americans have suffered financial difficulties due to identity theft. About one quarter of companies cheat on their books and in turn are cheated on by about a third of their employees. Add to these socioeconomic forms of cheating people who sexually cheat on their partners (about 50% according to some estimates) and persons who cheat on themselves—on their diets, exercise routines, etc., and we can see that cheating is almost a way of life in America.

While Callahan thinks that the cause of so much cheating is the "winner-take-all" competitive economy (which is surely part of the problem), I think a deeper understanding of why so many persons are cheating sees them as suffering from narcissistic vulnerability. Their selves are fragile and cannot endure setbacks; they would rather cheat than fail. Also, cheating is a way of getting something for nothing—of getting a reward without doing the work—and this is a sign of infantile narcissism, a regression to the time when we ought to have received loving care without working for it, without having to earn it. That is, cheating is a sign that the self is injured and fallen into a regressed state. Cheaters also seem to suffer from having vertical splits. I believe that most cheaters think of themselves as fine upright persons and offer excuses to themselves as to why their cheating is justified and not really indicative of who they are ("Everyone does it," "It is only this one time," etc.). That is, they refuse to own what they are doing and this, too, is a sign that the self is injured and cannot provide a basis for integrity (Riker, 2010).

When people cheat, they think that the rules don't apply to them—that they are above the rules. Such thinking is a symptom of pathological narcissism, a symptom that the self has been injured. What lies behind the voracious need to cheat seems to be both a confusion about what one's genuine self-interest is and a self suffering from fragmentation. The economic world identifies self-interest with personal pleasure (reaped mainly from money and status), while genuine self-interest resides in realizing one's organic ideals and being connected deeply with selfobject others. Hence, there lies behind the social phenomenon of cheating a triple relation to modern economic culture: it falsifies what genuine self-interest is, places everyone in a massive competition of all against all, and undermines the social institutions needed to develop strong selves.

While cheating is not a horrific moral crime like the genocides of Hitler or Pol Pot and often involves no physical violence, it is like a vicious hidden disease that is undermining the ethical health of both persons and society. That cheating is so widespread indicates that selves are being injured ubiquitously by the common social practices of the culture.

Racism: There are numerous causes for the persistence of racism and prejudice in America—causes that have been extensively explored in sociological and political literature. However, I think that these analyses are incomplete without a self-psychological understanding of narcissistic vulnerability.[3] Many of the accounts of why racism persists focus on how racist prejudices are passed down from generation to generation with such force as to constitute a fundamental structure of white Western (especially American) mentality in which white persons construct their worlds in a hierarchical way with themselves at the top and others ranked below them in order of color—the lighter are higher, the darker lower. What self psychology can add to this conceptualization of racism is an account of why white Western persons need to adopt and stringently hold onto this hierarchical structure of othering.

What we learn from self psychology is that we have primal narcissistic needs for empathic affirmation from selfobject others, borrowed strength from idealized others, and twinning from someone just like us. It seems that these needs can best be met by those with whom we share some crucial sameness, such as family, gender, social group, or race. Insofar as empathy involves a mirroring of affects, it seems best done by someone with whom one shares a sameness—the same feeling in the same kind of person. Likewise with idealization: we tend to idealize those with whom we share an essential likeness because we want to become *just like them*. It is even more evident that twinship requires some fundamental sense of shared sameness.[4]

We see this need to associate with sameness in young children who feel most comfortable in their families; in grammar school children who seem to feel most comfortable in relating to those of the same gender (whether that is biologically or psychologically produced); and to those in adolescence who seem to need small groups of like-oriented young persons with whom to merge. Especially in times of transition, such as first going to school, the arrival of puberty, and entering adulthood, self-structure tends to be fragile, as it must leave previous sources of selfobject nourishment and find new ones. At these crucial transitional times, sameness is comforting, soothing, and esteem-enhancing. For instance, when we turn adolescent, we can feel small and overwhelmed by our newly expanded worlds. If we can narcissistically support ourselves by merging with a group of like-persons (the athletes, the outcasts, the cheerleaders, the nerds, etc.), we then retain more narcissistic equilibrium. "I might not be great, but my group is the best, and I am a member of the group." Hence, the profound attraction of gangs for many adolescents and youth. The more vulnerable the self, the more there is a need to associate with a group that asserts some form of superiority or greatness. Groups will, in order to sustain their claim to superiority, tend to abject and demean others seen as different.

Kohut noticed that when we have healthy intact selves, we seek otherness, but when we have suffered traumas we retreat into worlds of sameness:

> Under certain circumstances we are interested in people who are very different from us. It is exciting to meet character types we have not known before, to see personalities that function very differently from ourselves. We will not want to see people who are very different from us when we are upset, when we are narcissistically disturbed, when we have suffered a narcissistic blow. We will naturally drift to people like ourselves, of our own cultural, emotional makeup. Then one feels enclosed again; one feels reinforced and supported.
>
> (1987, 70–71)

In sum, from a self psychological point of view, racism and other forms of prejudice tend to arise out of our narcissistic needs to immerse ourselves in sameness and abject those who are different. Group identity supports the grandiose sector of the self and gives self-esteem, especially in times when the self is fragile—as when one's status in the world is being severely disrupted. The crucial question arises as to why one of the chief forms of sameness is racial.

Is it by chance that racism arises in the West just as the economic era begins? There was widespread slavery in both the Roman and Greek worlds, but it was not based on race, but on whether or not a people were conquered. Racial slavery seems to appear with the discovery of the New World and the influx of wealth from these worlds, wealth that began to propel the economic revolution of Europe. For the white world to justify its use of black slave labor to help produce the new economic world in both hemispheres, it had to invent a theory of racial superiority. It is only a surmise, but it might be that with the creation of a middle class with all its insecurities that the West needed a class of humans to always be beneath them, thereby securing at least a base level of narcissistic superiority. We have seen this dynamic in working class white males who have been displaced from their former elevated place in the economy and have flocked to a racist and misogynist Trump as their hero (Hochschild, 2016). Here we see how narcissistic wounding can lead to an attempt to re-assert greatness by proclaiming that one belongs to a superior racial group: that of white males (along with women who are connected to them).[5]

Racism and prejudice are virulent, destructive social phenomena that have multiple roots extending deep into the swampy soil of humanity. What I hope to show in this book (and other writing) is the importance of our narcissistic needs in attempting to understand them. That economic culture is also a racially bigoted one is not by chance; the undermining of self-structure and the presence of a narcissistic sense of superiority in the white population are fully interwoven.

Obesity: Thirty-six percent of Americans are obese—not just overweight, but obese. There are many factors that go into the epidemic of obesity, including the super-availability of cheap fast foods, sugary drinks, and the unavailability of wholesome fresh foods in many lower income areas. There is substantially increased time sitting and watching TV or being on the Internet and less time moving and exercising. High amounts of stress in modern life also must be considered part of the cause. However, I think we must also consider the psychological feeling of inner emptiness being displaced into the stomach and having a compulsive need to keep filling the emptiness there. It is certainly possible that someone with a well-put-together self could live in a poor underserviced area, know little about nutrition, and become addicted to foods with high sugar and fat content; but I think that when one third of Americans are obese, we must add the cause of psychological emptiness being displaced into the stomach to this phenomenon.

Sexual violence: Sexual violence against both men and women in this country is immense. CDC research has found that nearly 20% of women have experienced completed or attempted rape; one third of women and one quarter of men have experienced physical sexual violence. Every 68 seconds an American is sexually assaulted. Again, there are multiple factors involved in sexual violence, but I think a major one—if not the major one—has to be men whose selves have been traumatized, who then sexualize their self needs (see Chapter 3) and fuse sexualization with narcissistic rage. In this way the eros of the self is transformed into sexual compulsiveness that has a sadistic/aggressive nature. When the ego's need for control and power is added to such a psychic configuration, then we have the makings of a male who is primed to be sexually violent. That is, persons with injured selves are implicated in this devastating social phenomenon, and, once again, we find that such persons come from non-nourishing (often violent) homes and social practices that do not recognize or confirm the needs of the self. And part of the reason why the needs of the self are not recognized is the modern ideal of the self-sufficient rational individual.

Gun violence: America has been experiencing an epidemic of gun violence. Mass-shooters, I assume, suffer from severe psychological disorders, which, from a self psychological perspective, means that their selves have been significantly traumatized. Put an AK-15 assault rifle into the hands of a severely traumatized young male who is filled with narcissistic rage and desperate for grandiose recognition, and tragedy is imminent. Most gun violence is, of course, not connected to mass shootings, but to everyday gang activity, domestic disputes, crime, etc. Yet, even in these less publicized cases, it is hard to imagine someone with a fully intact self wanting to murder someone else. Violence is typically the outcome of a history of suffering violence, the kind of violence that destroys self-structure. It is hard to imagine that someone who was lovingly raised as a child, empathically nourished, allowed to merge with idealized others, and encouraged to express themselves would be the kind of person who would want to rape and murder innocent others. In a horrendous fusion of variables, a country which is traumatizing persons' selves is also a country that has a constitutional right to bear arms and those arms include assault rifles.

I can see no end to this kind of violence, given the deteriorated mental health of the country combined with the easy access to guns.

Income inequality: The richest one percent of Americans have about the same amount of wealth as the lowest 90%. While this egregious disparity in wealth is due in part to Reagan's and subsequent Republican tax policies that allow the rich to become insanely richer, the modern concept of what it means to have the best of human lives is deeply implicated. Insofar as this concept posits that human beings are pleasure-maximizing organisms and that the amount of pleasure one can experience is seemingly limitless, it fosters greed for getting more and more and more. One can get pleasures from so many things in so many ways that this concept encourages one to seek ever greater wealth, despite research showing that once income level reaches $80,000, little extra happiness is gained from increased income (Summers, 2013). Modernity's emphasis on competition also comes into play as persons are primed to be "winners" and associate this with making more money than everyone else. When wealth is seen as that magic substance which will fill the emptiness in the psyche, then the intensity of greed increases and feeling a deep contentment with life vanishes. It is remarkable that those in the top 1% represent the paradigm for what we should all be striving to be. This is how insane the modern ideal for how to occupy our humanity is.

Global climate change: One can hardly blame humanity or an ideal of human excellence for one of the direst of humanity's problems: climate change. When humans discovered that fossil fuels could do most of the work required by modern life—heat us, cool us, transport us, run our machinery, etc., they became addicted to this kind of energy. Indeed, it is probably our deepest, most pervasive addiction and we will not give it up unless adequate substitutes come along, even if it dooms us to a very uncertain and uncomfortable future. However, all addictions are fueled by an inner neediness and the widespread denial about climate change reveals, once again, the fragility of self that needs to deny that anything is wrong with how we are living our lives. It takes a robust sense of self to deal adequately with radical change; too many in our world do not have this sense, given that the world has undermined the conditions for generating and sustaining self-structure.

Environmental problems are, of course, more than climate change and include the massive pollution of the earth, seas, lakes, and sky;

consuming the earth's non-renewable resources at an incredible pace, and the extinction of numerous species of plants and animals. These kinds of problems would not be occurring if first-world humans weren't consuming so much—goods, services, travel, etc. And this insatiable consumption is due in part to the feeling of profound emptiness that we carry in our psyches.

Political stasis: American politics, and, to some extent, the politics of the whole Western world, have become incredibly divisive with persons on the conservative side of the political divide refusing to listen to those on the liberal side and vice versa. Negotiated conversation in which there is respect for those who hold differing opinions has disappeared, and in its place we see hatred and even dangerous violence, as on January 6, 2021. While there are many political and historical reasons for this intransigence that threatens the very fabric of democracy, I, again, think that injuries to the self must be implicated. When the self is injured, the ego attempts to structure experience and one of the major structures is a political orientation. Since these structures are substituting for self-structure, they tend to be rigid. To challenge them is to threaten the cohesion of the psyche. Hence, the virulence and defensiveness of political discourse can be explained, in part, by contemporary persons having injured or absent selves. That is, insofar as democracy has taken on the form of an economic, capitalist society and constructed its ideal of the perfect market person, it is creating conditions that will undermine its viability.

7.4 Conclusion

This chapter has attempted to show how a misunderstanding of the self is implicated in many of the social/economic/political ills of contemporary society. While it is never the sole cause of any of these problems, it is, I believe, a crucial component without which many of the ills would either not occur or be significantly lessened. The social practices and institutions that have been constructed to generate the kind of human who can best operate, direct, and expand the economy have also either ignored or traumatized the self. As with global climate change, we could not have recognized this problem with the self until a scientific theory emerged that allowed us to see it. That is, we could not really understand the self and its needs until Kohut explored the patterns of narcissism he was finding in the consulting room. His analysis of narcissistic disorders uncovered a new, revolutionary concept of self—one not bent on independence, self-sufficiency, and pleasure optimization, but a fragile structure needing constant repair and nourishment from others to remain vitalized.

Recognizing our inherent vulnerability, fragility, and need for others is contra the West's insistence on autonomy, rationality, and self-sufficiency, which it has held as its highest values since Plato and Aristotle. We could not fully see how self-structure is formed and sustained through loving selfobject connectedness until we had a robust theory that explained how and why selves come into existence. With a Kohutian lens, we can now see why our misguided notion of self has been so devastating for persons raised in modern economic culture.

Many believe that these ills are collateral damage that we need to accept in order to have as productive a society as we do, but some of our most sensitive and insightful thinkers have found capitalist society to be so de-humanizing as to need to be abolished as a form of human existence. These critics claim that the exploitation of labor, incentives to greed, objectification of humans in terms of economic roles, destruction of the environment in terms of raping the earth for raw materials and polluting it with waste, etc., make capitalist economic society irredeemable. Marx and Engels called for revolution to overthrow the capitalists and their political cronies, as have many others. Despite these criticisms, capitalist economic culture has not only survived but expanded. It has solved a number of its internal problems in some countries through socialist adjustments and within itself in terms of more tolerable wages and better working conditions. But the profound problems of the objectification of persons, instability of institutions, reduction of life to "making a living," insane competition in which all are in strife against all and in which many are doomed to be losers, and, of course, the tendency to negate institutions that support the development and sustenance of self-structure all remain. Must we put up with these problems to have the productive capabilities of economic society, the great advances in medicine, the great increase in material well-being?

In the next part of this book, I want to address these questions by first exploring the paradigm that lies behind the construction of rational states and souls, namely, Plato's *Republic*, and then imagining what a society would look like if it focused its primary attention on the development and support of self-structure rather than the construction of persons governed by the ego and its quests for power, freedom, and self-sufficiency.

Notes

1 The statistics in this chapter are documented in the Appendix.
2 This quote is from Daniel Teplow's senior essay in philosophy, "The embodied self in the virtual era." Daniel's essay taught me a great deal about how the young experience the virtual world.
3 I have written about why human beings have a strong tendency to "other" human beings in several other works. See Riker 2010, 2018, 2022.
4 For a full article on the importance of sameness in acts of othering, see my "The Self and the Other: Hegel, Kohut, and the Psychology of Othering," *Psychoanalytic Enquiry*, *42*(2) Winter, 2022, 1–12.
5 One of the more important and controversial recent articles relating psychoanalysis and racism is Donald Moss' "On Having Whiteness" (2021) in which he compares "having Whiteness" to catching a disease that then infects one's whole way of being in the world. Whiteness is "a condition one first acquires and then *has*—a malignant, parasitic-like condition to which "white" people have a particular susceptibility.... Parasitic Whiteness renders its hosts' appetites voracious, insatiable, and perverse. These deformed appetites particularly target nonwhite peoples" (356). Moss describes persons who are particularly likely to be hosts for Parasitic Whiteness as those who map the world vertically (hierarchically), who are inclined to objectify those who are different, who have constant anxieties about threats from bad objects, and who have an authoritarian superego (359–360). I suggest that what Moss diagnoses as Parasitic Whiteness is mainly a narcissistic disorder in which the self has been injured and the persons who suffer from it are feeling a high degree of fragility. To compensate for the chaos caused by self-fragility, the psyche uses a superego authoritarian imposition to order itself and the world, treats others as objects, and locates a schema of understanding that grants the person a superior status based on race. That is, parasitic whiteness is a narcissistic disorder, one which reveals that selves have been injured by the society.

References

Brandshaft, B. (2007). "Systems of Pathological Accommodation and Change in Analysis." *Psychoanalytic Psychology*, 24, 667–687.
Callahan, D. (2004). *The Cheating Culture: Why More Americans are Doing Wrong to Get Ahead.* New York: Harcourt.
Case, A., & Deaton, A. (2020). *Deaths of Despair and the Future of Capitalism.* Princeton, NJ: Princeton University Press.

Foucault, M. (1979). *Discipline and Punish*. Tr. A. Sheridan. New York: Vintage Books.

Haynes, T. (2018). "Dopamine, Smartphones, and You: A Battle for Your Time." Cambridge, MA: Harvard University Blog (May 1, 2018).

Hochschild, A. (2016). *Strangers in Their Own Land*. New York: New Press.

Kohut, H. (1987). *The Kohut Seminars on Self Psychology and Psychotherapy with Adolescents and Young Adults*. Ed. M. Elson. New York: W.W. Norton.

Lewis, T., Armini, F., & Lannon, R. (2000). *A General Theory of Love*. NY: Vintage.

Moss, D. (2021). "On Having Whiteness." *JAPA*, *69*(2), 355–372.

Riker, J. (2010). *Why It Is Good to Be Good: Ethics, Kohut's Self Psychology, and Modern Society*. Lanham, MD: Jason Aronson.

———. (2018). *Exploring the Life of the Soul: Philosophic Reflections on Psychoanalysis and Self Psychology*. Lanham, MD: Lexington Books.

———. (2022). "The Self and the Other: Hegel, Kohut, and the Psychology of Othering." *Psychoanalytic Enquiry*, *42*(2) Winter, 1–12.

Summers, F. (2013). *The Psychoanalytic Vision: The Experiencing Subject, Transcendence, and the Therapeutic Process*. New York: Routledge.

Sweet, J. (2021). "The Loneliness Pandemic: The Psychology and Social Costs of Isolation in Everyday Life." *Harvard Magazine*, Jan/Feb, 31–35.

Turkle, S. (2011). *Alone Together*. New York: Basic Books.

Weissbourd, et al. (2021). "MCC Report, Loneliness in America: How the Pandemic Has Deepened an Epidemic of Loneliness and What We Can Do About It." Cambridge, MA: Harvard University Education Reports.

Part III

Plato's *Republic* and a New Self Psychological Society

Chapter 8

Plato's *Republic*
The Ideal of a Rational State and Soul

In 404 BCE the long and wearisome Peloponnesian War came to an end, as Sparta and its allies finally defeated Athens and installed 30 Sparta-friendly aristocratic tyrants to run the city. A mere five years later, Athens successfully revolted against the tyrannical government and reestablished its democracy. One of the very first acts of that newly restored democracy was to put Socrates on trial, find him guilty of corrupting the youth of Athens and impiety towards the civic gods, and execute him. Plato, who thought Socrates was the wisest person he had ever met, was so horrified that he would eventually write a long treatise, the *Republic*, on the kind of state that would not only not put Socrates to death but make him ruler. In its articulation of both the ideal state and soul, the *Republic* has become foundational for how Western culture constructs persons and polities.[1]

8.1 The Ideal of Rationality

One of the most dramatic claims Plato makes in the *Republic* is that the kind of souls humans develop mirrors the kind of state they live in. The reason that souls and states come in "kinds" is that different sectors of the psyche or factions of the state can control how a person lives or how a state is run. That is, to understand Plato's ethics, politics, and philosophical anthropology, we need to look at the foundation for all of it: his metapsychology, for it is in the metapsychology where we discover the different motivating sectors of the psyche and how these are responsible for the different kinds of both souls and states.

For Plato, there are three major motivational centers: the appetites, reason, and the *thumos*—the kind of energy a warrior has, often translated as spirit or anger. The appetites consist of all those motivations

DOI: 10.4324/9781003303657-12

that arise spontaneously and without rational deliberation: emotions, desires, drives, etc. Plato sees desires and emotions as "little tyrants," as each demands to have its way without regard for the general well-being of the person. They desperately need to be critiqued and organized.

Reason consists of motivations that result from careful deliberation, a deliberation that is grounded in objective knowledge of final truths. With this knowledge, reason has an ideal model for how to organize the soul and live a distinctively human life. To be rational for Plato is to set chaotic or disorganized things into order by hierarchically arranging them from the best at the top to the worst at the bottom. That is, to be rational for Plato is to impose a hierarchical structure onto the world. The forms are superior to matter because they don't change (are not chaotic in any way); the mind working according to eternal universal values is better than the mind moved by emotions because it is less changeable, less mutable. Aristotle will take this model and impose it on the universe: the unmoved mover is the highest being in the world as it has no matter and does not change; the heavenly bodies are next because they change only in space and in perfect circles; humans with rational minds are next. The mind is superior to the body, reason superior to the emotions, men are superior to women and slaves, women are superior to slaves and children, and so on. To be rational is to hierarchically rank everything.

While emotions and desires are spontaneously present from the beginning of life, reason needs to be developed through education— education that can last for decades until one can consistently grasp and understand fully abstract concepts and use these as a model for how to live well. Plato's ideal of rationality is not essentially pragmatic, but one which understands life and decisions from a universal perspective rather than an idiosyncratic personal one. Unlike Kohut's self-ideals, Platonic ideals are universals that are held to be true for all humans.

The *thumos* is the most difficult of the motivational sectors to describe, for while we can distinguish reason and appetites insofar as they conflict, *thumos* (spirit), has no natural antithesis. It is more of a pure energy that can align with either reason or the appetites. The example Plato gives is that of a man, Leontius, walking back from Piraeus to Athens and seeing that there are corpses on the side of the road. His desires want to see the corpses but his reason says it is wrong. "For a time he struggled with himself and covered his face, but, finally, overpowered by the appetite, he pushed his eyes wide open and rushed towards the corpses, saying, 'Look for yourselves, you evil wretches, take your fill of the beautiful sight!'" (440). The "overpowering" occurs because the *thumos* (spirit) sided with the appetites and gave them the energy they needed to win the fight against reason.

However, Plato also finds that spirit "sometimes makes war against the appetites" (440a), as when we get outraged at witnessing injustice. Hence, this spirit or aggressive energy can align with either the appetites or reason, and therefore is the major player in psychic dynamics, for the sector which the spirit supports will tend to gain the upper hand in the psyche. It is a kind of free-floating energy that can be used for either rational or irrational purposes. It seems to be inborn and to have different quantities in different people. "Even in small children, one can see that they are full of spirit right from birth" (441a). (In my Kohutian metapsychology, *thumos* is akin to the erotic energy of the self—more on this later.)

Each of these sectors of the psyche has a particular function: "isn't it appropriate for the rational part to rule since it is really wise and exercises foresight on behalf of the whole soul, and for the spirited part to obey it and be its ally?" (441e). The appetitive sector "is the largest part in each person's soul" (9442a), whose function is to motivate us with its wants, needs, desires, and emotions. However, it is the most chaotic sector of the psyche and needs to be organized and directed by a spirited rationality. For each sector to function well, it needs its proper virtue. (For the ancient Greeks, a virtue is any trait that helps a thing or person fulfill its function. For instance, the virtue of a knife is sharpness; the virtue of an eye is sight.) Reason needs the virtue of wisdom; spirit needs courage to follow what reason says is right; and the desires need temperance/moderation (sophrosyne) to be available for rational direction. The whole psyche then needs one more virtue: justice. A soul is just when each of its parts is doing its proper function and not usurping the functions of others. Hence, a just soul is one in which reason directs our choices supported by the spirit's energy and the appetites obey this leadership.

> One who is just does not allow any part of himself to do the work of another part or allow the various classes within him to meddle with each other. He regulates well what is really his own and rules

himself. He put himself in order, is his own friend, and harmonizes himself like three limiting notes in a musical scale—high, low, and middle. He binds together those parts and any others there may be in between, and from having been many things he becomes entirely one, moderate and harmonious. Only then does he act. And when he does anything, whether acquiring wealth, taking care of his body, engaging in politics, or in private contracts—in all of these, he believes that the action is just and fine that preserves this inner harmony and helps achieve it, and calls it so, and regards as wisdom the knowledge that oversees such actions.

(443d)

We could say that one does not even become a person until they have achieved a just soul, for before this integration, it is not a person that acts but a part. When we have unjust souls, we are ruled by our appetites—our emotions and desires—without wisdom or the good of the whole person in mind. Insofar as the harmonious integrated soul is psychologically healthy, we can equate the good soul with the healthy soul. "Virtue seems, then to be a kind of health, fine condition, and well-being of the soul, while vice is a disease, shameful condition, and weakness" (444e). It is good to become a just person because such a person will have the best kind of soul and be able to live the best kind of life. Although I will redescribe the healthy soul from a Kohutian perspective, I believe these stunning Platonic claims about the healthy soul being the same as a good soul and about people with the psychologically most healthy souls being able to live the best lives are profoundly true.

Good persons have the best kind of lives not because they get the most pleasures but because they are able to choose their lives rather than being tossed this way and that by irrational passions. That is, they can have organized lives. For Plato, the most profound evil is chaos—either in a state or a person. He saw what factions did to Athens in negating its strengths so that it lost to Sparta; and he saw how persons that lacked integrity and coherence in their psyches, such as Alcibiades, could engage in horrendous acts of self-and community-destruction. Good people with well-organized souls not only get to live the best personal lives but are also those who can best generate and sustain the community, for they live by rational universal standards of what is right rather than personal desires.

However, not everyone is capable of achieving enough wisdom to have the ideal soul and be a member of the ruling class. Indeed, those persons whose reason is not strong or developed enough to achieve wisdom are by far largest sector of the state. What about their souls? Plato says of such persons that if they have developed enough reason to accept the rule of those who do have wisdom (which will happen if the school system has educated them well), then they can live fine lives, even though they don't have perfect souls. The wise will set up social practices and ideals for such people, who, if they have moderated their passions, will be able to follow the rulers' wisdom and can get to live decent lives.

In sum, there are three different kinds of souls—those that are led by reason's wisdom, those who are highly spirited but who lack the ability to think abstractly, and those who predominantly live according to their appetites. The state needs all three. In the ideal state, the wise will rule; the spirited will perform police and military functions, and the appetitive will produce the material well-being of the state. Hence, the ideal state mirrors the ideal person: in both, wise reason rules with the help of the courageous spirit, and the desiring part or persons follow what reason says is best.

For such a state to develop, it needs to construct a model of excellence and develop social practices and institutions to actualize this kind of human being. For Plato, the key institution is the school, for it is responsible for evaluating all persons as to what realm of the state they need to occupy (workers, auxiliaries, rulers). The state will carefully censor myths, music, and gymnastics such that they help generate moderate, organized souls. The gods and heroes will be shown doing only good deeds (no rapes, no crying, no irrational desires); music that disturbs the soul will be banished; only those gym sports which make the body strong and harmonious will be allowed. In short, the ideal state is not democratic; it does not allow all kinds of literature, music, entertainment, etc., but restricts activities and discourse to those that promote cohesive order. The ideal society is much more like Sparta's military state with strongly imposed values and customs than Athens' open democracy. Likewise, the ideal person is not adventurous, open to change, or looking for innovation, but is someone who knows what is right and does just that.

Plato doubts that this ideal state can ever come into existence. Yet, he says that constructing his ideal is worthwhile, for it will lure humans to keep transforming their politics to get ever closer to the exemplar. Aside from the ideal rational state, there are three other kinds of states that either actually and/or potentially exist: the timocratic state based on honor (Sparta); the plutocratic state based on wealth (Corinth); and the democratic state based on the multiplicity of desires (Athens). Plato ranked these states in descending order from that which had the most coherence (the rational state) to that which had the least (democracy). What is important for us is that each kind of state tends to produce a corresponding kind of person: the timocratic state produces persons who hold honor as the highest value; plutocracy produces persons who value wealth above all (and, hence, aren't spendthrifts); and democracy produces persons who validate all their desires. In allowing a multiplicity of opinions, desires, and outlooks, democracy tends to produce persons who do not seek rational justification for their beliefs and do not try to rationally construct their lives towards what is good. They live by desires and pleasures, not standards.

Eventually, according to Plato, there will be so much discord in democracies that a minority faction will choose a champion and instantiate him as tyrant. Liberties will be squelched, and a strict order imposed—not a rational order, but a tyrannical order in which all is done to benefit the autocrat and his associates. (Given the January 6, 2021 insurrection in Washington DC and president Trump's refusal to admit he lost the election, Plato's analysis is frightening, to say the least.)

8.2 Socrates as the Ideal Human Being

To get a better understanding of Plato's ideal kind of human being, it will behoove us to look at the person Plato thought was ideal: Socrates. Socrates, at least in Plato's early dialogues, is known most for his dialectical questioning of important persons about concepts such as piety (*Euthyphro*), courage (*Laches*), friendship (*Lysis*), justice (*Republic*), erotic love (*Symposium, Phaedrus*), knowledge (*Meno*), and the nature of a good life (*Gorgias, Protagoras, Apology, Crito*, and others). In the *Euthyphro*, for example, Socrates asks Euthyphro, who has declared himself to be such an expert on piety that he is willing to prosecute his father for impiety, to give him a definition of piety, for he (Socrates) is about to go on trial for impiety and needs to defend himself. Euthyphro responds that what he is doing is pious, to which Socrates responds that this is hardly a definition and that he can't know if what Euthyphro is doing is pious until he knows what piety, indeed, is. While offering an example rather than a definition might look like a stupid error on Euthyphro's part, it is, in fact, the kind of answer that someone in a traditional society should give, a society which is not based on definitions but on traditional practices. If you want to know how to be a good doctor, follow one around. If you want to learn about piety, observe a pious person. In short, what Socrates does in this brief exchange with Euthyphro is to negate the epistemological basis of traditional society. By demanding a rational definition, Socrates refuses to follow the codes and practices of the world into which he was born.

His second exchange with Euthyphro is even more devastating for Athenian culture. Euthyphro now responds that being pious is doing what the gods love. Socrates then asks whether the gods can disagree among themselves, and Euthyphro responds that they can, to which Socrates retorts that the same act could then be both loved and hated, both pious and impious. Euthyphro is thus forced to say that the pious is that which all the gods love. However, if all the gods agree, then this is the same as if there were only one god. In this little exchange, Socrates annihilates polytheism as a viable religion. Humans cannot live in a coherent world if the universe is governed by gods whose values and powers conflict. Hence, the only kind of religion that makes sense for humans who want to live in an understandable, predictable world is monotheism.

This argument also seeks to replace Attic Tragedy as the fundamental way of orienting oneself towards life. Greek tragedy often involves an impossible conflict of ontological forces, such that if one is followed, the other is offended. Perhaps, the most famous is Sophocles' *Antigone* in which King Creon must refuse to have Polynices buried because he attacked the state, and Antigone, his sister, has to bury him because it is her duty as dictated by ancient custom and the gods. Creon must condemn Antigone, his son's fiancée, to death, but in so doing compels his son to commit suicide. In other dramas, such as Euripides' *Hippolytus*, gods (Artemis and Aphrodite) conflict with one another, dooming humans to tragic outcomes. Such a world of opposing divine forces is fully irrational to Socrates who thinks that whatever is divine must be unified, good, and make sense.

In questioning the basic concepts that grounded Athenian society, Socrates reveals how persons can free themselves from their embeddedness in the coded values of their cultural surround. However, Socrates was not the only person questioning the codes of the culture. When Athens went from being a local city-state to being the center of an empire after the Persian Wars, its socioeconomic world expanded exponentially, and possibilities arose that significantly disrupted the patterns of traditional society. Into this gap came the Sophists—a group of philosophers who typically came from city-states outside of Athens—to teach rhetoric to the upper classes, so that they could be convincing in political gatherings and court trials. They also taught that "man is the measure of all things" (attributed to Protagoras), by which they meant that each person should choose what they want to do with their lives without reference to codes or standards because all such values are arbitrary. Persons can use rhetoric to gain power and, hence, be able to satisfy more of their desires—especially their desire for power! The Sophists were not against reason, but favored pragmatic reason—reasoning for the sake of attaining power or the satisfaction of desire.

It is against this backdrop that Socrates and Plato offered a different alternative: not the life of social conformity nor the life of pleasure-seeking but an ethical life, a life based upon doing what is objectively right, not just on what is subjectively desirable or socially prescribed. When asked by the Sophists why anyone would want to choose an ethical life over one of pleasure, Socrates and Plato answer that it is only ethical persons who can have organized souls, and it is only persons with organized souls who can choose their own lives. That is, social conformity can be arbitrary because the customs and values of a society are not based in universal reason but on the happenstance of tradition; and desires and emotions are irrational and hence arbitrary. We don't choose what we desire—pressures from biology and society lie behind all unexamined desires and hence control us. It is only when our rational capacities choose what is right that we are not thrown this way and that by arbitrary forces.

The most famous example of this kind of life comes when Socrates is in prison awaiting execution and his friend Crito rushes in to tell him that his escape has been fully arranged. Everyone is paid off and the ship is waiting. Socrates replies that before escaping, he needs to determine whether it is the right thing to do. Crito, exasperated, says that of course it is—otherwise he will play into the hands of his enemies, and he was, after all, wrongly found guilty. Socrates then constructs an imaginary dialogue with the laws of Athens who proclaim that he was able to become a person only because he lived in a state that had laws. If he now breaks them, he will be committing injustice, and even if it is to pay back an injustice, it is still injustice, and, as such, would validate a principle that persons can be unjust whenever it is convenient for them. If everyone broke laws when they stood against their perceived interests, there would be no laws, and without laws, there is no state, and without a state there is no Socrates. To escape is to enter into a self-contradiction and violate the ground of rationality.

There is probably no stronger desire than that of self-preservation and, thus, in his refusing to escape prison and execution, Socrates is exemplifying a life of integrity—one based on principle rather than personal desire. It is more important to Socrates to have a good soul than to be alive. As he says in the *Apology*,

> I do nothing else except go around trying to persuade you, both young and old alike, not to care about your bodies or your money as intensely as about how your soul may be in the best possible condition. I say it is not from wealth that virtue comes, but from virtue comes money, and all other things that are good for human beings, both in private and public life.
>
> (30a)

For Plato and Socrates, it is only by living according to standards posited by reason that one can be free of arbitrary social or biological forces—that one can be free to choose what is good and right, that one can have an organized soul rather than a tyrannical one. Of course, what constitutes an objectively valid principle has changed dramatically over time, from Platonic Forms to God and God's will for religious people; to the laws of Nature for the Stoics, to categorical imperatives for Kant, to objective human rights in contemporary society, and so on.

Plato's depiction of Socrates and his construction of the ideal state and soul underlies much of how the West has gone about constructing human beings—with strong, questioning egos bent on expanding rational knowledge and seeking ever greater powers over the irrational forces of nature, society, and the human organism. This articulation of a form of life that is different from social conformity or desire-satisfaction—a form of life that is lived according to standards that should hold for all human beings and which can be used to critique irrational and prejudicial values in particular societies—is perhaps our greatest gift from the Greek philosophers.

8.3 Evaluation of the Ideal State and Soul

There is much to admire about Plato's vision of the ideal soul and state, a vision that lies behind much that has been positive in how the West—especially since the Enlightenment—has gone about constructing polities and persons. Plato's insistence that the state operate according to rational principles rather than custom and tradition has been extremely important in combatting practices and prejudices that could not stand up to the scrutiny of scientific rationality. The millennia-long discrimination against women, the unjust assessment and treatment of people of color, the discrimination against persons with different kinds of sexual preferences and gender determinations, along with other prejudices are being challenged as irrational. All institutions and social practices must now stand up to rational scrutiny; all customs and traditions need justification or they will be cast aside. Plato's ideal state in which justice reigns as the highest principle has been a powerful and positive model that has helped create a better world.

Plato is also right in thinking that we need to bring a critical rationality to how we go about living our lives. Without it, we are at the mercy of internal and external irrational forces that can leave us in a state of chaos or living lives that are not really chosen. And Plato is right that we need to develop the virtues that help moderate the passions and allow us to courageously live according to standards of excellence rather than whatever desires tend to gain ascendance.

Plato's vision is so grand, so hopeful, so full of transformed humanity that we want to affirm it, but it turns out to be highly problematical for a number of reasons, including the inability of reason to access final universal truths, the inability of reason to monitor and control unconscious psychic phenomena, the irrationality of reason itself (the inability of reason to rationally justify why it should be the predominant voice in decision making), and, of course, the failure of this psychology and politics to recognize the needs of the self. I will address each of these important problems in turn.

Plato's claim that reason has the ability to access ultimate universal truths—the Forms—has been shattered by Kant's and Hume's compelling critiques in the 18th century. The human mind is forever embedded in its own frameworks for interpreting and organizing experience. It does not have the power to overcome its situatedness to grasp truths that stand beyond the limitations of experience. What counts as a reason depends upon the framework one assumes. The Nazis had "good reasons" to eliminate the Jews; reasons that the liberal world found hideously irrational. In more recent times, the debate over abortion is impossible to resolve because each side has compelling reasons within its own framework for affirming or denying the rights of women to determine whether to have an abortion or not. There is no higher "objective rationality" that exists outside of frameworks that can resolve the debate.

Worse, the claim that there are eternally valid truths can provide a ground for institutions or persons becoming authoritarian. For centuries the Catholic Church claimed to be alone in its ability to access the truths of God and the divine realm, thereby setting up an epistemological and ethical autocracy. Others who have claimed that they knew these truths usually led to oppression of dissenting views. Plato's ideal state is not an open society; the great danger comes when authorities justify their values and practices in a way that claims absolute validity.

Of course, as we have already seen, the modern economic person still highly values rationality. We devote most of our education to the development of a highly-skilled, rational, quantitatively astute ego. However, this kind of rationality is different from Plato's metaphysical rationality bent on knowing ultimate truths of existence. It is a scientific and pragmatic rationality, centered on empirical experimentation and verification, keen logical argumentation, and focused on the "usefulness" of its rational decisions. This kind of rationality, freed from its metaphysical speculations, has radically transformed the world and continues to do so at a breathtaking pace. Yet, the problem with this kind of rationality is that it is not geared to think about final goods, ultimate values. This kind of pragmatic, scientific theory seems to hold that if it can be done, it should be done regardless of its effect on what is genuinely worthwhile for humans. In sum, neither Plato's metaphysical rationality nor the pragmatic rationality of modern persons seems adequate. What is called for is a pragmatic rationality that can be grounded in values that have an objective basis. I believe that self psychology offers us such a basis.

The second reason Plato's ideal person and state have failed to work is that Plato wrongly assumed that all psychic phenomena are conscious and thereby could come under the control of our rational powers. What we now know so thoroughly after Freud is that not only does the rational ego not know or control unconscious motivations and organizing principles for how we approach the world but is more or less at their mercy. It is the unconscious motivations that use rationality to get what they desire, not vice versa.

Although Freud and others conclusively demonstrated the power and extent of unconscious processes determining human decisions and behavior, the myth of the all-powerful rational ego remains dominant. Indeed, the preferred method for treating psychic disorders today is not psychoanalysis with its advanced therapeutic tools for transforming unconscious processes, but cognitive behavioral therapy—a form of therapy that still believes that one can consciously and rationally transform all that is pathological in the psyche.

There have been other devastating attacks on the rational ego. The Romantics proclaimed that the kind of life lived by the rational person is emotionally shallow, unconnected to the depths of existence, and has the tendency to petrify all that is living. Hawthorne's *Rappaccini's Daughter* chillingly describes the inhumanity to which objective rationality can go in its negation of the subjective reality of living human beings. Romantic poets such as Wordsworth, Byron, Shelley, Goethe, Emerson, and Whitman freed verse from its rationally ordered rhymed couplets and evoked strong affects and spontaneous intuition; rather than seeking a scientific knowledge of nature, they desired an emotional union with nature in all its beauties, forces, darknesses, and luminescence. The path into the deep truths of nature was not science, but poetry.

The Romantic critiques lie behind much of my own appraisal of the rational ego. The poets and psychoanalysts are right in claiming that emotion, connectedness, erotic longings, and aesthetic delights are where we feel most alive. If we have an intense eureka moment doing science, it is because we are erotically attached to this activity. It is not the ego but the invested self that feels so elated by a scientific discovery. I need to be clear that my position is not against scientific rationality— good heavens, no. We desperately need it; I just want the rational ego balanced with the erotic self and emotional vitality.

There is one more surprising critique of rationality, one best articulated by Nietzsche: when reason examines itself, it can find no compelling reason for claiming that rationality ought to be our highest value. That is, when reason turns its critical powers on itself, it cannot offer a rational argument as to why rationality is to be valued above all else without entering into circularity—without assuming that rationality is the highest value. The discovery of reason's inability to justify itself and its ability to be fooled by unconscious forces have led many into nihilism. As Nietzsche says, "What does nihilism mean? That the highest values devaluate themselves. The aim is lacking: 'why?' finds no answer" (1901/1967, 9).

Many today find themselves in nihilistic despair. After the great critiques of God made by Kant, Feuerbach, Marx, Freud, and others, and after the Holocaust, it is difficult to believe in a divine guiding presence or any objective meaning to human life. There is no right way to be human. No ultimate values to be striven for. As far as we know, our species is just a Darwinian chance mutation that has, so far, been successful (perhaps too successful) at surviving and reproducing. Human life means nothing more than that.

This fall into nihilism has been so devastating, especially in my field of philosophy, that it is one of the major reasons that I have become attracted to Kohut's self psychology. I could not dispel Nietzsche's claim that there are no metaphysically valid meanings but also could not fully affirm his contention that there is no basis for the creation of meanings. For Nietzsche, the act of creating values has no ground other than itself. We create for the sake of creating and will for the sake of willing. There is a deep attractiveness here—the acts of creating values and generating one's own world are exhilarating. But one also knows that there is no ground for the creating and, hence, can un-create at any time, especially when there are hardships to realizing the created values. How many Ph.D. dissertations have been cast aside after five years of toil because their authors realized that all their exasperating work was merely the result of an arbitrary choice?

While Kohutian self psychology also affirms the personal creation of values, these values are not arbitrary but the ideals that have grown organically in the structure of the self. Self psychology further affirms the validity of those ethical virtues that help create and sustain the self and selfobject connectedness. That is, self psychology offers an objective ground for the creation of value, namely, the self. This is not a metaphysics of value but one that is based upon the fact that as humans we all have a basic need to develop and sustain self-structure. Each self is unique; but the value of self-actualization holds for all.

And this leads us to the final reason for why the society of rational human beings is not ideal: it does not recognize the narcissistic needs of the self. The self is also a kind of irrationality as its ideals do not have a rational justification—they are just ideals that seem to be an unchosen destiny, a structure of who we are that seems to be given. Just as our likes and dislikes of food seem to be just what they are and do not need justification, so with the talents, traits, and predispositions that ground our organic ideals. The erotic eruptions of the self are spontaneous, not the result of a careful rational deliberation—although we can certainly deliberate about how best to actualize them. It is also difficult for the rational ego to admit and own the fragility of self-structure and its neediness to be embedded in a field of empathic responsiveness.

8.4 Reconsidering Democracy on the Basis of Self Psychology

Plato held that the greatest nemesis to the soul and state is chaos. He thought that the best soul and state were ones that were fully unified with no factions or dissentions. He sought a tight coherence, one that would allow for different kinds of persons and psychic motivations only if they were hierarchically ordered and controlled by a rational authority. For Plato, and most of the West that followed, rational organization of difference was hierarchical with those that were closest to the rational rulers being better than those who were dissimilar. This has been the basis for the discrimination against women, minorities, and others, given that privileged white men tended to be in positions of power (see the discussion of prejudice in Chapter 6). As African-American philosopher, Lucius Outlaw, says: "reason became whore to political expediency" (1987/1995, 313). The founders of America thought it rational to allow for the slavery of African-Americans because they were deemed incapable of the kind of rationality that white males had. Hence, even though Enlightenment reason proclaimed the universality of human rights and the dignity of all human beings, it also found it rational to enslave others (Outlaw, 1987/1995). As we discussed above, what counts as rationality is embedded in frameworks.

How are we going to move to a genuine form of democracy, one which allows for a real diversity of voices, one that is truly open-minded, one that does not attempt to control or hierarchically arrange discourse so that only one kind of voice dominates? For Jürgen Habermas (one of the premier political theorists of the later part of the 20th century), being open-minded involves bringing all the different stakeholders to the table and allowing them to engage in dialogue (1981/1983). This, of course, works only if the persons who come to the table are capable of listening to others, empathizing with their point of view, and adjusting their preferences in light of hearing the preferences of others. The key question now becomes, "What kind of human being is genuinely capable of being open-minded?" and its corollary question, "What kind of human being is incapable of being open-minded?" To answer both questions, we need to turn to self psychology.

We have found that persons who have intact selves tend to feel secure in themselves and do not need their egos to bind them together with tight cognitive structures of values and political ideologies. When persons have injured selves that cannot provide an inner gyroscope, there is a tendency to hold themselves together through cognitive structures and ego defenses. As these defensive structures are vital to the sense of psychic coherence, they tend to be rigid and brittle. Such a psyche does not tend to be open-minded but to be ideological and dismissive of other points of view.

Further, as we have seen, all persons have a tendency to surround themselves with those with whom we share some important sameness. These "same" others have a kind of automatic mirroring and obviously satisfy our narcissistic need for twinning. Hence, there is a normal tendency to group with those who are like us and abject those who are different. However, this tendency is countered by the healthy self's need to be expansive, developmental, and exploratory. When we feel secure in our self-structure, we can venture out into diversity more easily. In metapsychological terms, when persons have coherent, vitalized selves at the core of psychic functioning, their egos can be free to entertain different points of view, different perspectives, different kinds of human beings from themselves.

However, when persons have injured or displaced selves, the tendencies will be to identify more intensely with a selfsame group and develop rigid ego ideologies. Jonathan Lear identifies closed-mindedness with "knowingness" (2000). Knowingness occurs when one refuses to question or inquire, because they already know the truth. Such persons are the opposite of Socrates insofar as they think they know what life is all about, what politics are correct, what religion has the truth about God, etc. This kind of person cannot be swayed by facts—which they claim are not facts—or by the viewpoints of others, as these others are already condemned as wrong, for their psychic cohesion depends on their belief-structure remaining intact.

Adding to these problems is the fact that persons with injured selves harbor narcissistic rage and have strong tendencies to identify a set of others as the evil ones who need to be destroyed (Terman, 2010). The combination of the rageful urge to victimize, compulsive need to identify with one's selfsame group, and the totalizing conviction that one's position is right make injured selves grave dangers to the open-mindedness needed for democracies to function. Many Western democracies—not just America—have seen these narcissistically wounded persons start to undermine democratic procedures and bring violence, lies, and hatred rather than peaceful voting procedures to elections.

Not only do democracies need persons with strong selves, but selves have the best chances of developing, *ceteris paribus*, within democratic polities. Democracy is the one form of government that can recognize and validate difference and set up institutions (law courts, etc.) and procedures (voting, etc.), in which disputes between diverse parties can be solved without violence. As John Dewey says, "Can we find any reason that does not ultimately come down to the belief that democratic social arrangements promote better quality of human experience, one which is more widely accessible and enjoyed, than do non-democratic and anti-democratic forms of social life" (1938/1973, 513). By "better quality of experience" Dewey means experience that is more lively, more open to experimentation, more future-oriented rather than repetitious, more aesthetic, more under the control of the individual—the kind of experience persons with strong self-structure rather than defensive structures value and seek. This does not mean that all socio/political systems ought to be democratic. We have witnessed the foolhardiness of attempting to export democracy to societies that were neither ready nor able to sustain democratic procedures and institutions. Nor does it mean that all democracies are favorable to the development of the self—indeed, the major theme of this book is to show how American democracy, having succumbed to market economics, has developed institutions and practices that hinder the development of self-structure.

Insofar as economic society is producing persons with injured selves, it is undermining the democratic politics it needs to exist. If market economics needs democratic forms of government to flourish, and democracies need persons with coherent selves, then we are witnessing a profound contradiction at the heart of American culture. If only for the sake of saving democracy and with it a robust economics, we need to be far more sensitive to how we are or are not nourishing selves. It is not only crucial for the sake of personal happiness to start to determine how to change social practices, but crucial for the future of democratic forms of government. In the next chapter I will try to imagine what a different kind of ideal state would look like, one that emphasizes above all the construction of persons with strong selves. This will not be Plato's rational state nor the current economic state but a state based on the findings of self psychology.

Note

1 Unlike Plato's *Symposium* in which eros was put forth as the most human of motivations, in the *Republic* eros is not only not validated but proclaimed to be the most tyrannical force in the psyche to be avoided at all costs (573b). How does one get these preeminent Platonic dialogues together? I see the *Symposium* as exploring what Kohut will later call the self and the *Republic* as exploring what a soul would look like if a rational ego could achieve preeminence in the psyche. For the most part, the West has been enamored of the *Republic* and the possibility of constructing both rational persons and rational states. In my advocating a soul with both a highly developed rational ego and a highly developed erotic self, I hope to show how Plato's two great dialogues can fit together.

References

Dewey, J. (1938/1973). *Experience and Education*. In Ed. J. McDermott, *The Philosophy of John Dewey*. (pp. 511–523). Chicago: University of Chicago Press.

Habermas, J. (1981/1983). *The Theory of Communicative Action. Vol 1: Reason and the Rationalization of Society*. Tr. T. McCarthy. Boston, Beacon Press.

Lear, J. (2000). *Open-Minded: Working Out the Logic of the Soul*. Cambridge, MA: Harvard University Press.

Nietzsche, F. (1901/1967). *The Will to Power*. Trs. W. Kaufmann & R. Hollingdale. New York: Random House.

Outlaw, L. (1987/1995), "Philosophy, Ethnicity, and Race." In J. Lee & F. Hord, Eds. *I Am Because We Are: Readings in Black Philosophy*. (pp. 304–328). Amherst, MA: University of Massachusetts Press.

Plato. (2016). *Republic*. Tr. C. D. C. Reeve. In *Readings in Ancient Greek Philosophy*. Eds. M. Cohen, P. Hurd, & C. D. C. Reeve. (pp. 234–418). Indianapolis, IN: Hackett.

Terman, D. (2010). "Fundamentalism and the Paranoid Gestalt." In *The Fundamentalist Mindset*. Eds. C. Strozier, D. Terman, & J. Jones. (pp. 47–61). Oxford: Oxford University Press.

Chapter 9

The Ideal Self Psychological State

A New *Republic*

Let me commence this chapter with several important disclaimers. First, the chapter attempts to parallel Plato's vision of an ideal society and concerns only what is needed for an ideal society to attend primarily to the needs of persons' selves. As such, it does not deal with how to transform the drastically important problems of current society—problems such as global warming, income disparity, social injustices, the suffering of the poor, political stasis, etc. Second, while I will make a number of suggestions for how to alter social institutions and practices to help bring about a self-psychologically oriented society, I am not a sociologist and confess to having little empirical knowledge in this area. However, what I am advocating is not based on how society is currently constructed but how it ought to be constructed were it to have the development and sustenance of self-structure as one of its top priorities. Third, it is an ideal that arises in relation to American institutions and practices and might not be applicable at all to cultures and societies that have very different kinds of social institutions and practices.

9.1 From Plato's Rational State to a Self-Psychological Society

As we saw in the last chapter, Plato thinks that the democratic state and soul are so factionalized as to be fully inept. Yet, our new self-psychological society must be democratic, for this is the only kind of polity that attempts to integrate diversity and affirm persons' freedom to choose how best to live their individuated lives. The healthy self-psychological soul must also be democratic in the sense of allowing all the various motivational sectors of the psyche to speak. Hence, to imagine

DOI: 10.4324/9781003303657-13

an ideal self-psychological state and soul, we must replace the ancient model of rational hierarchy, as it inherently lessens the voices of those sectors not in power, especially those seen as irrational.

I think that we can use an ecological pattern of organization rather than a hierarchical one for understanding how both the psyche and the state can achieve a functional order without structures of domination and control.[1] Ecological organization consists of interdependent relationships among its components without one being dominant and the others subordinate. As we have discovered, when persons have intact selves at the nucleus of psychic functioning, there is a natural ecological organization that appears in the psyche, for the other motivational sectors—the ego, id, and social unconscious—will revolve around the self's values, but not be dominated by them. The desires, emotions, and drives will be unconsciously modulated, regulated, and prioritized by the self so that they do not disorganize the psyche but find ways to be satisfied that are syntonic with the self. The ego, for sure, will come increasingly into play as we mature and help us with its powers of rational organization, but it is the self that does the initial sorting, regulating, and prioritizing of psychic motivations. Since selves are singularized to individuals, the organization of the various psychic components will be unique for the person and situation. Such an ideal relieves us of the problem of everyone's having to attain a universal ideal, as is posited in rational ethics. In short, we do not need a rational hierarchical ordering of our irrational motivations to get out of psychic chaos; psyches that have strong selves at their core can attain a psychic harmony and coherence without the imposition of a ranked codification.

When the ego, self, social unconscious, and id are ecologically interrelated, their various voices can be heard, balanced, and given priority depending on the situation. While a full intertwining of the self and the ego is optimal, there are times when the ego needs to take the lead; others when the self does; others when our biological needs will take precedence; and still others when we need to act and behave in socially coded ways without rational questioning or the self's expressing its narcissistic needs. While having a strong vitalized self at the core of experiencing is crucial, it is not to be conceived of as hierarchically superior to the other motivational sectors. It is a polestar around which the others can revolve; not a monarch asserting dictatorial control over the psyche. The ecological organization is not democratic in asserting that each voice is equally important regardless of situation or developmental trajectory. An ecosystem is functional to the extent that it can survive and meet the needs of all its members in an appropriate balance. Situations count, as do natural temperaments. Some people are overly rational; others overly emotional; others overly concerned with bodily needs, others overly concerned with being socially proper; and still others can be too full of themselves. So long as all the voices of the psyche are given legitimacy and the self is intact, the ecological structuring of the psyche can take myriads of different forms.

Like an ecologically balanced psyche, a robust democratic state will allow all the voices of its various constituencies to be heard; not just those that are privileged or historically more powerful. If the state functions more like an ecosystem than a hierarchy of power, it will respond to those populations most in need at different times. The diverse populations will work in harmony without losing their different values, ways of being human, or ways of constructing social life. The more a community can allow for vitalizing differences and yet retain an ecological harmony, the healthier it will be. The kind of democratic society that truly attempts to achieve "liberty and equality for all" will emerge into existence only when its citizens develop selves at the cores of their psyches.

While Plato's measure for the health of a society is the degree of its unity, contemporary economic society measures its well-being by assessing its GNP—that is, its productivity—especially the rate at which productivity is increasing. In the capitalist world, the economy must be expanding to be healthy, and this, of course, is one of the great problems with capitalism—an ever-expanding economy is unsustainable in terms of depleting the earth of its valuable resources and polluting the world and its atmosphere with wastes. The capitalist expansive economy has as its endpoint doom. I believe that for the economic world to transform into a sustainable one, the society needs to balance economic values with those of psychological well-being. That is, it will need to measure the well-being of society, corporations, and personhood not simply in terms of productivity and profit, but in terms of the psychological well-being of its members. I believe that in focusing on psychological well-being, the society will still be highly productive (as its workers will be happier) and will also attain a coherent harmony, insofar as persons with coherent selves can listen to and deal with diversity without repression or degradation.

It would not be that difficult for our social scientists to develop a well-being inventory scale based on self psychology. It would attempt to measure (a) how meaningful persons find their lives to be—how much they find themselves able to be striving for their ideals; (b) how strong their self-esteem is; (c) how vitalized their sense of agency is; (d) how connected they feel with others—how much they feel they can count on others to be there for them in times of difficulty; (e) how much they think of themselves as good persons able to be empathic and caring for others, and (f) how much they think that the others who surround them are good persons.

While I am advocating the demise of economic culture and the assent of a self-psychological society, I am not advocating any kind of Marxist revolution. As far as I can see from my limited knowledge of the history of revolutions, violence tends to promote violence. Czarist violence is replaced by Communist Party purges; the French monarchy's violence is replaced by the Terror of Robespierre; the American revolution eventually leads to a land full of gun violence. Further, the competitiveness and profit-seeking motives of capitalism have produced a world of economic well-being unimaginable a mere 300 years ago. It is not only that we have an undreamed-of plethora of goods and services, but we have such an explosion of possibilities for work, recreation, and social engagements that there are now an extraordinary number of opportunities for persons to find activities and relationships in which they can realize their selves. That is, given the wide variety of idiosyncratic talents, predispositions, and traits that persons have, the economic world has created a vast variety of activities in which individuals can satisfy their selves. In this way, the economic modern world is the best that has ever existed for self-realization. What needs to happen is not an annihilation of the dynamic nature of this world exploding into ever expansive possibilities for self-realization, but a curbing of the anti-self tendencies that we have uncovered, especially the ideal of the self-sufficient rational individual.

I think that the amalgamation of economic culture into a self-psychological society can take place non-violently if we can change certain key practices in the society's most important institutions—home, school, and work. While I will make some suggestions for changes that the culture needs to make to transist to a psychological society, I need to qualify my claims by saying that I am not a sociologist and will be making concrete proposals without a full knowledge of the variables in play.

9.2 Revitalizing the Home

The most important social institution for developing selves is the home, as it is the crucible in which selves are forged in early childhood. Kohut often describes the kind of parent who most damages a child's ability to develop a self as being cold, distant, unavailable, or caught up in disciplining the child into a standardized ideal rather than responding to the child's singular needs, capacities, and traits. The ideal parent is just the opposite: warm, available, empathically responsive, calm without being cold or distant, delightfully playful (twinning the playfulness of the young), and able to affirm the singularity of the child rather than its ability to fit a social norm. Empathic responsiveness is undoubtedly the most important trait for a caregiver in the child's very early life; empathy is the psychic protein out of which selves are built.

In our ideal self-psychological world, caregivers will affirm the child's need to express its infantile grandiosity but also attend to the need to transform its sense of greatness to one based on accomplishment—always treating the child, whether in success or failure, as being special, as being a wonderful little person who is wanted and loved. They will be highly reluctant to ever shame displays of greatness or failures of accomplishment. They will not impose rigid ideals of proper behavior but will gently socialize the child to live with and respect others in a world constructed around social codes. They will not only allow themselves to be idealized but cherish the idealizations of their children.

These practices are, I believe, natural for caregivers who themselves have vitalized selves. Good parents lovingly adore their children and get substantial narcissistic nourishment from them. They replenish their own sense of grandiosity and perfection by identifying with the baby as a chip off the old block—myself reborn with aspirations and hopes for the greatness the child will be. As Freud says, "His Majesty, the Baby ... The child shall fulfill those wishful dreams of the parents which they never carried out" (1914, 91).

Again, being a warm, caring, responsive, playful parent is, I believe, how we are naturally inclined, if we have healthy selves and are not excessively burdened by demands from the outside world—especially the demand that we not be in the home because we need to be at work. Caring for infants and very young children is one of life's most demanding tasks—it is incredibly time and energy intensive, as any parent knows. For caregivers to devote themselves to the child as much as the child needs, they should be largely free from having to leave home for work. However, in our current world, among married families with children, over 70% of households have at least one employed parent outside the home, and in about 50% of these families, both parents are employed (Bureau of Labor statistics). It is extremely difficult to be a warm, relaxed, loving caretaker when parenting must be done in one's precious spare time.

In our ideal self-psychological society, one or both parents will be relieved of the burden of having to leave home for work. Other countries, such as Finland and the Netherlands, have much more beneficial parental-leave policies than the United States. It would not be that difficult to have the premier parental-leave program in the world, with both parents having at least two years of parental-leave and one even longer. In the long run, the financial support for this program will more than pay for itself, as children who have well-developed selves will be far less likely to be criminals or cheaters later in life, thereby relieving the disproportionate amount of money spent on the judicial system. Other kinds of adjustments are possible: each of the parents works a part day during different times of the day. Much non-physical work can be done by computer from home. I think that there are myriads of imaginative possibilities for solving this problem of work and childcare. We have not explored them in depth due to work having such a dominating role in contemporary life.

Of course, disburdening parents from outside pressures does not relieve them from inside pressures, if they have injured or traumatized selves. Those with injured selves are going to have problems being parents, as their children are likely to re-traumatize them in various ways, if only to remind them of their own childhood injuries when the traumas likely occurred. Of course, it is not just parents that need relief from the internal pressures of an injured self. If I am right about economic culture's severely undermining self-structure for many of its members, then in the transition to our ideal self-psychological community, the community will need to offer subsidized self-psychological therapy for all who need it.

The home is not the only place where young children will be nourished. Even if parents are mainly at home (with some doing work from home), there will be occasions in which parents will need to use day-care centers for their children. These will need to be delightfully warm, empathic places whose employees have a substantial knowledge of the psychological needs of young children and provide them with the mirroring and idealized strength they need. The positions in these centers should not be considered low-level, underpaid ones, as they are now; for in a society whose primary aim is the development of strong vitalized selves, they should be high status, well-paid positions.

Children, of course, need more than empathy and the ability to merge with idealized others. They need stimulation, and this is where storytelling comes in to excite the imagination and, I believe, nourish both the self and soul. Unlike in Plato's *Republic* where stories are censored and only morally correct tales and myths are told, in our self-psychological community, fairy tales, myths, and stories of all kinds will delight children and help them deal with difficult emotions and situations. As Bruno Bettelheim has shown in *The Uses of Enchantment* (1976) and Marcia Dobson in her *Metamorphoses of Psyche in Psychoanalysis and Ancient Greek Thought* (2023) the symbols and emotional engagement with fairy tales and myth can both help organize the psyche and open it up to imaginal/liminal realms of experience. The new self-psychological world will be one teeming with stories, art, and myths from around the world to nourish and expand psychic possibilities.

9.3 Revitalizing Primary Schools

Schools are where a child gets a first and lasting impression of what the big world is like and what it means to engage with institutions. Since much of our lives will be lived in institutions—schools, corporations, etc., this initial engagement is of the utmost importance for setting unconscious expectations about what life beyond the family can mean. The aim of schools has been, and must be, the development of the cognitive powers of the ego. However, while the ego needs substantial development during the school years, so does the self.

Schools present children with their first significant environments in which they are challenged in numerous ways—as being good or poor students, as being popular or unpopular, as being capable or not on the playing fields, etc., and their self-esteem will depend in part on how they do with these challenges. Since these challenges are often competitive and produce both winners and losers, they tend to cause significant anxiety, especially for a child whose self is not well-formed. Such children often want to retreat back to the safety of home; others seem to accept that they are not as good as others.

The sense of failure that occurs in schools is often the result of a hierarchical ranking of performance in all areas. Those who succeed well at the tasks of school life—academics, sociality, sports—are likely to have solidified self-esteem but also be prey to the social codes that govern these aspects of life. In short, school presents a very difficult time for budding selves. Insofar as it places everyone in a hierarchical scheme, it has the tendency to either overstimulate or crush our narcissistic grandiosity. While losing can be devastating, so can winning, for often the price one pays for being successful is a tendency to lose the self by becoming overly attuned to social expectations. The question arises as to how one can retain, mature, and foster one's ideals and unique singularity while in school.

Even in our new self-psychological world, schools will undoubtedly have competitions, rankings, and difficult tasks to perform. To counter what might be devastating experiences for many children, primary schools need to provide a warm inviting ambiance in which children feel cared for and special. Their teachers, administrators, and counselors will be empathic and nurturing, but also boundary-setting, self-discipline enhancing, etc. They need to understand the toxic consequences of shame and rarely use it. They need to attend to each child as special, which they can do if the classroom size is small. Researchers claim that optimal classrooms are no larger than 18 students—I think that 15 might be best for each child to get the attention they need and feel special. I believe that if this optimal ambiance is achieved, it will greatly lessen the blows to self-esteem and ideals that can occur in this new, competitive world.

What children's selves need most during the primary school years is a solidification of self-structure in terms of modulated (age-appropriate) self-esteem, and continued abilities to idealize others and transmutingly internalize their functions and character. The early school years are also a crucial time for developing the moral virtues—for practicing generosity, justice, courage, temperance, empathy, etc. These traits need to develop if children are going to become persons who can thrive in reciprocal selfobject relationships, the kind of relationships that are the key to sustaining self-structure in adolescence and adulthood. As primary narcissism does not disappear suddenly but is slowly matured, having help (re-enforcement, modeling) developing these character traits in school is crucial. If the self continues to gain esteem and solidify idealization during the primary school years, then children will typically develop a love of accomplishing through engagement with the world. This contrasts with many young persons' having a deep anxiety about entering today's highly competitive society in which one can so easily be cast aside and become lost.

Primary school is also the time in which children develop an expanded ability to partake in friendships—especially those in which there is substantial twinning. While parents can playact twinning, the friendships developed in school are crucial in getting this primary narcissistic need met. And with budding friendships, children further learn how to negotiate their narcissistic self-centeredness with that of others, thereby maturing their narcissism without crushing it. It is also a time when singularity needs to assert itself in the sense of finding just those friends that somehow you connect with. Schools can set up opportunities for different groups of students to do projects, explore, etc., and hence enhance opportunities for finding special others. The search for twinning friends contrasts with what often happens today: the quest for popularity—a pursuit that compels one to forsake one's self and adopt the kind of social persona that makes one popular.

The other aspect of primary schools (and secondary schools) that I would advocate for helping young persons solidify self-structure is offering rich, variegated curricula. The more children can explore possibilities in all forms of creativity and different environments—art, nature, music, storytelling, etc., along with developing their analytic and linguistic skills—the more they will be able to locate the predispositions and propensities of their selves.

After parents and close family members, primary school teachers are often the most important factors in whether children's selves develop and become solidified during these years. These teachers should have extensive education in self psychology, the ability to recognize and address the narcissistic needs of children and have gifts of empathic responsiveness. Society needs to recognize the extreme importance of teachers by making these positions well-paid and given significant status.

9.4 Revitalizing Secondary Schools

Secondary schools need to support self-structure by continuing to have variegated curricula, small classrooms, empathic teachers, etc. This is the time when minds (the full psyche) can blossom and come alive if students encounter some field, work of literature, work of art, or scientific methodology that speaks to them so deeply that it opens genuine possibilities for how to orient oneself to the world. I will never forget reading Dostoevsky's *Crime and Punishment* as a high-school junior, as it transported me out of the banal understanding of human beings that dominated middle-class American culture in the 1950's into a depth of complex psychology, longing for love and redemption, and the dark despair of human life that I had been experiencing. It propelled me to shift the whole direction of my life. Others come alive in history classes or chemistry labs. What is needed is teachers whose minds are still alive and who cherish witnessing their students' minds catch fire. There is little worse in schools than to be in a classroom with a teacher whose mind has gone to seed. We need to stop attempting to standardize education and start imagining ways for teachers to stay vitalized and adventurous in what and how they are teaching. It is not only students who need to feel special but also teachers, and they cannot feel this way unless they are allowed to be unique.

The major psychosocial problem that needs to be solved in these teenage years is the integration of sexuality with one's self. As many have noted, the teenage years bring with them a return of some aspects of primitive narcissism, insofar as teenagers are desperately concerned with who they are, how they appear, how well they are liked, and so on. This return of self-centeredness has to do with the onset of puberty and the development of sexual bodies. While Freud is surely right in saying that our sexuality commences when life begins and has extremely important early stages, it is really with the onset of adult sexuality that we need to integrate our gender identity, sexual preferences, and sexual desire with our selves.

This task has probably always been difficult, but with the opening of society to gender fluidity, de-normalized sexual preferences, and variations of sexual desire, this time of life has become highly anxiety-provoking for many. Given that these anxieties and confusions are occurring at a time when the self is shaky due to a disruptive transition from the home to the outside world—a transition to different selfobjects—we can see how tumultuously difficult this time of life is. The more sexual explorations and experimentation can occur within committed relationships that offer some stability of selfobject reciprocity, the more self-cohesion will be available to negotiate the tempestuous waters of adolescence.

Unfortunately, there is a strong trend in American culture to isolate sex and sexuality to its own realm without relation to other needs of the person. When sex occurs mainly in hook-up relations that give sexual enjoyment without commitment, it is unlikely that sexuality will be integrated into the purposes of the self and serve its needs. What a committed intimate relation adds to ordinary selfobject friendships is that it allows for the exploration of one's sexuality within the safety of a relation in which someone loves and cares for you. However, even committed relationships among the young tend to be ephemeral—as they need to be for crucial psycho/social/sexual explorations to occur. Youth is a time for experimentation, for exploring the possibilities of life. In short, there needs to be some balance of exploration and commitment, with better defined rituals for initiating and uncoupling relationships.

What can schools do to help this difficult transitional period? They provide a secure structure while the hormonal chaos is going on and keep the ego on its cognitive developmental curve. More than this, I would love to see high schools and colleges offer courses in psychoanalysis introducing the complexities of unconscious motivation. Such theoretical knowledge can lead to more self-understanding and psychic cohesion. Teachers in our new world will have a fine grasp of the narcissistic needs of their adolescent students and be empathically attuned to their experiences. I would add lots more counselors, especially those educated in depth psychologies, who are highly empathic, and who are non-judgmental—especially about sexuality and gender formation.

9.5 Revitalizing Colleges and Universities

The fundamental task during the college years is to solidify an ego identity that can incorporate, express, and find ways to realize the ideals and ambitions of the self. While forming an ego identity has probably been going on for most of adolescence, college is a time to go from "I might be a this, or I might be a that" kind of identity experimentation to firming up what Erikson calls "identity formation" as opposed to "identity diffusion" (1960/1980). This is a time of life in which the young need to "find themselves" rather than getting lost or succumbing to general social ideals and choosing a persona that has little connection to the self. One of the key acts in constructing an ego identity is choosing a major, and this is when students experience an overwhelming pressure from the economic society (and quite often from their families) to choose a "practical" major—one that will help them get a job right out of college. This is a powerful way in which the economic society colonizes the psyches of young persons (especially those in the middle/upper classes) to use them as vehicles for its goals of productivity and profit. Almost 80% of college students today are in pre-professional programs; only about 20% choose a liberal arts education. For those in a liberal arts education, a substantial percentage are choosing to major in STEM disciplines or economics. It used to be that English and History were the most popular majors. No longer. They do not map onto the quantitative, computational, and analytical skills most in demand in the economic world.

In short, college education today is not for the exploration of the different realms of human creativity (the arts), human history, ways of experiencing language, or ways of thinking in order to find what is most syntonic with the self. College education today is mainly about preparing one for the economic world. Education is being replaced by training. This is sad, because many young persons choose a major or pre-professional program before they know who they are. One of the great benefits of a liberal arts education is that it allows one to creatively explore what really interests them and what bores them. I went to college expecting to follow my father into business, but when I took my first economics class, I couldn't stay awake. I was utterly bored. I switched into a philosophy class (not knowing quite why), and, even though the professor was moderately incompetent, I became awake and enthralled as never before. I found a lifelong friend—Socrates. Had I chosen to go to a major university and proclaimed myself to be a business major, I might have spent my professional life doing something that had little relation to myself.

Colleges and universities are eliminating positions in the Humanities as these are now out of favor in an age in which the young are so anxious about getting positions in the economic world that they often think that courses in the Humanities are a waste of time. And yet, it is courses in the Humanities that concern ultimate questions about what it means to be human and offer unique ways of exploring the human psyche and self in literature, language, the arts, and theory.

What colleges and universities can do to foster the discovery of self and the integration of self with ego identity is to resist the commercial pressures to sell only what students are buying and to hold steady in the belief that college education ought to foster a love of the Humanities and the exploration of different ways humans have constructed their humanity. This can be instituted in general education requirements but also in the ambiance of the school in which professors, hopefully, will be able to tout not just their specialties but a well-rounded education. And it would help if career centers let students know that statistics show that humanities students—especially philosophy majors—are doing better in terms of salary and position 20 years after graduation than those in pre-professional programs. Humanities majors might be slow out of the gate, but the skills of interdisciplinary thinking, communication of ideas, and seeing the complexities of human beings will stand them in good stead when executive and management positions arise.

Self psychology would advise students to choose a major whose subject matter they love, that makes them feel alive, that has somehow touched their selves. What if students don't really fall in love with any subject-matter (not an unusual occurrence)? They can still examine their experience in different disciplines to see what made them more engaged and what less. These are hints as to what the self's ideals truly are and, if followed, can lead to hypotheses of where in the non-academic world one might find oneself. Quite often the self for the young comes most alive in recreational activities. In this case, choice of location and its access to the recreational activity (for Colorado College students, skiing) takes precedence over seeking to establish a professional identity. That will come in time.

Aside from choosing a major, other essential aspects of identity formation that need to be dealt with during college are how one relates to their gender, race, ethnicity, sexual preferences, etc., and how one responds to how their cultures impose prejudices on various of these identities. In this realm colleges and universities can be of immense help in exposing racial, sexist, and non-binary prejudices and providing tools for how to respond to these prejudices in such a way that they do not lower self-esteem.[2] We would hope in our ideal self-psychological society that persons with strong vitalized selves will be far less likely to discriminate against those seen as different or other than happens in our current society. Indeed, those with strong selves seek to relate to what is different because such relations open up expansive possibilities for self-growth.

There is one other major problem for developing and maintaining self-structure during the college years: graduation. While graduation is universally proclaimed to be a great achievement to be thoroughly celebrated, it is also highly traumatic to the self. It is not uncommon for students to exhibit many traits of a traumatized self during senior year: they increase their drug and alcohol usage, often become less productive then when they were juniors, break up stable love relationships, and report higher levels of anxiety and depression. These symptoms arise because students are anticipating the end of life as they have known it: the end of two decades of school. With graduation not only do they lose the social arena in which they have demonstrated success (and, hence, gained self-esteem), they lose the web of selfobject friendships they have spent four years developing. If selfobjects are an intrinsic part of the self, then graduation literally breaks the self apart—and seniors are anticipating this as the day of celebration comes closer.

The difficulties with identity formation, relationships, and graduation are being experienced today by students who enter college with substantial psychological vulnerability. The mental health of college students has, for many reasons, greatly deteriorated over the last quarter century. The California Endowment reports that for 75% of young adults (18–24) experience significant anxiety, 50% experience depression, and 31% experience suicidal ideation. Many college students are on various kinds of psychotropic medications. In short, our best and brightest young adults are in crisis—and the crisis is occurring just as they are about to enter the difficult world of adult work and love, a world overshadowed by global climate change, a fiercely competitive economy, and crushing issues of social inequity. And many are entering this new difficult world alone, having left behind their selfobject friendships or love relationships, in part because they have accepted the misguided ideal of the self-sufficient independent individual. They believe they are supposed to do life on their own without depending on others.

What can colleges and universities do to help students sustain and develop self-structure during the college years? In general colleges need to devote far more resources to their mental health facilities. The pandemic, of course, was traumatic for many, as students had to take online classes isolated from fellow students, professors, and the healthcare services on campus. Because many students had no chance to develop new selfobject relationships during the pandemic years, their mental health declined. While I would love the counselors at colleges to be deeply versed in self psychology, any kind of increased psychological support would help.

In relation to self psychology, I have the following recommendations, some of which I have attempted to carry out at Colorado College. First, it is important for students to hear about what the self needs during the college years—how to go about finding who one is, how to integrate self-ideals/ambitions into an ego identity, and the importance of close selfobject relationships—the importance of friends and committed love relationships during the college years. A careful training of dorm leaders to look for disturbances of the self and know what kinds of interactions are likely to shore up self-structure will help. I would love for there to be several courses students could take that would teach them psychoanalysis and self-psychology so that they might be better able to probe their own depths and help their friends. I think that it would be wise to find ways to inform seniors of how difficult and psychologically threatening graduation is and offer strong advice about watching out for increasing drug and alcohol use, shattering relationships, and finding little motivation for their schoolwork.

9.6 Revitalizing Adult Life: Work and Home

After graduation, persons will spend most of their adult lives in places of work and at the homes they establish for themselves. It is primarily in these two places that persons need to find both activities in which to realize the self and receive selfobject nourishment. In the modern economic world, it is the workplace that is the fulcrum around which life revolves and, for it to be more attentive to the needs of the self, it needs to complexify its aims and values.

When a worker/employee joins a company there should be some deeper form of commitment than now exists with workers free to leave at any time, regardless of what the company has invested in them in terms of education, training, etc., and companies are free to let their workers go if their productivity isn't high enough, their specializations are no longer needed, or competitive market conditions demand layoffs. In a self-psychological world, working conditions would increasingly emphasize the values of giving employees as much security and psychological support as possible. And I believe that with this kind of loyalty to workers, they will respond with increased loyalty and productivity on their part, as it seems to have happened in Japan.

Most of all, the workplace needs to foster selfobject connectedness among its employees, including executives. That is, workplaces need to foster warmth, caring, empathy, and friendship. While this increase in emotional presence might get in the way of productivity, efficiency, the ability to fire employees, and could increase the possibility of sexualization entering the workplace, these problems need to be overcome if we are going to have places of work that genuinely enhance one's sense of well-being because the self is being nourished.

Hegel, in the first third of the 19th century, recognized even then the extreme importance of corporations in modern life for families and individuals.

> In the corporation, the family not only has its firm basis in that its livelihood is guaranteed—on condition of its possessing a certain capability, but the two [i.e., livelihood and capability] are also recognized, so that the member of a corporation has no need to demonstrate his competence and his regular income and means of support—i.e. the fact that he is *somebody*—by any further external evidence.
>
> (1821/1977, sec. 253)

What this dense Hegelian passage says is that corporations are crucial in providing its members with security, income, and a sense of belonging.

It also grants them an identity—it makes them "somebody" by being recognized as part of a corporation. This recognition grants the person *"honor"*—that is, stabilizes and affirms their self-worth. In Hegel's view of corporations, they are institutions that help sustain the selves of their members—they are "a second family." It is a concept that seems to be prevalent in Japan and is one to which American corporations should return.

Of course, corporations must survive in the market and hence make decisions along economic lines. But in our new self-psychological world, these economic values will be balanced by values promoting self-cohesion. I think that the more corporations can achieve this sense of being a second home for those who work in them, the more adult life in modern societies will be satisfying and enlivening. Further, I believe that a corporation's caring for the selves of its employees will, in fact, make them highly productive, for persons with vitalized selves tend to have more energy and commitment available for accomplishment. Rather than being ambivalent about where they work and what they do, workers will cherish the workplace, if it relates to their narcissistic needs.

The second and most important institution that needs to sustain the self is the home—the home that one now creates as an adult rather than the original parental home. Even if the workplace is attuned to the needs of persons' selves, it has traditionally been the home where, after the toils of the day, one can find warmth, love, and renewal. I would hope that the home has a partnership and is not a home with a single head of household, as an increasing number of homes are today. A loving partner in life is undoubtedly the most important source of selfobject security and nourishment. Just knowing that when you wake up in the morning and collapse in the evening there is someone there who has loving eyes for you and for whom you are the most wonderful being on earth sustains self-esteem and buoys erotic energy as little else can.

One's own home is also a realm in which a person or a couple can express their selves' erotic singularity in how to furnish it, arrange it, fill it with personal treasures, especially ones that carry memories of special experiences. Eros, as we have found, is aroused by beauty. The more one can create a home space that flows with the kinds of beauty that delight one and carry meaning, the more it can feel like an environment that holds and nourishes our deepest selves. I think that homes (apartments, condos, etc.) need art, for art carries the creative verve of the artist—a novel way of perceiving and producing meaning—and this reminds us that we, too, are unique centers of perception and initiative. Art arouses the erotic vitality of the self and sustains it.

Especially for those who have been injured in childhood and for whom the world has a feeling of danger, having a safe, warm, special home can make a great deal of difference. To choose to fill one's home with children is a more difficult choice that involves the taking on of enormous responsibility and the willingness to sacrifice some of one's own goals to attend to the needs, hopes, and delights of one's children. As hard as children are, they can add more to one's life's journey in terms of love and enriched narrative complexity than any other constituent of life.

9.7 Revitalizing General Social Practices

The changes that I am suggesting for the institutions of homes, schools, and the workplace are, to me, both essential in transforming to a self-psychological world and also quite possible. All the suggestions need not cause a major disruption to the beneficial patterns of economic society, although replacing the ideal of the autonomous individual seeking wealth with the ideal of attempting to realize and sustain one's self is, indeed, a radical disruption that might have far-reaching consequences that are not predictable. What I am going to suggest in this section is somewhat more far-reaching, but still within the realm of possibility. At least the suggestions can act as lures for beginning social transformations.

In our ideal self-psychological society, there will be three crucial social practices that occur independently of the changes to homes, schools, and the workplace, namely, the practices of almost everyone's seeing a therapist on a regular basis; intensely engaging with natural and cultural beauty; and engaging in love relationships through rituals that provide the most amount of self-growth and the least amount of anxiety.

In earlier cultures, families living together and understanding the need for connection and mutual understanding also had older women, grandmothers, old wise "women," or "crones," serving as the holders of the wisdom of the ages and turned to for advice. Extended families and small villages could also provide numerous selfobjects other than those in the nuclear family. Life has become far more complex, selves have become more fragile, and self-sustaining networks have largely disappeared. These facts suggest that we need to establish a new social practice of a person's having a psychotherapist they can see either on a regular basis or in times of crisis. Just as we have personal physicians, dentists, eye doctors, etc., we need to have our personal therapists—persons who know us, know our histories, and are empathic with our inner turmoil and struggles.

Three things stand against this kind of practice being put into place right now: the ideal of self-sufficiency which tells us that if we have a problem, we should handle it by ourselves; expense; and the lack of well-trained therapists. In our ideal self-psychological world, we would have a different understanding of ourselves and be much more ready to accept therapeutic help, and the society would find adequate ways to subsidize therapeutic visits. I believe that persons who receive fine therapy will have healthier psyches, and this in turn will alleviate other medical expenses and make them far less likely to turn to criminal behavior, thereby relieving monies which nowadays are spent in other areas. If persons who have had extensive and effective psychotherapy are shown in general to have much lower medical bills, then the insurance companies or a national healthcare insurance organization ought to be happy to fund therapy more than they do now.

Life is tough for humans. Oftentimes those who are most likely to shatter our psychic equilibrium are those closest to us—our partners, family, and friends. Even in our ideal self-psychological world, there will be narcissistic blows, illnesses, deaths of beloveds, failures, broken relationships, and so on. How wonderful it would be to have a consistent, empathic therapist ready to steady the ship with unproblematic selfobject support. Just as we take our automobiles in for gas when their tanks are empty, why not our souls when they are depleted? Change the ideal; show insurance companies the math, and this becomes a very possible change. However, there is one more problem with it. There are not enough good therapists to go around. We need far more institutions and better training to produce the number of therapists that will be needed.

The need for modern persons' having therapy for injured selves is obvious; however, the recognition of this need goes largely unrecognized. To the degree it is recognized, treatments tend to center around short-term CBT, a therapy that does not reach into the depths of the unconscious where the self resides. Psychoanalysis has come a long way since Freud first articulated the nature of psychoanalytic treatment. His objective surgeon stance has been replaced with a two-person, intersubjective, empathic therapy that can reach into the depths of the unconscious and throw a lifeline to the injured self. There is a need; we now have a powerful method for working with injured selves. All that is needed is a recognition of the problem and the right way to deal with it, and we are on our way to becoming a more ideal society. Not long ago there were no computer experts, a need appeared, now there are many thousands. The same can be true for well-trained therapists.

The second social practice I would hope to encourage in our new self-psychologically informed world is the habit of enriching our souls with natural and cultural sources of beauty. We previously found that the erotic self is nourished by aesthetic experiences. Its needs for harmony, coherence, and creativity are all related to beauty. Plato, Emerson, Whitehead, and many other thinkers claim that it is beauty, more than any other value, which gives vitality and meaning to life. Our economic society has downplayed the aesthetic in favor of efficient, cost-effective productions, and while the clean, mechanical look can be quite pleasing to the ego, the emotional textures, chiaroscuro, and spontaneous eruptions of the self need a different kind of reverberating environment. The economic culture has also forced the poor and disenfranchised to live in squalid, ugly conditions. Before the modern era, the poor were usually tenant farmers who at least were living close to nature and in quaint villages; in the industrial and post-industrial worlds, they often must live in slum conditions. In our new self-psychological world, the state would require that the living environments for all persons be constructed with aesthetic values, not just efficiency and profit values.

I would encourage the purchasing of art that speaks to the self and having it fill our homes with beauty and vibrancy. We will need many kinds of art that can speak to the many different kinds of selves that are being developed, and we need to resist ranking the various artistic expressions in a hierarchical way. Let us bring back the crafts that made so many of our buildings and homes warm, beautiful places in which to dwell. Such a shift would give those who erotically thrill at woodworking, iron-smithing, architecting, etc., creative outlets for their self-expressions.

I hardly need to speak a word for the beauty of nature, as there is such a strong American literature proclaiming its transformative powers on the soul. Emerson, Thoreau, Whitman, Leopold, Robert Frost, and so many others (along with several scientific studies) have shown us how being in nature can relieve us of stress and nourish our sense of well-being. I believe that nature can perform selfobject functions in terms of soothing the emotions, arousing us to our "natural" singularity, offering us metaphorical meanings that take us out of social triviality into the depths of metaphysical existence, and giving us a deeper sense of belonging (see Riker, 1992, ch. 7).

However, many of us live in urban centers, surrounded by concrete, reflective glass, and electric lights that drown out the stars and moon. Parks, green swards, forest preserves, and public gardens are crucial for the well-being of city dwellers. And we hope that our cities and suburbs are surrounded with great forests, lovely fields, or vibrant deserts, within easy access to those living in them. And we should protect as much nature as we possibly can from developmental greed and the intrusion of humans onto every square inch of the planet.

The more beauty we encounter in the world, the more our eros is evoked. That is, the more beauty we find ourselves experiencing, the more we will find our selves loving—loving our selves, our significant others, nature, our culture, life itself. While experiencing beauty sustains the self, erotically creating beauty actualizes it. Creating need not be a work of art or poetry or architecture; sometimes it can be re-arranging a room to be more aesthetically pleasing, planting a garden, doing a skateboard maneuver that you've never done before. We have occasions to create beauty all the time, and the more we can approach life with a creative aesthetic eye, the more enlivened life will be.

One further social change I would make applies mainly to adolescents and young adults: an instantiation of dating rituals. I believe that we mature our narcissism most when we negotiate our lives, bodies, values, and selves with intimate others. These intimate others, as has often been said, replace the devoted love of our early caretakers—except that the new relation is (or ought to be) fully reciprocal.

The sparkle in the lover's eye replaces the gleam in the mother's eye. The mother's tender stroking of our bodies is replaced by our lover's sensuous touch. We are once again thoroughly enmeshed with another human being. The glow of our early narcissism returns, but without the infantile self-centeredness. To learn how to recognize our intimate others as individuals in their own rights with their own values, viewpoints, agency, etc., rather than reducing them to objects for our use is one of the crucial tasks in becoming a mature narcissist.

Indeed, Freud said that the only way to fully overcome the problem of retaining too much narcissistic libido is to engage in reciprocal love relations in which we send our love out to others, thereby depleting our self-love, but are loved back in return, thereby replenishing our self-love. As blood circulating through the lungs gets replenished with oxygen, so our eros circulating through a beloved becomes re-invigorated. As Freud says, when reciprocal intimate relations go well, narcissistic love and object love become so fused as to be indistinguishable.

> Loving in itself, in so far as it involves longing and deprivation, lowers self-regard; whereas being loved, having one's love returned, and possessing the loved object, raises it once more... The return of the object-libido to the ego and its transformation into narcissism represents, as it were, a happy love once more; and, on the other hand, it is also true that a real happy love corresponds to the primal condition in which object-libido and ego-libido cannot be distinguished.
>
> (1914, 99–100)

Many adolescents and young adults today are, as I have previously said, wary of committed love relationships. They are often seen as baggage limiting choices and mobility, and as dangers insofar as a failure in the relationship could be traumatically devastating to fragile selves. Part of the problem with engaging in serious love relationships is that the culture seems to have lost a set of ritual practices for easing gently into relationships, testing the waters without raising expectations, and terminating relationships without guilt when they are not working.

While I dislike sounding nostalgic, I thought that the dating practices of the mid-20th century had some merit insofar as they had set ritual practices for initiating and leaving various degrees of relational commitment. If we wanted to casually meet up with someone, we would gather at parties at someone's home or as a group at the local sweetshop for a coke. If we wanted to test the waters further, we would go on a date in which there was an actual invitation and acceptance to go to the movies or to a dance. A date meant that there was an intent to get to know the other—but nothing physical, other than maybe holding hands (a truly sensuous selfobject experience!) at least on the first couple of dates. That is, there was a bit more investment than the initial meeting, but nothing that would create the expectation of a more committed relationship. One could disengage without guilt or remorse. Then, if all went well with some more dates, there might be "going steady," a relationship that involved a commitment to an exclusive relationship and some physical intimacy—although rarely more than kissing and light petting (this was pre-pill). It was not expected that these relationships would result in engagement and marriage, although they sometimes did. What was expected was that there would be a commitment to work through problems in the relation until they couldn't be solved. Typically, the problems were not deep—getting bored with one another or finding yourself more attracted to someone else. If the relationship occurred in college, then there was "pinning," which typically was a precursor to becoming engaged to be married. While this scenario was quite strictly heterosexual in the 1950's, it could be expanded to include all kinds of different relationships.

I rehearse this scenario because it allowed young human beings to explore their complex and budding sexuality in relationships that had at least a bit of security and commitment. The reason why commitment is important from a self-psychological point of view is that it means that one is dedicated to working through problems until they are unsolvable. It is in working through problems that we grow out of our self-centered narcissism and learn how to negotiate our existence with another human being, a negotiation that typically involves being empathic with and sensitive to the viewpoint of the other. I believe that the more the culture can generate new rituals for entering, sustaining, and ending committed relationships, the more it will help persons develop vitalized selves.

9.8 An Ideal Self Psychological Society

I believe that the above suggestions for how to construct homes, schools, workplaces, and social practices are genuine possibilities for our current society. That is, I do not think my suggestions for making the society more attentive to the needs of the self are entirely fanciful, for they leave the economic world more or less intact. What follows is a fantasy—a play of ideas—in which major structures of the economic world are displaced.

In our ideal self-psychological society, there will be a wide variety of vocational, recreational, and social activities in which persons can realize their selves and establish patterns of human connectedness to help sustain their selves. In this ideal world, society will not be structured around socioeconomic identities and the insane competition to get those positions that are the most lucrative in terms of money and status. Instead, each person will try to find those niches in which they can achieve a high degree of self-realization. In our ideal world, everyone will have guaranteed for them some place of labor, recreation, or social interaction in which they can most develop their self's ideals. All those who want to be artists will be able to be artists. All those who want to be biological researchers can be. All those who love to make music will be able to be musicians. At present, only about one tenth of those who would love to teach philosophy or literature at a college level are able to do so. In our new world, this will not happen. From the moment we are born we will have an abiding sense that there will be a wonderful place for us in the world when we grow up. This is a radically different mindset from the current one in which we think that we must have one of the best socioeconomic positions to be successful in life and need to enter an anxiety-inducing competition in which there will be some winners and many losers. This anxiety will disappear in our new self-psychologically constructed world, as everyone will be assured of a place in which they can do what is most important in life: realize their self's ideals.

One of the great benefits of the shift from identifying the worth of life by the amount of wealth one has to how much one is able to realize ideals and connect with others is the destruction of class society. While people will have differing amounts of wealth, this will not be the primary way in which they achieve status or a sense of self-worth. We will no longer think in terms of the rich and poor, no longer base life on the achievement of an exalted socioeconomic status. The whole class structure will disappear—just what Marx and the communists have advocated, but without a violent revolution or the destruction of a viable economy.

Obviously, this new self-psychological world demands a great deal of what Leibniz calls "pre-established harmony" (1989). That is, there will need to be enough people wanting to learn philosophy for those who want to teach it. There will need to be enough persons wanting to hear live music for those wanting to create it. At present, the economics of supply and demand plus cost effectiveness governs work: where there is demand, there are jobs; regardless of whether the work is self-satisfying. Rather than having many professors teach philosophy to small classes, too often there is a large lecture hall with hundreds of students needing only one professor. Very cost effective, but hardly optimal for the growth of minds or for allowing those who would love to teach philosophy to teach it. This shift from a supply/demand model to a model in which positions are created to satisfy self-longing is so huge as to seem impossible. However, the diversity of interests in people is vast, and much could be accomplished without social engineering. It amazes me how many people love to work with machines—something I abhor. I have met plumbers, electricians, carpenters who get great self-fulfillment from labors many, if not most, would detest. They, on the other hand, can hardly understand why anyone would spend their time reading abstruse philosophical texts. I suspect that a great deal of our basic needs could be satisfied just by people expressing their preferences.

We would need to add a few more principles to make this new world workable. First, I think everyone should receive a base livable salary so that no one must work but can, if they want to, add to the base salary. (The idea of a base livable salary for all has been proposed any number of times, including by such important economists as John Kenneth Galbraith and Milton Friedman.) If persons can find self-fulfillment in activities that are not salaried, they can still have decent material lives. And the lack of material abundance will not bother them much, for it is now not an economic society, but a psychological one. Those positions that require an immense amount of education and exceptional intelligence (physicians, lawyers, etc.) will be able retain their high salary levels, and those positions that need to be filled but which are not self-fulfilling to enough people will also have a high salary rather than a menial one, as they do now. There is no need for most jobs to take eight hours plus per day; much self-realization can occur in recreational and social activities, such as hiking, playing games and sports, gardening, knitting, dancing, bridge clubs, etc. Would-be philosophers could be part of small groups that gather to talk about philosophical problems; they don't have to be paid professors; musicians could play for friends, not just paying audiences. People could hang out and not think it was wasting time; for it might be solidifying selfobject relations.

Right now, activities do not seem to have much worth unless one is paid for them. This mindset would change drastically. Socrates proclaimed that if he got paid for doing philosophy, it would distort and even co-opt his ability to do it freely and with integrity. The same probably holds true for many artists. Once we disconnect the worth of activities from their economic status, I think a great deal of the "forced labor" of the society would cease and persons would attain their happiness in doing what they truly love rather than in what pays well.

In today's world, college education is centered on pre-professional programs; in our new self-psychological world schools will have liberal arts-based curricula in which students are exposed to the worlds of music, art, drama, literature, poetry, social science, languages, the sciences, etc., so that they might both live more expansive lives and become audiences/consumers for those who want to practice in these fields. Persons with expansive interests are likely to discover realms of beauty that help sustain the erotic energy of their selves. Professional education will be fully available afterwards, as we need highly trained professionals in all fields, but they will not be narrow persons whose horizons are limited to their profession.

The most important change will be giving up the ideal of radical individualism and replacing it with an ideal of connectedness and mutual selfobject reciprocity. We will not think about going it alone, heroically conquering the obstacles of life; rather we will affirm friends, family, and lovers as high priorities. We will give up our obsession with mobility and be more concerned with establishing deep connections to place, communities, and those who are most important to us and we to them. That is, in our new world, there will be more stability, more human interconnectedness, less adventurous pursuits of economic positions. There will still be adventures—life requires them to be alive— but they will be more for the sake of self-enhancement rather than income enhancement. We will adventure into new forms of beauty; new ways to be creative; new explorations of our self-possibilities.

Obviously, such a new world cannot come into existence without a great deal of social engineering that would attempt to balance the needs of the economy with those of self psychology. What I am suggesting is not the revolutionary overthrow of the values of profit and production but a complexification of values, such that corporations, persons, and the society at large measure their well-being not simply in terms of material production, but in terms of how meaningful and vivacious persons experience their lives to be.

9.9 Conclusion

In sum, our ideal self-psychological community will foster the development and sustenance of self-structure as its highest priority. It will still have a robust economy, but the economy will be for the sake of selves, not selves for the sake of the economy. If in general people find activities in which to actualize the ideals and ambitions of their selves and construct stable selfobject matrixes to support self-structure, then our new society will be erotically alive, aesthetically attuned, highly creative, and its members will act from the depth of their selves rather than surface motivations.

What I am advocating in our new society is nothing less than a different way of occupying our humanity. The shift from an economic society to a self-psychological one is based on a conceptual revolution, a revolution in the ways we think about who we are as human beings, what we most need, and what gives the most fulfillment to our lives. The ideational revolution is grounded in Heinz Kohut's discoveries about our narcissism, how it transforms into self-structure, and what our selves need to flourish. It negates modernity's concept of the abstract, economically inclined, autonomous individual.

This change of how we think about ourselves and our priorities will deeply affect patterns of economic life but will not destroy it. There will still be jobs, the production of goods and services, profits and innovations, professions, etc. Persons like having and enjoying a robust material life and I have no intention of ruining it. However, persons will no longer sacrifice their selves on the altars of profit and economic status as modernity has encouraged; nor will they demand that others sacrifice their selves in order for the upper classes to have inexpensive goods. Our homes and schools will still produce persons with highly functional rational egos, but they will be balanced by a recognition of the needs of the self. How such persons will alter the fabric of the economy I do not know; but it should be exciting.

The politics of our new self-psychological state will be democratic rather than aristocratic, as in Plato's *Republic*. It will consider all forms of meritocracy to be suspect insofar as they are based on hierarchical rankings that necessarily involve certain prejudicial presuppositions. How our current politics, which are a mixture of oligarchy and democracy, will transform with the de-emphasis on money, is, again, hard to say. However, the politics must have as its guiding ideal promoting policies that foster as many persons as possible having chances to achieve deep forms of self-satisfaction. It will be a person-oriented politics rather than one based on the economy. I am not a political scientist and have not studied all the ramifications of countries, such as the Scandinavian states, that balance social welfare with capitalism, and so feel uncertain about deducing conclusions about the structure of governments. However, such countries point to a viable fusion of economic and social concerns, and they tend to rank among the happiest countries in the world, whereas the United States tends to lag far behind on the happiness scale.

Plato said that it did not matter that his ideal world would probably never come fully into existence. What mattered was that it was an ideal to strive for. Likewise, my ideal self-psychological world might never come fully into existence, but this ideal can help us make changes to the current society and guide it towards a more humane way of constructing humans. And it is not such an outrageously abstract ideal that it cannot motivate us to do better now. Indeed, much of what I suggest is already being done in numerous places. There are many warm, empathic homes in which parents have decided to stay home to be with children. Schools are starting to be more attentive to the mental health of students, and some businesses—typically small and not in the spotlight—have a deep concern for their employees. Despite the ideal of the autonomous self-sufficient individual, most people highly value and seek friendships and love relationships. What seems to be lacking is not the values or desire, but the kind of self-structure that can participate deeply in intimate connectedness. That is, the psychological revolution asks us to create better conditions for becoming the kind of human beings we, in our hearts, truly want to be.

Revolutions in how to occupy our humanity often start in seemingly insignificant, imperceptible ways. The small numbers who first followed Socrates, the Buddha, Confucius, and Jesus, for example, helped generate new worlds, new ways of being human. Perhaps the small groups of humans—the analysts, therapists, patients—who are exploring how to integrate the unconscious into the fullness of being human are the cadre that is opening up a new possibility for how we can better inhabit our humanity. I truly believe that this is the future of humanity.

Notes

1 See my *Human Excellence and an Ecological Conception of the Psyche* (1992) for my initial attempt to use an ecological model for organizing the psyche.
2 See Chapter 6 for an exploration of racist and sexist prejudices embedded in the economic ideal of autonomy.

References

Bettelheim, B. (1976). *The Uses of Enchantment: The Meaning and Importance of Fairy Tales*. London: Thames & Hudson.

Dobson, M. (2023). *Metamorphoses of Psyche in Psychoanalysis and Ancient Greek Thought: From Mourning to Creativity*. New York: Routledge.

Freud, S. (1914). "On Narcissism." In *Vol. 11 of Standard Edition of the Collected Works*, tr. & ed. James Strachey, et al. London: Hogarth Press (1953–1974). pp. 219–230.

Erikson, E. (1960/1980). *Identity and the Life Cycle*. New York: W.W. Norton.

Hegel, G. (1821/1977). *Elements in the Philosophy of Right*. Tr. H. Nisbet. Cambridge: Cambridge University Press.

Leibniz, G. (1989). *Philosophical Essays*. Tr. R. Ariew & D. Garber. Indianapolis, IN: Hackett.

Kohut, H. (1985). *Self Psychology and the Humanities*. Ed. C. Strozier. New York: W. W. Norton.

Riker, J. (1992). *Human Excellence and an Ecological Conception of the Psyche*. Albany, NY: SUNY Press.

Chapter 10

Transcending the Self

Metaphysics, Spirituality, and the
Meaning of Life

I have elucidated Kohut's notion of the self, how it stands in dire opposition to the regnant concept of individuality, and how we might use it both to critique contemporary society and propose a culture better able to meet the needs of persons' selves. However, our psyches can open to wider horizons of meaning than the self's ideals and ambitions that ground personal life. Kohut points to these realms of meaning when he says that the final transformation of our narcissism is one in which we enter a stage in which the individual self merges with universal values (1966/1985; 1971) and attains a stage of wisdom, a stage he terms "cosmic narcissism." While I discussed this final transformation of narcissism at the end of Chapter 1, I now want to expand on the possibilities that our psyches have both needs and powers to extend into realms of meaning beyond those that characterize ordinary self-experience. I will explore this "spiritual" dimension by inquiring into the epistemological powers of the soul that extend beyond the usual boundaries of experience, examining the metaphysical moods which color all experience, and sketching Whitehead's cosmological understanding of reality in which the mind/body problem can be resolved, in which there is a non-omnipotent, poetic, divine presence, and in which creative experiencing is the fundamental activity of every being that exists. It is a metaphysics that shows how our humanistic search for meaning can unite with a scientific understanding of reality. I will conclude by extending my thoughts on what constitutes an ideal self-psychological community by relating it to Raanan Kulka's vision of a spiritual self-psychological community.[1]

DOI: 10.4324/9781003303657-14

10.1 Strange Powers

Even when the self is fully present in subjectivity, the ego tends to organize experience into structures of space/time regularities and predictable patterns of causation for us to optimize pragmatic control over the vicissitudes of existence. As such, the ego disallows various aspects of experience that might open us to vastly different realities and ways of being in the world. As William James said, experience at its base level is a "buzzing, booming confusion"—a stream of consciousness with focuses and fringes, penetrated with emotional moods, flowing into and out of recognizable patterns, and never fully set or organized. Such a world of "pure experience" seems unwieldy to our pragmatic needs, and so the epistemological capacities of the ego organize it by turning what we experience into stable objects and patterns of causation. Such structuring allows us to act in the world with direction and definiteness.

However, as some psychoanalysts and philosophers have shown, our experience can retrieve its original connectedness to a world of flowing presences and extend to realities beyond the empirically given, to mysteries that resist explanation with our usual epistemic theories, without a loss of wholeness or integrity. Marcia Dobson calls these "liminal experiences"—experiences that reveal presences and depths of connectedness unavailable in ordinary ego experience (2023). She finds that they characterize what is called "the third" in psychotherapy, inexplicable visions of hidden truths, and the experience of the characters we meet in pre-Platonic Greek literature who have interchanges with gods and goddesses and for whom nature is filled with spirits—every stream seems to be a kind of god and the woods are teeming with nymphs, satyrs, and other spirited beings. Rather than seeing these experiences as infantile fantasies, Dobson posits that these pre-classical Greek persons had much more permeable and fluid psyches than we allow ourselves. For persons with this kind of pre-ego-controlled subjectivity, there is no careful delineation between a private interior and an objective exterior world. Subjectivity flows into the world and the world into subjectivity. For instance, rage is not a personal feeling but Ares invading our psyches; falling in love is not a subjective state but a divine gift from Aphrodite. For Dobson, the language through which we can engage liminal spaces is not that of empirical description, but that of symbol, metaphor, myth, and analogy—poetic language—just the language Freud says characterizes primary process thinking. One might say that for these Greek characters the ability to organize the world according to secondary process has not yet been fully developed.

Other authors write about powers of the psyche that extend beyond what we ordinarily think of as possible. Internationally acclaimed psychoanalyst, researcher, and clinician, Elizabeth Lloyd Mayer, Ph.D. in her remarkable *Extraordinary Knowing: Science, Skepticism, and the Inexplicable Powers of the Human Mind* (2007) documents her own experience in encountering persons who know things that they supposedly can't possibly know (such as a dowser who located the whereabouts of her daughter's precious cello although she was thousands of miles away) and scientifically examines evidence for such powers being real. Her careful analysis of claims for extra-sensory knowledge is so strong that it invalidates most of the contemporary models of the human mind. Carl Jung and his followers believe, based on cross-cultural studies of myths and symbols, that our unconscious minds can open to a realm of universal archetypes and a collective unconscious.

I mention these different and extraordinary ways of experiencing and thinking about reality to acknowledge that there is substantial evidence that the mind has powers beyond those recognized by psychological science and to suggest that an openness to these kinds of experiences can expand the horizons of our understandings of who we are as humans. Exploring them further is far beyond the limits of this book.

However, there are two ways in which delving into metaphysics is important in understanding how we can bring everyday experience to an optimal intensity of aliveness. The first is to look at philosophers, especially William James, who believe that we all have a semi-conscious set of beliefs about what is ultimately real, and these issue into a kind of "metaphysical mood" that colors our experiences. The second is to suggest a speculative metaphysics that helps overcome the intractable mind/body problem by allowing us to see how physicality and mentality can be thoroughly interfused and offering an original theory of what a non-omnipotent divine presence might be. For this excursion, I will give a thumbnail sketch of the remarkable metaphysics of Alfred North Whitehead.

10.2 Metaphysical Moods

As humans, we seem innately drawn to questions of what ultimately exists, who we ultimately are, why we ultimately are, whether there is some ultimate purpose to life, whether there is a divine being present in the universe, and so on. These ontological questions seem to spring upon us involuntarily, and how we respond to them—even if we ignore them—will affect what I call "the meaningfulness of our existence." For most peoples in most of human history, religions have provided answers to these questions and generated a generalized framework for making sense of human experience. However, since Hume and Kant in the 18th century argued convincingly that the human mind cannot extend beyond the realm of empirical experience and science claimed that we did not need any non-physical causes to explain why the world is the way it is, metaphysics has generally been abandoned—even forbidden—among the intelligentsia. Nietzsche and Freud went further in showing how metaphysical beliefs were fantasies, wish-fulfillments, or desperate attempts to give a meaningless human existence a contrived meaning. Positivism concurred and helped deposit metaphysical thinking into a graveyard of abandoned ways of explaining the world to join astrology, phrenology, and other mistaken explanatory theories.

The problem is that scientism is also a metaphysics, for it tells us what is real and what we can believe, and, as such, generates a kind of metaphysical mood that affects how we experience life. What I mean by "metaphysical mood" is best understood within William James' concept of experience. For James, experience, which always occurs in a stream of consciousness, has a focus and a fringe, with elements of the fringe capable of becoming the focus and vice versa. Part of the fringe is a metaphysical penumbra, which, like a misty cloud surrounding the sun, is a vague general mood through which we experience the meaning of our lives. That is, it makes a difference to our general sense of well-being whether we think that science has the final say about what exists in the universe or whether there might be ontological presences other than material entities that exist.

For James there are three basic kinds of metaphysical moods: those that characterize "healthy minds," those that characterize "sick souls," and those that acknowledge the complexities of existence with a sense of solemn hope (1902/1985). The healthy-minded, according to James, believe that God's presence penetrates everything. Such people think that human life is fundamentally good and that a divine being is watching over us. They can relax and enjoy life knowing that God is in control. They seem to be innately optimistic about life. Although James calls such people "the healthy-minded," he denies that this is the best way to be human.

> [H]ealthy-mindedness is inadequate as a philosophical doctrine, because the evil facts which it refuses positively to account for are a genuine portion of reality; and they may after all be the best key to life's significance, and possibly the only openers of our eyes to the deepest levels of truth.
>
> (1902/1985, 163)

We can say that the experience of healthy-minded persons tends to be shallow and not intensely alive because they deny too much reality. If intensity of experience is produced by the harmonic integration of contrasting elements, the healthy-minded do not allow the most profound of contrasts to enter their experience, and, hence, cannot experience the highest levels of intensity.

The "sick-souled" are those whose metaphysical outlook is one of gloom. They are predisposed to see evil and darkness everywhere and, as such, tend to live in a state of despair and/or depression. A significant variation of this sick-souled person is what James experienced and fought most of his life—a belief that science has the final truth about the universe and, as such, human life is more or less causally determined and fully meaningless. From science's point of view, the human species has come into being as the result of a series of chance mutations and when we die, we become food for worms or carcasses to be mined for organs. We exist for the minutest blip of time and then disappear into infinite nothingness. The metaphysical mood that best resonates with this set of beliefs is one that accepts it as our fate and attempts to carve out what bit of meaning one can by finding local causes for which to fight. A kind of stoic resignation takes over the soul and we suffer from a "metaphysical melancholy." This kind of sick-soul also does not have the most intensity of experience because it can find no compelling reason why life counts for much of anything.

The third metaphysical mood James describes is one of "solemn hope." James responds to the question of whether life is worth living by saying, "Maybe.... It depends upon you, the *liver*" (1895/2000, 238–239). What the hopeful soul believes is that "the so-called order of nature, which constitutes this world's experience, is only one portion of the total universe, and that there stretches beyond this visible world an unseen world" (1895/2000, 233). James does not want to go further than this, being distrustful of all theologies that attempt to characterize what a divine presence might be. The metaphysically hopeful soul recognizes that the world contains both wondrous beauty and goodness but also the darkness of evil and senseless destructiveness. It can accommodate the contrasting elements because it has a firm hope that beyond the hard facts of this world, another invisible world is present that will salvage what is good, including us. James further says that it is the belief in a divine presence that can lead to experiences that provide evidence that there is a world beyond the one of hard facts.

In short, our metaphysical beliefs constitute a set of meanings that color and penetrate our everyday experiences of the world. They generate a kind of metaphysical mood that grants us a profound sense of well-being or a kind of "in vain" attitude as we wander through the mists of life, not really knowing who or what we are. While I fully believe that actualizing the ideals of the self in a way that brings narcissistic recognition is largely responsible for our sense of happiness and well-being, I think that James is right is thinking that this kind of joyful self-actualization takes place within a wider realm of the meaning of life, and that our metaphysical outlook adds an inescapable dimension to our experience. The most important way to give meaning to life is by discovering and enacting the erotic self; but having hope and belief that there are mysteries in this world that point to our lives having meaning beyond our small insignificant accomplishments can add a layer of meaningfulness and well-being to ordinary experience.

There are two great obstacles that thoughtful persons must face in order to accept a mood of solemn hope: scientism and a misconception of God as an omnipotent monarch of the universe. "Scientism" claims that the only realities which exist are the physical realities studied by science. That is, scientism turns science into a metaphysics by claiming that science offers a complete understanding of ultimate reality. Since scientific methods can discover only physical entities, this position is a circular one. Just because science by its very nature cannot discover non-physical entities does not mean that they do not exist. However, science can claim that it can explain all the events in this world without reference to any non-physical causes. And this is where the evidence from extraordinary knowing comes in—for there are numerous experiences that science cannot yet account for, including the appearance of self-consciousness and the realm of meaning.

The second obstacle to adopting a mood of solemn hope is a conception of divine presence as a God who is all-powerful, all-knowing, and who, as such, can control all that happens in the universe. This conception arose mainly in Christianity and was constructed during the Roman Empire in which the theologians thought of God as a divine Caesar and granted Him the qualities of an absolute monarch. For many, belief in an omnipotent divinity is impossible after the Holocaust. If God can control everything, how could He possibly allow the slaughter of millions of innocent people? Hence, if we must conceive of divinity as omnipotent, then we cannot believe in God. However, the conception of divine presence as omnipotent is only one possible way of thinking about divinity. Some of our deepest religious thinkers of the 20th century such as Buber, Tillich, and Whitehead offer us very different ways to think about divine presence than as a patriarchal absolute monarch. I will sketch Whitehead's understanding in the next section, as I find his conception of divine presence makes the most sense of our world.

10.3 Metaphysical Speculations: Whitehead

While James did not want to engage in metaphysical speculations beyond having a hope in an unseen world, it is natural for the human mind to seek to understand what this unseen world might be and how it intersects the visible world. Having a theory as to why and how the universe makes sense can lend a deep sense of coherence and purpose to life. We cannot, I believe, ever have knowledge of what constitutes ultimate reality, but this does not mean that speculation about what ultimately exists cannot provide meaning—cannot offer us a satisfying way of making sense of it all. That is what happened to me in college when I first read Whitehead. His incredibly complex metaphysical system made sense of the world, divine presence, and how minds could emerge from bodies enlivened me in a way like no other speculative metaphysics. I was so elated that I had to write a monumentally long senior thesis on Whitehead and have carried his metaphysical philosophy with me ever since. It underlies everything I have written about ethics, self psychology, and psychoanalysis, although it says almost nothing about these discourses. Achieving a feeling that the world, indeed, makes sense has given an aura of meaningfulness to my experience that grants a kind of solemn hope.

Whitehead was a world-famous mathematician who grasped almost immediately the philosophical implications of quantum mechanics and Einstein's relativity theory. He interrelated them with both the phenomenological insights of lived experience and some of humanity's deepest religious intuitions. He says that his theory is fundamentally based on the idea "that the energetic activity in physics is the emotional intensity entertained in life" (1938, 231–232). Unfortunately, Whitehead's *Process and Reality* (1929a) came out just as positivism was coming to dominate European and American philosophy and with it the rejection of all metaphysics. Hence, the most brilliant (and difficult) metaphysical system ever elaborated has gone largely unnoticed. Strangely, Whitehead begins *Process and Reality* with the claim that metaphysics can only be a speculative discourse—not a knowledge-producing one, but one which nonetheless needs to be engaged, for otherwise we fall into "the benumbing repression of common sense" (1929a, 10).[2] That is, he answers the critique of positivism that metaphysics cannot produce knowledge by agreeing with it but then arguing for why it is still necessary to engage in metaphysical speculation.

This is hardly the place to explicate Whitehead's complicated metaphysics, as that would require a full book, but I can give the bare rudiments. For Whitehead, everything in reality is in process—each entity is a drop of process, the universe as a whole is an ongoing evolutionary process, and even God is moving and changing. The universe is made up of "real individuals" which Whitehead calls "actual entities" or "actual occasions," each one of which is a unique quantum of space/time but which is intrinsically related to all the other actual entities in the universe. Hence, this philosophy is one of atomism (the world is made up of discrete individuals), organism (all the individuals are intrinsically interrelated), and process.

Because both what we call matter and mind are made up of events, Whitehead can overcome the dualisms that have haunted philosophy since Descartes. For Whitehead, each sub-atomic particle is a series of events that has a high degree of repetitiveness. An electron is a series of electronic events, each of which passes on to the next certain crucial properties such as a negative charge. Material things such as atoms and molecules are organizations of these elementary particles and can initiate new series of events (such as the nucleus of a cell).

Every event is caused to come into existence by the world of preceding events. Physical causation is real. However, what causation generates is only the first phase of an event (a phase Whitehead terms the physical phase or conformal phase). After this first phase, each event initiates an interiority of experiencing in which it can creatively adjust the elements that entered it. That is, if subjectivity is the same as creative experiencing, then every entity in the universe has a subjective dimension. In short, each event has an interiority in which it takes the materials forced into it by causation and creatively adjusts them to produce a satisfaction which is that harmonious integration of elements that produces the greatest intensity of experiencing. Once the event has completed its integration, it ceases to be active and becomes a fact in the universe, a fact that will influence all future facts. It re-enters the world as causation. Hence, we can say that every entity in the universe is a data-processing event, a creative experiencing in which data are synthesized into a new entity which then effects all succeeding events. In sum, every being in the universe participates in both physicality (causation) and mentality (creative adjustment of the physical prehensions). The difference between events in the inorganic world and those that occur in living organisms is that the creative adjustments in the inorganic world are minimal—hence, material entities have a great deal of predictability and stability.

The world in which we live—the world of humans, animals, plants, mountains, air—is made up of things which are highly complex interconnections of events. Mammals tend to be organized in such a way that they channel energy to a central nervous system and especially the brain. The brain of humans is such a rich, dense environment of channeled energy and data that it can evoke a string of events that achieve consciousness and self-consciousness. Whitehead says that the mind is a string of events winding through the interstices of the brain, gathering its richly processed data, and organizing it into lived experience. That is, our minds are not made of a different kind of substance than our bodies—both are ultimately sets of events. The body is that set of interconnected events that funnels data and energy to a central stream of events that is conscious, and which can then influence the events of the body in terms of action, meaning, and emotion. In short, we have misconceived of matter as being an inert, dead substance and mind as being a self-contained mental substance. Everything in the universe engages in the production of meanings and everything in the universe is involved in acts of physical causation.

For Whitehead, the universe is an ongoing evolution in which ever-more intensely experiencing organisms are being created. He thinks that evolution as happening solely by chance mutations makes no sense, as there is a clear direction from an inorganic world to one that has produced living beings with ever-greater abilities to experience higher levels of intensity. Whitehead thinks that this kind of evolution, along with the presence of genuinely novel forms of creativity, indicate a divine presence influencing the world. This divine presence is not conceived of as omnipotent, for the events of the world have their own energy and creative initiative. However, God, who prehends all the events as they complete themselves, can offer suggestions for how events can integrate material to generate the most intense unifications. That is, Whitehead says that God "does not create the world, he saves it; or, more accurately, he is the poet of the world, with tender patience leading it by his vision of truth, beauty, and goodness" (1929b, 183). For Whitehead, God is an event, like all other entities, but an event that is everlasting. What distinguishes God is his/her envisionment of the infinity of pure possibilities (he calls them "eternal objects"—they are akin to Platonic forms). It is this envisionment that allows God to suggest creative possibilities to the world as it is coming into being.

I relate this brief thumbnail sketch of Whitehead's metaphysical theory in hopes that it lures the reader to think that there are alternative ways to imagine what is real, other than an incomprehensible Cartesian dualism or the reduction of everything to physical entities that are conceived of as things with no possibility of having interior experiencing. Whitehead's concept of the universe as an unfolding process guided by a non-omnipotent divine presence in which everything is both a subject and an object allows us to have hope that the world is, indeed, rich beyond measure in meaning and purpose.

10.4 Spiritual Self Psychology

Raanan Kulka, the founder of the Human Spirit Psychoanalytic-Buddhist Training Institute at Lod in Israel, finds psychoanalysis in general and Kohutian self psychology in particular as leading humanity into a "realm of spirit." By "realm of spirit" Kulka envisions a world in which human beings recognize and affirm our interconnectedness with all other human beings—indeed, all beings—in a kind of loving embrace and affirmation (2020).

> A republic infused with the spirit of self psychology is a human vow, a promise of loving goodness, for joyful and wise compassion, immersed continuously and ceaselessly in the Other, the very other that cannot live without me devoted to him, without my fully committed selfhood, without total fraternity.
>
> (2020, 326)

Kulka thinks that self psychology needs "to respond to the summons of a **serving leadership**" guiding us to

> the creation of a **supra-contextual web of empathy** that will embrace the personal and the general, the similar and the different, the multiplicity and the oneness. Such a gigantic task calls upon us to raise the Kohutian legacy to its final lofty destination, to the shores of **self object psychology**.
>
> (2020, 324, bolded by Kulka)

In this selfobject realm of the spirit, humans "would create an infinite platform of ideals and ideas, devoted to the welfare of all comers to the universe," and "would maintain an internal dialogue of fraternal solidarity with a philosophy that grants exclusive priority of infinite ethical responsibility amongst humans of the world" (2020, 325). In short, Kulka is envisioning an ideal world of human solidarity and the overcoming of divisions caused by difference—an ideal even loftier than the self psychological community I envisioned in the last chapter. To bring this "realm of spirit" into being, Kulka, I think, would recommend that we engage in two fundamental Buddhist practices: meditation and compassion. Buddhist meditative practice can be of great help in enhancing our abilities to be empathic by quieting the mind and clearing it of incessant presuppositions that distort our relations to others and the world. That is, our minds are always at work projecting concepts and frameworks on what we perceive. Meditation is a practice that allows the mind to slow down, quiet the onrush of ideas, and allow what is before us to appear with less presuppositions distorting the experience. Empathy now has an easier time locating the inner experience of others and being there with it.

Buddhist compassion is not a "feeling sorry for" as this comes out of a place of superiority rather than fellowship; in its Buddhist formulation, compassion extends care and concern to all creatures, including ourselves, because we all participate in the endless "perpetual perishing" of the universe. Buddhist compassion probably should be included as an aspect of Kohut's notion of cosmic narcissism insofar as it embodies wisdom and universality. Compassion is not just a universal ideal, but a metaphysical mood, rather like James' solemn hope, that both colors experience and directs activity. It is a metaphysical mood that not only hopes that in the end good will prevail but helps that good prevail. Compassion for all beings grants them dignity and worth, and in this granting the world becomes a more loving and livable place. In addition, becoming a compassionate person gives a profound sense of meaningfulness to life. One recognizes the impermanence of existence, the suffering this transience causes, and offers compassion as an optimally meaningful way to dwell on the earth.

Raanan Kulka's Human Spirit Institute is grounded in a vision of what kind of human being will most sustain humanity as we venture ever further into our very uncertain future. The more we develop the empathy and understanding of self psychology, become meditatively compassionate, develop our own core selves, and nourish our souls with the beauty of the art, literature, and philosophies that have been created by our cultures, the more we become the kind of person who can foster a genuinely loving, caring, and enriched humanity.

Notes

1 The last chapter of Strozier et al.'s *The New World of Self* deals with Kohut's spirituality. Unlike what I attempt to do in this chapter, their chapter focuses on Kohut's own sense of spirituality and the relation between empathy and spirituality. My chapter asks about the relation of the psyche to metaphysical matters, matters that transcend the self.
2 *Process and Reality* is so dense as to be almost unreadable. I strongly suggest Donald Sherburne's *A Key to Process and Reality* in which he re-organizes the key ideas and concepts of Whitehead's text into a much more readable format. But it is still tough!

References

Dobson, M. (2023). *Metamorphoses of Psyche in Psychoanalysis and Ancient Greek Literature: From Mourning to Creativity*. New York: Routledge.

James, W. (1895/2000). "Is Life Worth Living?" In *Pragmatism and Other Writings*, Ed. G. Gunn. New York: Penguin.

———. (1902/1982). *The Varieties of Religious Experience*. New York: Penguin.

Kohut, H. (1966/1985). "Forms and Transformations of Narcissism." In *Self Psychology and the Humanities*. Ed. C. Strozier. New York: W.W. Norton.

———. (1971). *The Analysis of the Self*. New York: International Universities Press.

Kulka, R. (2020). "Selfobject Psychology for a Troubled World." *Psychoanalysis, Self, and Context*, 15(4), 324–337.

Mayer, E. (2007). *Extraordinary Knowing: Science, Skepticism, and the Inexplicable Powers of the Human Mind*. New York: Random House.

Whitehead, A. (1929a). *Process and Reality*. New York: MacMillan.

———. (1929b). *A Key to Whitehead's Process and Reality*. Ed. D. Sherburne. Chicago: University of Chicago Press.

———. (1938). *Modes of Thought*. New York: MacMillan.

Appendix 1

Internet Sources of Statistics as produced by Macie Aronski

1. Homelessness
   a. What is the % of people in the US who are homeless?
      - 0.2% as of 2022. That's 552,830 people.
      - About 17 people per every 10,000 are homeless each day
        https://policyadvice.net/insurance/insights/homelessness-statistics/
        o How has this increased in last 10 years; last 25 years?
      - It has not increased or decreased
        o 2008: 664,000 homeless (0.2%)
          https://www.huduser.gov/portal/sites/default/files/pdf/2008AHARSummary.pdf
        o 2012: 633,782 homeless (0.2%)
          https://nlihc.org/resource/us-homelessness-declined-2012-part-due-federal-programs-now-risk
        o 2022: 552,830 homeless (0.2%)
          https://www.huduser.gov/portal/sites/default/files/pdf/2008AHARSummary.pdf
   b. What is the % of homeless who suffer from severe mental illness?
      - 30.25%—almost a third of all homeless suffer from mental illness
      - 38% alcohol abuse—roughly 4 out of 10
      - 26% drug abuse—over a quarter
      - Chronic homelessness:
        o 31.23% of all homeless US individuals
        o Almost a quarter of the homeless population experience a disabling condition (disability, mental illness, substance abuse)

  o   Unaccompanied individuals
  o   Homeless for over a year straight or experienced
      homelessness multiple times
      https://policyadvice.net/insurance/insights/homelessness-
      statistics/
c. What are the major reasons people give for being homeless?
  •   I have found the following reasons for homeless to be con-
      sistent across many studies and articles:
  o   Poverty due to insufficient income, unemployment
      (and a lack of employment opportunity), stagnant
      wages and/or a lack of available public assistance
  o   Lack of affordable housing
  o   Lack of affordable healthcare
  o   Lack of access to mental health treatment/addiction
      facilities
  o   Domestic violence/family conflict
      https://homelesslaw.org/wp-content/uploads/2018/10/
      Homeless_Stats_Fact_Sheet.pdf
      https://www.humanrightscareers.com/issues/root-
      causes-of-homelessness/
      https://nationalhomeless.org/about-homelessness/
  o   90% of homeless women have been severely physically
      or sexually abused in their lives
      https://nnedv.org/wp-content/uploads/2019/07/
      Library_TH_2018_DV_Housing_Homelessness.pdf
2. Loneliness
a. What is the % of people in the US that report acute or chronic
   loneliness?
  •   Over 1 in 3 Americans face "serious loneliness"—36% are
      lonely "frequently" or "almost all the time or all the time"
  •   An additional 37% feel lonely "occasionally"
b. Age distribution of the lonely
  •   A 2018 study found that young adults struggle with loneli-
      ness the most: 40% (ages 16–24), compared to the elderly
      with 27% (ages 75+)
      https://www.bbc.co.uk/programmes/articles/2yzhfv4Dvq
      Vp5nZyxBD8G23/who-feels-lonely-the-results-of-the-
      world-s-largest-loneliness-study

- According to a 2020 study:
  - o   51% of mothers with young children
  - o   Over 61% of young adults (aged 18–25)
  - o   43% of young adults have felt significantly more loneliness since the pandemic
  - o   "About half of lonely young adults in our survey, for example, reported that no one in the past few weeks had 'taken more than just a few minutes' to ask how they are doing in a way that made them feel like the person 'genuinely cared'" (Weissbourd et al., 2021). https://static1.squarespace.com/static/5b7c56e255b 02c683659fe43/t/6021776bdd04957c4557c212/1612 805995893/Loneliness+in+America+2021_02_08_ FINAL.pdf

  c. Percentage of households that have single adult in them
  - In 2021, 28% of all US households (37 million) were single-person households
  - In 1960, only 13% were single-person households
  - The statistic more than doubled half-a-century later
  - Over the past decade:
    - o   50% of adults live with a spouse (2021) compared to 52% (2011)
    - o   37 million adults/14% ages 18+ lived alone (2021) compared to 33 million/13% (2011)
    - o   8% of adults live with an unmarried partner (2021) compared to 7% (2011)
  - Families living with their own children
    - o   2021—40%
    - o   2011—44%
    - o   2001—48%
      https://www.census.gov/newsroom/press-releases/ 2021/families-and-living-arrangements.html#:~:text= Other%20Highlights&text=There%20were%2037%20 million%20one,only%2013%25%20of%20all%20 households

3. Divorce
   a. What is the % of marriages that end in divorce?

- Almost 50% of marriages in the US end in separation or divorce
  - o   41% of all first marriages
  - o   60% of all second marriages
  - o   73% of all third marriages
- 15% of adult woman in the US are separated or divorced today, compared to less than 1% in 1920
- On average, there is one divorce every 42 seconds in the US
- For ages 50+, the divorce rate has doubled in the past two decades
  https://www.wf-lawyers.com/divorce-statistics-and-facts/#:~:text=Almost%2050%20percent%20of%20all,first%20marriages%20end%20in%20divorce

b. What is the rate of persons in marriages that cheat on their partners?
- 26% of married people experience infidelity in the marriage (2020)
  https://hellorelish.com/relationship-health-report-2020/
- 20% of men, compared to 13% of women
- That's 11.3% on average—significantly more than 1 in 10 people will cheat on their spouses
- The data is from self-report surveys; the numbers are likely higher in reality
  https://www.brides.com/what-percentage-of-men-cheat-5114527
- "56% of men and 34% of women who commit infidelity rate their marriages as happy or very happy" (2021).
  https://laintelligence.com/infidelity-the-cold-hard-truth-about-cheating/

c. What % of marriages break up because of cheating?
- 55% of marriages that end do so because of infidelity
  (https://www.wf-lawyers.com/divorce-statistics-and-facts/#:~:text=Almost%2050%20percent%20of%20all,first%20marriages%20end%20in%20divorce)

d. What is the average time married couples talk with one another?
- 2010:
  - o   Directly after marriage: 40 min per day
  - o   20 years into marriage: 21 min per day

      o   30 years into marriage: 16 min per day

      o   50 years into marriage: 3 minutes per day
https://www.oprah.com/relationships/have-you-and-your-spouse-stopped-talking#:~:text=Twenty%20years%20into%20marriage%2C%20the,three%20minutes%20in%20an%20hour!

e. How many married persons complain of not receiving enough empathic responsiveness?

- Only 1–2% of the population are true "empaths" (https://www.wellandgood.com/empath-vs-empathic/#:~:text=Despite%20the%20great%20many%20people,population%20consists%20of%20true%20empaths), yet 98% of people have the ability to empathize "wired into their brains" (https://www.bbc.com/news/magazine-33287727)
- Empathy declined 48% between 1979 and 2009 https://greatergood.berkeley.edu/article/research_digest/empathy_on_the_decline

4. Addictions: gambling, alcohol, drugs, sex, shopping

    a. % of people who are addicted to each.

- 2 million US adults (0.6%) are addicted to gambling https://behavioralhealthnews.org/the-impacts-of-problem-gambling/#:~:text=There%20are%20many%20people%20who,on%20Problem%20Gambling%2C%202020
- 14.5 million people in the US ages 12+ (4.4%) have Alcohol Use Disorder (AUD) (2019) https://www.niaaa.nih.gov/publications/brochures-and-fact-sheets/alcohol-facts-and-statistics
- 23 million people in the US (7%) have a drug addiction (including alcohol) https://www.firstrespondersfirst.com/post/how-many-people-are-addicted-to-drugs-in-the-us https://projectknow.com/blog/are-you-one-of-americas-20-million-shopping-addicts/
- 3–5% of US adults experienced sexual addictive behavior https://www.therecoveryvillage.com/process-addiction/sex-addiction/sexual-addiction-statistics/
- 6–7% of US adults (20 million) are addicted to shopping https://projectknow.com/blog/are-you-one-of-americas-20-million-shopping-addicts/

b. % of people who are drug- or alcohol-dependent, even if not addicted.

- 3.3% of US adults (1 in 30) are alcohol-dependent, and 1 in 3 are excessive drinkers
  https://www.cdc.gov/media/releases/2014/p1120-excessive-driniking.html
- 10% of US adults have experienced a drug use disorder (dependence/abuse are terms no longer used in the context; different levels of severity of the disorder are noted instead)
  https://www.nih.gov/news-events/news-releases/10-percent-us-adults-have-drug-use-disorder-some-point-their-lives

5. Credit card debt: what is the average amount of debt for each American?

- Average credit card debt: $6,270
  https://www.valuepenguin.com/average-credit-card-debt
- The average American has $92,727 of debt
  o includes credit card balances, mortgages, personal, auto and student loan
  https://oportun.com/financial-education/how-much-debt-does-the-average-american-have/#:~:text=According%20to%20a%202020%20Experian,personal%20loans%2C%20and%20student%20loans

6. Obesity

a. What is the % of Americans who are obese; fat? Significantly overweight?

- 36% or 1 in every 3 people are obese
- 500,000,000 adults are obese in the world
- By 2030, 20% of the world's population will be obese (if unaddressed), including 1 billion adults
  https://www.singlecare.com/blog/news/obesity-statistics/

b. What factors are experts saying lie behind this epidemic of weight-gain?

- 42% of US adults reported unwanted weight-gain since the beginning of the pandemic
  o Stress and isolation
- Marginalized communities such as lower-income populations and people of color have seen great weight gain
  o Obesity is more common for people in these communities, and the pandemic amplified these disparities

- o Healthy food became even less accessible for people who live in places where access to fresh food is accessible
- Child obesity: 13.7% pre-pandemic vs. 15.4% during the pandemic
  - o High stress > food cravings, poor sleep, too much screen time
  - o Screen-time recommendation for children at risk of obesity is two hours or less, but virtual school requires seven to eight https://www.apa.org/monitor/2021/07/extra-weight-covid
- Our "obesogenic environment" says, eat more, exercise less
- Environmental causes are the driving cause of obesity and its dramatic increase
  - o These factors more significantly impact weight-gain than genetics
  - o How much we sleep and stress levels impact obesity
- We impact the obesity of future generations
  - o Babies born to smoking or obese mothers are more likely to develop obesity themselves
  - o How we raise our children matters: childhood habits stick
- Food:
  - o Increased portion-sizes, availability, and high-calorie foods
- Exercise:
  - o Recommended: an hour a day
  - o Less than 25% of Americans meet this goal
  - o Exercise is not a priority in school. There have been cuts in PE classes
  - o Cars have replaced the exercise we would have normally gained from going place to place
  - o Household appliances reduce the effort (physical activity) behind chores
- TV:
  - o Watching TV is a habit positively linked to obesity
  - o The average American spends four hrs/day watching TV
  - o Watching TV has taken the place of doing activities that burn more calories

- o On average, there are 11 food advertisements for a one-hour episode of TV
- o People are stimulated to eat more calories (particularly calories from fat) when watching TV than when doing other activities
- Stress:
  - o The cycle: emotional disorders can promote weight-gain, and weight-gain can lead to emotional disorders
  - o Today, working long hours and taking less vacation time is common
  - o Violence in the world makes parents less likely to allow kids to walk/bike to places so they drive them, causing less physical activity for children and more stress for parents
  - o Time pressures > lack of sleep and eating on the run > stress and weight gain
  - o Neurologically, irregular eating disrupts the appetite control center (closely connected to the brain's pacemaker) and contributes to obesity
    https://www.health.harvard.edu/staying-healthy/why-people-become-overweight

7. Racism/prejudice: how many racially motivated killings or acts of violence against Blacks, Asian-Americans, Hispanics have occurred in the last five years?
   - CSUSB data:
     - o Hate crimes rose 44% 2020–2021
     - o Hate crimes against Asian-Americans rose 342% 2020–2021
     - o Hate crimes against Asian-Americans rose 124% 2020–2021
       - ▪ (Data discrepancy between CSUSB and FBI may be due to differing definitions of "hate-crime")
     - o Hate crimes' spike against Blacks began in 2020 following the murder of George Floyd
       https://www.ny1.com/nyc/all-boroughs/news/2022/02/14/hate-crime-increase-2021-asian-american-
   - FBI data: 2020 FBI hate crime stats:
     - o 62% motivated by race/ethnicity/ancestry
       - ▪ 5,227 acts: 32% increase since 2019 (3,969)

- o   Anti-Black or African-American
  - ▪   2,817 incidents in 2020: 49% increase since 2019
- o   Anti-Asian
  - ▪   279 reported incidents in 2020: 77% increase since 2019
- o   Anti-Hispanic or Latino
  - ▪   517 in 2020 and 527 in 2019
    https://www.justice.gov/crs/highlights/2020-hate-crimes-statistics
- 2020 incidents reported:
  - o   Anti-Black or African-American
    - ▪   1,930
  - o   Anti-Asain
    - ▪   158
  - o   Anti-Hispanic or Latino
    - ▪   527
- 2019 incidents reported:
  - o   Anti-Black or African-American
    - ▪   1,930
  - o   Anti-Asian
    - ▪   158
  - o   Anti-Hispanic or Latino
    - ▪   527
- 2018 incidents reported:
  - o   Anti-Black or African-American
    - ▪   1,943
  - o   Anti-Asian
    - ▪   148
  - o   Anti-Hispanic or Latino
    - ▪   485
- 2017 incidents reported:
  - o   Anti-Black or African-American
    - ▪   2,013
  - o   Anti-Asian
    - ▪   131
  - o   Anti-Hispanic or Latino
    - ▪   427
      https://ucr.fbi.gov/hate-crime

- Rise in Asian hate is correlated with COVID and blaming Asians for the pandemic
  https://www.cnbc.com/2021/08/30/fbi-says-hate-crimes-against-asian-and-black-people-rise-in-the-us.html

8. Sexual violence: what is the % of women who have suffered unwanted sexual aggression, molestation, rape, etc.? Same question for men.
   - CDC research:
     o Nearly 1 in 5 women experienced completed or attempted rape
     o Nearly 1 in 38 men experienced completed or attempted rape
     o More than 1 in 3 women experienced physical sexual violence
     o Nearly 1 in 4 men experienced physical sexual violence
       http://www.cdc.gov/injury/features/sexual-violence/index.html
   - 90% of adult rape victims are female
     o 82% of all juvenile victims are female
     o 17.7 million adult American women have been raped since 1998
   - Every 68 seconds, an American is sexually assaulted
   - 463,634 (aged 12+) victims of S/A on average in the US each year
     https://www.rainn.org/statistics/victims-sexual-violence

9. Cheating: has Callahan updated his "The Cheating Culture" book with new statistics? No. If not:
   a. What is the % of college students who cheat at least once?
      - 2021:
        o 60% of US college students say they've cheated this year
        o 31% say they've cheated more than once
          https://thecheatsheet.substack.com/p/new-survey-60-of-us-college-students?s=r
      - 2021: 75–98% of college students surveyed each year admit to having cheated at least once throughout their academic careers
        https://bestaccreditedcolleges.org/articles/75-to-98-percent-of-college-students-have-cheated.html#:~:text=75%20to%2098%20Percent%20of%20College%20Students%20Have%20Cheated

- 2021: 59.8% of college students say they've cheated during their studies
  - o The US has the highest cheating rate in this context compared to all English-speaking countries
    https://fixgerald.com/blog/cheating-and-plagiarism-statistic#:~:text=Cheating%20and%20Academic%20Dishonesty&text=59.8%25%20of%20students%20there%20admitted,least%20once%20during%20their%20studies
- 2017: 86% of college students say they've cheated
  https://www.cleveland.com/metro/2017/02/cheating_in_college_has_become.html

b. What is the % of people who cheat on income taxes?
- US tax evasion convictions:
  - o 2020: 593
  - o 2019: 848
  - o 2018: 1,052
- There's a clear downward trend
  https://spendmenot.com/blog/tax-evasion-statistics/#:~:text=In%202020%2C%20there%20were%20593%20tax%20evasion%20convictions%20in%20the%20US.&text=In%202019%2C%20848%20people%20were,there's%20a%20clear%20downward%20trend
- 2019: less than 2,000 people were convicted of tax crimes in a recent year (0.0022% of taxpayers)
  - o But the IRS estimates that 15.5% of people don't comply with tax laws in some way
    https://taxattorneydaily.com/tax-law/fraud-and-tax-crimes/#:~:text=It%20is%20a%20crime%20to,in%20some%20way%20or%20another
- 2020: IRS identifies $2.3 billion in tax fraud
  https://www.irs.gov/newsroom/irs-criminal-investigation-releases-fiscal-year-2020-annual-report-identifies-2-point-3-billion-in-tax-fraud
- 2021: tax cheats cost the US $1 trillion each year, according to Charles Retting, IRS Commissioner
  https://www.nytimes.com/2021/04/13/business/irs-tax-gap.html

   c. How widespread is identity theft?
- 47% of Americans experienced financial identity theft in 2020
- 68% increase in data compromises over 2020
  https://www.iii.org/fact-statistic/facts-statistics-identity-theft-and-cybercrime

   d. % of companies that cheat on their reports
- Small-business fraud: 28%
- Larger organizations: 22–26%
- Small-business corruption (<100 employees): 32%
- Larger organizations (>100 employees): 43%
  https://businessfraudprevention.org/fraud-statistics/#:~:text=The%20small%20businesses%20have%20ranked,at%20a%2022%2D26%25

10. What is the % of Americans in jail. How does this rank with other first-world countries?
- 2.19 million prisoners (2019)
  - o (~0.67%)
- The US has the world's highest incarceration rate
- 25% of the world's imprisoned population is in the US (2019)
  https://worldpopulationreview.com/state-rankings/prison-population-by-state

11. How happy are Americans? Breakdown by wealth.
- Americans usually are happier when earning a higher pay, but the correlation is only steady up until an annual salary of about $60,000
  - o Happiness levels begin to plateau or decrease once you reach this number
    https://hqhire.com/how-much-money-to-be-happy/
- Happiness and wealth used to be negatively correlated, but now it's positively correlated
  https://www.fastcompany.com/40544341/america-desperate-for-happiness-is-getting-less-and-less-happy

Index

Pages followed by "n" refer to notes.

For Product Safety Concerns and Information please contact our EU
representative GPSR@taylorandfrancis.com
Taylor & Francis Verlag GmbH, Kaufingerstraße 24, 80331 München, Germany